Assessing and Managing Security Risk in IT Systems

A Structured Methodology

OTHER INFORMATION SECURITY BOOKS FROM AUERBACH

Asset Protection and Security Management Handbook
POA Publishing
ISBN: 0-8493-1603-0

Building a Global Information Assurance Program
Raymond J. Curts and Douglas E. Campbell
ISBN: 0-8493-1368-6

Building an Information Security Awareness Program
Mark B. Desman
ISBN: 0-8493-0116-5

Critical Incident Management
Alan B. Sterneckert
ISBN: 0-8493-0010-X

Cyber Crime Investigator's Field Guide
Bruce Middleton
ISBN: 0-8493-1192-6

Cyber Forensics: A Field Manual for Collecting, Examining, and Preserving Evidence of Computer Crimes
Albert J. Marcella, Jr. and Robert S. Greenfield
ISBN: 0-8493-0955-7

The Ethical Hack: A Framework for Business Value Penetration Testing
James S. Tiller
ISBN: 0-8493-1609-X

The Hacker's Handbook: The Strategy Behind Breaking into and Defending Networks
Susan Young and Dave Aitel
ISBN: 0-8493-0888-7

Information Security Architecture: An Integrated Approach to Security in the Organization
Jan Killmeyer Tudor
ISBN: 0-8493-9988-2

Information Security Fundamentals
Thomas R. Peltier
ISBN: 0-8493-1957-9

Information Security Management Handbook, 5th Edition
Harold F. Tipton and Micki Krause
ISBN: 0-8493-1997-8

Information Security Policies, Procedures, and Standards: Guidelines for Effective Information Security Management
Thomas R. Peltier
ISBN: 0-8493-1137-3

Information Security Risk Analysis
Thomas R. Peltier
ISBN: 0-8493-0880-1

Information Technology Control and Audit
Fredrick Gallegos, Daniel Manson, and Sandra Allen-Senft
ISBN: 0-8493-9994-7

Investigator's Guide to Steganography
Gregory Kipper
0-8493-2433-5

Managing a Network Vulnerability Assessment
Thomas Peltier, Justin Peltier, and John A. Blackley
ISBN: 0-8493-1270-1

Network Perimeter Security: Building Defense In-Depth
Cliff Riggs
ISBN: 0-8493-1628-6

The Practical Guide to HIPAA Privacy and Security Compliance
Kevin Beaver and Rebecca Herold
ISBN: 0-8493-1953-6

A Practical Guide to Security Engineering and Information Assurance
Debra S. Herrmann
ISBN: 0-8493-1163-2

The Privacy Papers: Managing Technology, Consumer, Employee and Legislative Actions
Rebecca Herold
ISBN: 0-8493-1248-5

Public Key Infrastructure: Building Trusted Applications and Web Services
John R. Vacca
ISBN: 0-8493-0822-4

Securing and Controlling Cisco Routers
Peter T. Davis
ISBN: 0-8493-1290-6

Strategic Information Security
John Wylder
ISBN: 0-8493-2041-0

Surviving Security: How to Integrate People, Process, and Technology, Second Edition
Amanda Andress
ISBN: 0-8493-2042-9

A Technical Guide to IPSec Virtual Private Networks
James S. Tiller
ISBN: 0-8493-0876-3

Using the Common Criteria for IT Security Evaluation
Debra S. Herrmann
ISBN: 0-8493-1404-6

AUERBACH PUBLICATIONS
www.auerbach-publications.com
To Order Call: 1-800-272-7737 • Fax: 1-800-374-3401
E-mail: orders@crcpress.com

Assessing and Managing Security Risk in IT Systems

A Structured Methodology

John McCumber

AUERBACH PUBLICATIONS

A CRC Press Company
Boca Raton   London   New York   Washington, D.C.

Library of Congress Cataloging-in-Publication Data

McCumber, John, 1956-
    Assessing and managing security risk in IT systems : a structured methodology / John McCumber.
        p. cm.
    Includes bibliographical references and index.
    ISBN 0-8493-2232-4 (alk. paper)
    1. Computer security. 2. Data protection. 3. Risk assessment. I. Title.

QA76.9.A25M4284 2004
005.8—dc22
                                    2004050274

Visit the Auerbach Publications Web site at www.auerbach-publications.com

© 2005 by CRC Press LLC
Auerbach is an imprint of CRC Press LLC

No claim to original U.S. Government works
International Standard Book Number 0-8493-2232-4
Library of Congress Card Number 2004050274
Printed in the United States of America 1 2 3 4 5 6 7 8 9 0
Printed on acid-free paper

DEDICATION

As my personal growth and professional challenges have evolved with the rapid pace of technology, there has been a constant element in my life that continues to be my unwavering source of inspiration. My wife has always been there for me regardless of the daunting obstacles we have faced. Linda is both my life partner and best friend. She and I have now shared more of life together than we have ever known apart. She provided moral, emotional, and editorial support to this project and ultimately made it a reality. Linda continues to amaze and inspire me with her intelligence, creativity, and tireless work ethic. To her and her alone is this book dedicated.

John McCumber

CONTENTS

SECTION II THE McCUMBER CUBE METHODOLOGY

SECTION III   APPENDICES

FOREWORD

In 1988, a young graduate student at Cornell University released the first destructive Internet worm. Late one night in November of that year, it crashed thousands of connected computer systems and startled computer administrators and government officials alike. Shortly after that incident, I learned about it from my supervisor who was also this young man's father.

As I sat with Bob Morris in his office that early morning, he motioned me to shut the door so he could try to get away with smoking in the government office building. He always got caught, but he fought the rules anyway. After I returned to the side chair, he spoke for a few minutes about his mixed feelings of filial pride and parental frustration. But after only a few comments, we both found ourselves lost in personal reflection. Bob slowly twirled the unfiltered cigarette in his nicotine-stained fingers and stared at the smoke rising from the end. We were both aware a line had been crossed and the world we inhabited had changed. I am sure he wished the security industry contributions had been his alone and not something for his son to use for notoriety.

I had arrived for work at the National Computer Security Center several months earlier. I had been a young military officer and had volunteered for this assignment because I was intrigued by the security challenges I had encountered while managing data centers for the U.S. Air Force. I wanted to specialize in the field despite the ridicule heaped on me by peers.

"Why the devil would anyone want to get that deep into computer security?" mused a confidant that year of 1987. "No one will ever really care about it except a handful of secret government organizations. Your career is so over!"

It was with these words of confidence and support ringing in my ears that I started making career choices that landed me in Bob Morris's office the morning after the news broke about his son's activities in the computer laboratory at Cornell University. I wanted to be in the center of all the action and I realized I had arrived.

Shortly after this incident, the people at the National Computer Security Center began trying to change the name of the business we were engaged in. Until the late 1980s, we were all happy to explain to colleagues and relatives alike that we worked in the computer security field. Colleagues would stifle a yawn, family members would look at us through incredulous eyes, and then return to their discussion of U.S. versus Japanese cars.

Back in the 1980s, the government bureaucrats even anointed my career with an approved acronym: COMPUSEC. This moniker was coined to differentiate my line of work from the decades-old science of COMSEC, or communications security. Even at that time, scientists and mathematicians known as cryptographers dominated the information security business. They protected secret communications by the deft application of cryptography, the science of encoding data so that only specific individuals or systems can decode it.

Computer security arose when the government needed to establish a new discipline that did not rely solely on encryption. Computers had added a new wrinkle to the age-old cryptographic solution of encoded communications. Computers could not process encrypted information, it had to be in plaintext. Information was still ones and zeroes, but these ones and zeroes had to be in a machine-readable format. If they were machine readable, they would ultimately be human readable using the same technology.

Once the industry graybeards realized they needed a broader approach to a solution than cryptography to deal with information security threats, they sought to integrate the two fields by calling them information security. In the spirit of making it sound appropriate for a highly technical agency, they also gave it its own government-approved acronym: INFOSEC. The name was advanced to aggregate and categorize government agency responsibilities, but no one had actually defined exactly what the science of INFOSEC was going to be. At the time, the best one senior government administrator could do to describe the new discipline was to depict two water pitchers — one labeled COMSEC and the other COMPUSEC — emptying their contents into a common bowl labeled INFOSEC.

I always felt this pictorial representation was lacking, so I published a paper in 1991 that has since been called the McCumber Model or McCumber's Cube. It was developed in response to the INFOSEC scientists and researchers of that era who were busy trying to develop special secure operating systems and complex formal models for verifying security requirements. Others were publishing thick standards and requirements for security that had to be revamped every time the technology changed.

Moore's Law and the inevitable evolution of technology ultimately doomed these efforts to obscurity.

My subsequent papers represented my desire to move my chosen career field back toward science and away from the black art it was apparently becoming. As computing and networking technology advanced rapidly in the early 1990s, much of computer security in the public domain was relegated to computer geeks in windowless offices seeking convoluted, and mostly undocumented, means to circumvent standard security mechanisms of the day.

Several years ago, the government started to adopt the term *information assurance* to help clarify the nebulous and idyllic connotation of security. Most commercial businesses and the media seem content with the terms *computer security* or *network security* that the government had already deemed archaic. In military circles, another term, *information superiority*, was coming into vogue.

At the dawn of the 21st century, the distinct elements of art and science are still prominent features of the information security discipline and are still at odds. Add in the issues of national security, antiterrorism, digital rights, e-mail management, malicious code, and personal privacy and it becomes easy to see we are still far from a consensus on the science of protecting digital property and privacy in a networked world. Even the infamous Internet bubble and subsequent bust of recent memory has done little to change the ever-broadening landscape for data security practitioners.

Almost every book I own on the subject of computer security is currently obsolete. In fact, most were obsolete by the time they ultimately arrived at the publisher's desk. That is because these books (many are how-to guides) were based on the authors' intimate knowledge of specific operating systems, computer implementations, or technical vulnerabilities. These aspects of computer and telecommunications systems technology are always changing and changing quite rapidly. New systems are being deployed every day. And just as soon as an operating system patch or a security add-on eliminates a technical vulnerability, two new vulnerabilities are identified in networking protocols or a new wireless device. To be an effective security practitioner, you have to work diligently to remain current.

Principles and models that are not solely technology-driven are key elements that have been missing from the field of information systems security. Security vulnerabilities in information systems are not just technology problems; so technology-only solutions are not the answer. Security practitioners need a process, a methodology that does not change with every new operating system upgrade or application. To achieve that goal, we need a process that is information-centric, not technology-centric. The McCumber Cube is a security assessment and implementation tool designed to provide a structured methodology to assess and implement safeguards in any information systems environment.

This guide builds on the original model to provide a structured methodology that does not need to be discarded or altered as technology evolves. The model was first published in 1991. It has witnessed the personal computer (PC) revolution, the advent and explosive growth of the World Wide Web, and the Internet economic bubble and bust. It has withstood the test of time.

I have used this process to assess, structure, design, and implement security in several large-scale projects. It provides system developers, security analysts, auditors, policy makers, and managers a common security lexicon and approach for addressing their security requirements. It is now available in this text and guide for your use. I trust you will be able to use it to help make our shared digital world a safer and more profitable place for all of us.

John McCumber
Washington, D.C.

INTRODUCTION

HOW TO USE THIS TEXT

To effectively assess and implement security in information technology (IT) systems, it is vital that a structured, information-centric process is followed. This text encompasses several chapters that define an information-based process and the various elements and activities that make up that methodology. This text also contains a variety of charts you can employ to help assess and implement security in your IT systems. It will be easier for you to make use of the information herein if there is an overview of the entire process. I have included it here.

Previous standards and methodologies to define security requirements have all had one fatal flaw—they were technology-based models. Technology-based models were fine as long as the technology components in question were to remain unchanged. Unfortunately, technology development and deployment has been rapid and intense. By the time security standards could even be codified, let alone find their way into commercial products, the technology had advanced beyond the environmental and technical bounds envisioned by the security researchers.

This was the case with the National Security Agency's (NSA) "Rainbow Series" of security standards for computing and telecommunications systems. The requirements set forth in the foundational document in the series, the *DOD Trusted Computer System Evaluation Criteria*,[1] were technology-based standards that were unable to adapt to rapid changes in technology capabilities. To try to keep up, various clarifications and subsequent interpretations were published to endeavor to keep the requirements current and applicable to this dynamic environment. Of course, these documents then required a significant amount of upkeep to continue to maintain their relevancy as technology brought us to the reality of a World Wide Web of interconnected computer and telecommunications systems.

To realize the promise of these criteria, the government encouraged technology vendors and information systems integrators to certify their products and systems to these standards. This process, however, became so costly and time-consuming that the systems undergoing certification testing and analysis were often technologically obsolete long before they achieved their certificate of compliance. The other challenge to this process has been the seeming inability to force government entities to purchase and deploy these certified products — even by fiat. Most agencies and departments did not want to be handcuffed to aging or out-of-date technology to meet uncertain security requirements. Ultimately, vendors became incensed when their expensive security-compliant systems collected dust as agencies and organizations rushed to purchase less expensive (and more functional) components to deploy — often from other vendors who may not have incurred the time and expense of undergoing an evaluation.

These centrally dictated security requirements were often misunderstood and misapplied because many decision makers could not map the requirements of the security criteria to their operational environment. The terminology used by the government's criteria eventually centered on the concept of trust (instead of security) with the implementation of a security policy, a security model, and a security kernel to enforce the trust to the degree required in the applicable standard. The trusted computing base concept called for the development of protection mechanisms that included the totality of the hardware, firmware, and software responsible for enforcing the security policy. However, it became difficult, if not impossible, to equate the requirements of a trusted computing base to the security requirements of networks made up of a variety of subsystems and components including commercial operating systems, network protocols, numerous applications, and a wide variety of hardware types.

Central to these issues was the problem of mixed models and unmet expectations. What most system purchasers and implementers wanted (whether they knew to ask for it or not) was a risk assessment methodology where they could make decisions on how much they needed to invest in security safeguards, what they needed to implement, and where to implement it. The Rainbow Series criteria and now the Common Criteria (from "Common Criteria for IT Security Evaluation")[2] are not risk assessment processes; they are simple security functionality evaluation criteria. Without the ability to factor in the threat, systems environment, and the value of the information in the information system, the best a set of evaluation criteria can define is a functionality assessment of the security-relevant attributes of a particular component. Perhaps those seeking to establish the Good Housekeeping Seal of Approval for information systems and security safeguards will ultimately recognize this fact and content themselves with a process that works within their model. As long as their efforts are perceived as defining what is secure from what is not, these approaches will not be successful.

An oft-cited Holy Grail of information systems security evaluation has been to build a computer system that is secure out of the box. Such an objective is laudable on its face, but with a little deeper scrutiny, it is obvious such a goal is neither practicable nor even desirable. Security is not a binary notion — something is secure or it is not. It is a matter of degree. The more important question is: Does this component or information system have adequate safeguards for my security requirements? This question can only be answered by a risk assessment. However, there is still a need for determining what security functions need to be employed. That is the purpose of this text.

Another long-sought magic pill for security practitioners was a method to provide sound return on investment (ROI) numbers for their outlays in an information systems security program. There is really no ROI calculation for information security. The investment in security is more akin to purchasing insurance: you invest in it because bad things may happen. The fact that some of these unwanted consequences do not occur does not mean your investment in security was or is unwise.

The McCumber Cube methodology is not a risk assessment process, but a security implementation and assessment methodology. This distinction is critical. A risk assessment process includes a complete operational analysis of the four major elements — threats, vulnerabilities, assets, and safeguards. The McCumber Cube methodology does not assess or account for the implementation-specific threats and assets elements of this analysis. The structured methodology included herein is designed as a process to analyze and implement security safeguards that are effective in mitigating risks inherent in system and component vulnerabilities. Only the broader risk assessment process can define the elements necessary to define what amount and type of security is most effective for a particular environment.

The McCumber Cube methodology works cooperatively with the risk assessment process by providing a deeper appraisal of the security-relevant functionality of the system and its components. It can be employed as an important precursor for a structured risk assessment or as a stand-alone process to evaluate the security functionality of systems and components. In either case, this information-centric structured methodology is what is required to accurately ascertain the appropriate security attributes for any type of information system.

The McCumber Cube methodology is exactly what is required to define and implement security requirements at all levels of abstraction. When applied against global-scale systems of interconnected networks, it can be employed and analyzed to make assessments about the security environment and relative risk. By defining the information states of transmission, storage, and processing, and following the flow of information through the system, a security practitioner has a structured way to look at the environment and the effectiveness of security controls.

When the McCumber Cube methodology is applied to organizational and local area networks (LANs), it again provides a structured approach for assessing, implementing, and enforcing security safeguards and controls. As with global systems, the first step is to define information flow. The security practitioner continues by assessing the safeguards necessary to provide confidentiality, integrity, and availability during each state phase. By seeking out safeguards from the three categories of technology, policy and procedure, and human intervention, the analyst can define the amount and extent of safeguards necessary as weighed against the value of information.

The McCumber Cube methodology is also easily adapted to making assessments of security functionality within subsystems and network components. The process is nearly identical to both the global and organizational approach, except for the scale. The process itself focuses on more minute state changes that take place within the component under review. The elements of security are also identical. Although more emphasis will logically fall on technical safeguards, the analysis is information-based to ensure consistency and universal applicability.

The value the McCumber Cube brings to the science of information systems security is the application of an information-based approach that is applicable irrespective of the specific technology implementation employed. It can be used in every information systems environment and can be adapted to every level of abstraction — from global internetworked systems to silicon chips. By following the structured methodology, analysts, security practitioners, and decision makers all have a common data set for their use in making critical risk management choices for effective security.

WHAT YOU WILL NOT SEE

This text does not include categorization by technology or safeguards such as authorization, intrusion detection systems, firewalls, access control, and others. Industry trade groups and industry analysts tend to prefer these groupings. They are adequate for them to portray the landscape of security technology vendors and are important for use in technology development. However, their use in assessing and implementing a broad-scale information systems security program is insufficient. These terms and categories also do nothing to advance the science of defining and assessing security features for subsystems and network components.

Too often, security technologies are bought and deployed simply because of the how they are marketed and sold. Labels and defined categories such as firewalls and intrusion detection systems are often used to encourage a purchase without a detailed understanding of their specific risk mitigation capabilities. When new technologies are developed, many are forced to languish indefinitely as the market evolves to create the appropriate niche environment where IT implementers and purchasers can feel comfortable buying and deploying these capabilities. Some badly needed tools and technology solutions have been unable to get funding and support to complete development and deployment activities for this same reason. It is my hope that a structured methodology like the McCumber Cube will accelerate development of advanced technologies to enforce security and privacy controls, while mitigating the risk for all of us who rely on information for our professional livelihood.

This is also not one of the many vulnerability-centric how-to security books that are available. These books are almost all based on the penetration and patch model of security that will be discussed in detail in this text. Suffice it to say that vulnerabilities are constantly evolving. As soon as one is retired, two more arise to take its place. Additionally, some organizations never get the word and even old vulnerabilities with widely published patches or remedies are exploited with surprising frequency.

This text is based on the fundamental principles of information systems security; the methodology presented here can be applied effectively even as technology changes. For a fun challenge, try applying the McCumber Cube methodology to an antiquated information system such as a rudimentary telegraph system using Morse code or the management of military command and control information between Napoleon and his generals. You will discover the model is relevant and can be effectively applied to assess the security attributes of the system under review irrespective of the actual technology used. It could be used to implement a vastly improved security environment as well.

The McCumber Cube can be applied to information systems that existed before the advent of modern computer technology and will also retain its applicability for information systems not yet envisioned. This unique capability is predicated on the fact that the model is information- (or asset-) based. This is critical for formulating a process (or set of criteria) for an assessment and implementation methodology that does not have to change with every change of technology.

ACKNOWLEDGMENTS

The concepts and processes outlined in this text are the result of years of applied research and technical experience. Numerous academic, technical, and policy initiatives have contributed to advancing the science of information security, risk management, and information valuation that support the McCumber Cube methodology. I would find it daunting, if not impossible, to include all the appropriate references and acknowledgments here. I will focus on several seminal publications to give credit and acknowledgment to these pioneering efforts.

The McCumber Cube methodology itself has evolved from the initial paper published in 1991. This paper was entitled "Information Systems Security: A Comprehensive Model"[3] and was published in the *Proceedings of the 14th National Computer Security Conference*. The paper was reprinted in the *Proceedings of the 4th Annual Canadian Computer Security Conference* and also reprinted with the author's permission in *DataPro Reports on Information Security*.

Derivative papers followed. These included "Application of the Comprehensive INFOSEC Model: Mapping the Canadian Criteria for Systems Certification"[4] and "Developing and Implementing Principle-Based Information Technology Security Policy."[5] These papers focused on *The Canadian Trusted Computer Product Evaluation Criteria* (CTCPEC), Version 3.0.[6] The CTCPEC improved the criteria process dramatically and helped launch the effort to create the Common Criteria, Version 2.0 published in 1998. I owe a great professional and personal debt to the primary author of the CTCPEC, Eugen Bacic, for his mentoring and technical insights.

The risk assessment process and threat models presented in this text were derived primarily from the research efforts of Trident Data Systems — a company of outstanding information security professionals that I had the privilege to work with many years ago. The empirical risk assessment process was first outlined in the T-RAP study, the Trident Risk Assessment Process. This study was sponsored by the U.S. Air Force and was formally published as *Risk Management Theory and Practice*.[7] I also draw on this study for the structure of the threat metrics used throughout the text.

THE TEXT

The book is divided into three primary sections. Section I is designed to provide an overview of the subject of information systems security. It contains chapters about the science and myths of information security, some historical perspectives, and a chapter on the elements of determining the value of information. The definition and underpinning theories of information security are also explored. This section concludes with an overview of theory of risk management. None of these chapters is designed to be a complete exploration of the subject matter. They were written to provide the appropriate perspective for understanding and applying the McCumber Cube methodology.

The chapters that discuss the valuation methodologies for information are an outline for developing your own information valuation techniques and processes. As yet, information is not a corporate asset that finds its ultimate expression on the balance sheet. The McCumber Cube methodology will employ the rather simplistic information valuation metric of low, medium, and high to demonstrate the application of the model. However, adapting more discrete and accurate metrics for information valuation will only improve your risk management capabilities using this approach. There is not one process for assigning value to information that has yet been developed and adopted for use among a broad range of industries and applications. Until such methods are developed and adopted, it is recommended you use those metrics that best reflect your use and valuation of information resources.

The final chapter in this section is one on the nature of risk and its application to information systems security. Risk management is ultimately the science necessary to make intelligent, operational decisions on the nature and amount of safeguards for a specific environment. All your decisions about how to assess and implement security in your environment will boil down to the concept of risk management. To be both effective and efficient, IT security must provide for the prudent remediation of risk to information assets and resources. This chapter is central to understand the trade-offs between security and functionality.

Once this stage has been set for the overriding issues of risk management, Section II will cover the McCumber Cube methodology. The first chapter in the section captures the original paper from 1991. The following chapters will outline the methodology and provide you the tools and understanding necessary to employ this information-centric process. You will learn how to accurately map information flow in modern computer and telecommunications systems by the use of simple yet comprehensive examples.

After you learn to track information as it moves through information systems, you will need to take the information states of transmission, storage, and processing and chart them against the information security attributes of confidentiality, integrity, and availability. Once these are charted, you can then assess the security policy implementation using the categorization method that accounts for technology, procedures, and human intervention. The examples primarily used are those of medium-sized organizational information systems, although guidance is given for applying the methodology to global systems.

A separate chapter has been included to show how the McCumber Cube structured methodology is applied to individual systems components and subsystems. In this chapter, the methodology is used to assess security functionality of the more basic elements of information systems. It demonstrates the universal applicability of the methodology and proposes its application for government and private industry-sponsored criteria to evaluate security functionality of computer system components such as workstations, routers, and any other type of subsystem.

Section III is included as a resource for analysts and security practitioners who would like to investigate and employ more detailed information on technical vulnerabilities and risk assessment analytics. There is a comprehensive body of knowledge already available on this subject and I have cited The MITRE Corporation's Common Vulnerabilities and Exposures (CVE®) library[8] as the most complete reference on this subject area. I have extracted information from this resource and show how it is applied both to the McCumber Cube methodology and to the more comprehensive risk assessment process.

TERMS AND DEFINITIONS

Normally, definitions are included in the reference sections of a text. However, there are many terms and phrases used in information systems security parlance that are grossly misused. It is important to use the terminology accurately because our words define our understanding of the topic. For that reason, I felt it important to include these definitions at the beginning of the book. I have included here the most recent and accurate definitions in use in the industry. These definitions are taken from the initial public draft of the National Institute for Standards and Technology's *Standards for Security Categorization of Federal Information and Information Systems:*[9]

- Authentication — security control designed to establish the validity of a transmission, message, or originator, or a means of verifying an individual's authorization to receive specific categories of information.
- Authenticity — the property of being genuine and able to be verified and be trusted. See authentication.
- Availability — ensuring timely and reliable access to and use of information.
- Confidentiality — preserving authorized restrictions on information access and disclosure, including means for protecting personal privacy and proprietary information.
- Countermeasures — synonymous with security controls and safeguards.
- Executive agency — an executive department specified in 5 U.S.C., SEC. 101; a military department specified in 5 U.S.C., SEC. 102; an independent establishment as defined in 5 U.S.C., SEC. 104(1); and

a wholly owned government corporation fully subject to the provisions of 31 U.S.C., Chapter 91.

- Federal information system — an information system used or operated by an executive agency, by a contractor of an executive agency, or by another organization on behalf of an executive agency.
- Information resources — information and related resources, such as personnel, equipment, funds, and IT.
- Information security — the protection of information and information systems from unauthorized access, use, disclosure, disruption, modification, or destruction to provide confidentiality, integrity, and availability.
- Information system — a discrete set of information resources organized for the collection, processing, maintenance, use, sharing, dissemination, or disposition of information.
- Information technology — any equipment or interconnected system or subsystem of equipment that is used in the automatic acquisition, storage, manipulation, management, movement, control, display, switching, interchange, transmission, or reception of data or information by the executive agency. For the purposes of the preceding sentence, equipment is used by an executive agency if the equipment is used by the executive agency directly or is used by a contractor under a contract with the executive agency, which (1) requires the use of such equipment or (2) requires the use, to a significant extent, of such equipment in the performance of a service or the furnishing of a product. The term *information technology* includes computers, ancillary equipment, software, firmware, and similar procedures, services (including support services), and related resources.
- Integrity — guarding against improper information modification or destruction and includes ensuring information nonrepudiation and authenticity.
- National security system — any information system (including any telecommunications system) used or operated by an agency or by a contractor of an agency or other organization on behalf of an agency, (1) the function, operation, or use of which involves intelligence activities; involves cryptologic activities related to national security; involves command and control of military forces; involves equipment that is an integral part of a weapon or weapons system; or is critical to the direct fulfillment of military or intelligence missions (excluding a system that is to be used for routine administrative and business applications, for example, payroll, finance, logistics, and personnel management applications); or (2) is protected at all times by procedures established for information that

have been specifically authorized under criteria established by an Executive order or an Act of Congress to be kept classified in the interest of national defense or foreign policy.

■ Nonrepudiation — assurance that the sender of information is provided with proof of delivery and the recipient is provided with proof of the sender's identity, so neither can later legitimately deny having processed, stored, or transmitted the information.

■ Residual risk — the portion of risk remaining after appropriate security controls have been applied.

■ Risk — a combination of (1) the likelihood that a particular vulnerability in an agency information system will be either intentionally or unintentionally exploited by a particular threat resulting in a loss of confidentiality, integrity, or availability, and (2) the potential impact or magnitude of harm that a loss of confidentiality, integrity, or availability will have on an agency's operations (including mission, functions, image, or reputation), an agency's assets, or individuals (including privacy) should the exploitation occur.

■ Risk assessment — a key component of risk management that brings together important information for agency officials with regard to the protection of information and information systems including the identification of: (1) threats and vulnerabilities, and (2) the potential impact or magnitude of harm that a loss of confidentiality, integrity, or availability would have on agency operations (including mission, functions, image, or reputation), agency assets, or individuals (including privacy) should there be a threat exploitation of information system vulnerabilities.

■ Risk management — the process of identifying, controlling, and mitigating risks. It includes risk assessment, cost benefit analysis, and the selection, implementation, testing and evaluation of security controls.

■ Safeguards — synonymous with security controls and countermeasures.

■ Security controls — the management, operational, and technical controls (safeguards or countermeasures) prescribed for an information system that, taken together, satisfy the specified security requirements and adequately protect the confidentiality, integrity, and availability of the system and its information.

■ Threat — any circumstance or event with the potential to intentionally or unintentionally exploit a specific vulnerability in an information system resulting in a loss of confidentiality, integrity, or availability.

■ Vulnerability — a flaw or weakness in the design or implementation of an information system (including the security procedures and security controls associated with the system) that could be intentionally or unintentionally exploited to adversely effect an agency's operations (including mission, functions, image, or reputation), an agency's assets, or individuals (including privacy) through a loss of confidentiality, integrity, or availability.

REFERENCES

1. Department of Defense Directive 5200.28-STD, *DOD Trusted Computer System Evaluation Criteria* (Rainbow Series Orange Book), Washington, D.C., December 1985.
2. National Institute of Standards and Technology, Common Criteria for IT Security Evaluation, 1996 [updated 1998 and 1999; available at www.csrc.nist/gov/cc/index; accessed October 2003].
3. McCumber, John, Information Systems Security: A Comprehensive Model, *Proceedings of the 14th National Computer Security Conference,* Washington, D.C., October 1991; reprinted in the *Proceedings of the 4th Annual Canadian Computer Security Conference,* Ottawa, Ontario, May 1992; reprinted in *DataPro Reports on Information Security,* Delran, NJ: McGraw-Hill, October 1992.
4. McCumber, John, Application of the Comprehensive INFOSEC Model: Mapping the Canadian Criteria for Systems Certification, *Proceedings of the 5th Annual Canadian Computer Security Conference,* Ottawa, Ontario, May 1993.
5. McCumber, John, Developing and Implementing Principle-Based Information Technology Security Policy, *Proceedings of the 7th Annual Canadian Computer Security Conference,* Ottawa, Ontario, May 1995.
6. Canadian System Security Centre Communications Security Establishment, *The Canadian Trusted Computer Product Evaluation Criteria* (CTCPEC), Version 3, Canadian government, 1993.
7. Trident Data Systems, *Risk Management Theory and Practice: An Operational and Engineering Support Process* [report], March 30, 1995.
8. The MITRE Corporation, Common Vulnerabilities and Exposures [www.cve.mitre.org, accessed October 2003].
9. National Institute of Standards and Technology, *Standards for Security Categorization of Federal Information and Information Systems,* Gaithersburg, MD: Department of Commerce, December 2003 [available as FIPS PUB 199 at www.csrc.nist.gov].

I

SECURITY CONCEPTS

1

USING MODELS

INTRODUCTION: UNDERSTANDING, SELECTING, AND APPLYING MODELS

In the late 17th century, as the story goes, Sir Isaac Newton observed an apple fall from a tree. This mundane event caused him to ponder the essential elements of gravity. He struggled to understand the forces that pulled the apple from its position high in the tree toward the ground. Sir Isaac theorized that the two objects were attracted to each other and that the larger mass, the Earth, had the greater exertion causing the apple to fall toward the ground.

This revelation allowed him to extrapolate his thesis to the planets in orbit around our sun. Once he measured the elements involved, he developed mathematical models to explain the way the planets moved around in our solar system. His mathematical models became the basis for our modern understanding of the forces of gravity. He used his models to explain how planets stayed in their orbits. His models also explained the fact that orbits were not perfectly circular, but elongated. Less than a century before he was born, the prevailing wisdom of leading scientists was that an invisible shield was at work to keep the planets in their orbits.

Newton's mathematical models were relatively simple, yet they went a long way to create the foundation for not only solar study, but also rocketry and manned space exploration. The equations he developed 300 years ago were foundational to an entire realm of scientific achievement. Today, space travel is possible through those same time-tested models he developed.

Maps represent a different type of model. A map is simply a representation of the topographical features of a defined area. I use the state maps that I keep in my car to locate and identify routes and distances. By following the map, I am assured of knowing where I am in relation to my destination. In the case of a road map, the terrain representative model I use allows me to see far beyond my natural field perspective.

Before maps, early man most likely ascended a hill or climbed a tree to reconnoiter and establish his position. By using a model such as a map, a modern traveler can have an even greater and more accurate understanding of the world around him in a convenient, portable format. Technological advances such as the global positioning system greatly enhance the value of these maps by providing pinpoint location data and automated tracking capabilities.

There are some necessary elements of planning, however, that may not be represented in the model. For example, I may wish to take roads that will minimize my chances of being trapped in rush hour traffic or caught up in roadwork. No paper road map can yet provide me that level of dynamic detail. I can interpret information on the map to give me clues, but the map only represents a static view of the road system itself. To answer these more detailed questions, I may need to seek out information from radio announcements or other travelers to add to the information I obtained from the map.

Both mathematical and representational models enhance our ability to analyze and comprehend large, complex systems like the roadways in the United States. By applying these models to solve problems such as defining which roads to take to get from Washington, D.C. to New York City, we can tackle a large area with thousands of roadways and select the optimal route for our trip.

The most important aspect of applying models to complex problems is to assess and employ the best model or sets of models for the job. You may use mathematics to calculate distances and travel time for an automobile trip, but the route map is usually the key for managing your journey. You can draw pictures of spatial orbits, but for precise knowledge of planetary behavior, space scientists apply Newton's mathematical models. The proper model will provide us the data we need to be successful.

UNDERSTANDING ASSETS

Before describing the application of various models in security, we need to understand the key attribute for any security analysis — the asset. An asset can be anyone or anything that requires protection. Undoubtedly, people are a key asset. So are facilities, equipment, inventory, and most certainly information and data.

Assets always must be considered in the broadest sense. When asked to define our personal assets, we will undoubtedly mention money we have in the bank, brokerage accounts or retirement plans, home furnishings, jewelry, and vehicles we own. However, we may not consider assets like family photographs, important records, or clothing. After a tragic fire, burglary, or other dramatic loss, we realize the list of our personal assets is long and varied.

Most people apply common, prudent safeguards to protect their family assets. We insist our banks insure checking and savings accounts against losses. Deadbolt locks, security lighting, alarm systems, and fences can be used to deter those who would steal from our homes. Car alarms, key systems, and garages can help protect expensive investments in automobiles and boats. Ultimately, many of us also carry various types of insurance to help shield us from catastrophic loss such as natural disasters, lawsuits, or the untimely death of a key wage earner.

In each of these cases, we make an evaluation of the risks we face as property owners and family members. We then make a decision about how much to invest in safeguards to offset the likelihood of undesired consequences. Much of this decision process is based on our experiences and personal tolerance for risk. In the case of insurance or large investments, we sometimes seek the advice of professionals.

Corporate assets also comprise a broad range of tangible and intangible resources. In addition to easily identified property and cash reserves, assets can include trade secrets, customer lists, and even a company's reputation. Each of these assets can have a value placed on it and security controls commensurate with its worth to the organization.

Most everyone agrees information has both strategic and tactical corporate value. However, determining how much protection these assets require is the difficult problem. Historically, sensitive information that requires protection has always been a challenge for those responsible for security. A complex variety of tangible and intangible safeguards have been employed. For example, employees given access to sensitive information resources such as product formulae, trade secrets, and company methodologies are asked to send legally binding documents regarding their access and further use of this information. Even though these controls cannot physically prevent the exploitation of the information, the threat of legal action is used as a deterrent to abuse of the company data.

Many other information safeguards have been designed and used to protect sensitive intangible assets. The ancient use of cryptographic systems attests to the demand to control and manage secrets and sensitive information. Loyalty oaths, implied threats, and access control lists have all been employed as mechanisms to control information resources.

For assets like money and property, there are comprehensive rules and guidelines for establishing current value. Information and data have been known to have value, but the advent of mass digital storage and processing has created many problems with determining and assigning appropriate value to these intangible assets. Assigning value to information resources deserves its own treatment and will be discussed in a separate chapter in this book.

LAYERED SECURITY

Layered security is a key security principle that will be addressed throughout the book. It is a fundamental element of any comprehensive security program and is absolutely vital for designing and managing security in large IT systems environments. We need to address the issue here before we turn to security models in order to define and outline the development and application of layered security. It is perhaps easiest to understand layered security in the context of protection of physical assets like money.

A good example of physical implementation of security layers to protect tangible financial assets would be a branch bank. The corporate security officer would want to review construction plans for the new branch office. He or she would make determinations about the need for site-specific safeguards such as window placement, parking, and lighting. Even relatively minor issues like the placement of ornamental shrubbery and walkways have security implications that must be evaluated.

The value and beauty of designing security into the entire development process should be obvious. At the outset, the architect, bank managers, builders, and subcontractors are all aware of the security implications of their design. Interior spaces are built with security as a centerpiece. Officers of the bank either sit out in the open or within glass rooms designed to discourage furtive or clandestine activities. Bank employees can easily scan all people in the bank. This design not only thwarts armed robbery, but also encourages the employees to conduct their activities in full view of their colleagues. The psychological implications are overt and were built into the physical structure of the bank itself.

The exterior blueprint of the bank is also a key part of the security environment. Large windows and glass doors expose the activities in the bank to passersby and ultimately to law enforcement personnel. These same windows are usually made of high-strength materials to resist intrusion. Areas below these potential access points are planted with thorn bushes and thick vegetation to make intruders think twice before deciding to enter through a window.

The parking lot and pedestrian areas also contribute to the security of the bank's assets. Curbs, cement planters, and architectural details are often used as barriers to prevent thieves and terrorists from using cars and trucks as a means for breaching the bank's security perimeter. The heavy cement bollards containing lights to illuminate the walkway at night also serve a more important security function by preventing vehicles from coming close to the building. A security practitioner can quickly see that

an ornamental stone bench has more functions than as just a mainte-
nance-free convenience for foot-sore pedestrians and customers.

Layered security principles call for security to be built into the entire
project with an eye toward increasing the risk to an intruder or potential
thief as they come closer to the assets being guarded. After assessing
security risks at the outer edges of the physical space, the physical security
analyst will work inward through concentric rings of protection. At each
stage, the security analyst will apply appropriate safeguards for each layer
of security (Figure 1.1). This process of layered security is critical to
implement structured, comprehensive security architectures in physical
space.

The example of the branch bank is instructive. As you model the
environment in relation to assets, it is easy to see how the bank implements
stronger security controls the closer one comes to the bank's most significant asset — its cash. If exterior security lighting and windows open to
public view do not discourage a burglar, then the door locks and alarm
systems designed to catch an intruder will be employed. If these systems
are either breached or initially ignored, the safe room with its armored
door and complex locking device should thwart a stealthy attempt at theft.

A knowledgeable security professional will employ these various safeguards in a way designed to minimize risk to the bank's assets. Each
safeguard is used to reduce or eliminate specific vulnerabilities. If eliminating a specific vulnerability is not cost-effective, a safeguard is usually
employed to notify someone that it has been exploited.

The bank's security officer is certainly aware that it would be foolish
to completely eliminate the chances of a break-in at a branch office. The
building would have to resemble a bomb shelter. Customers may be
turned away. In this case, special glass is used to eliminate the likelihood
of a quick entry and alarm systems are often embedded in the glass to

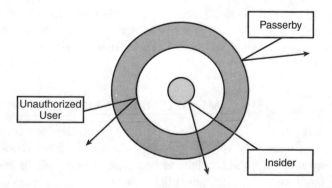

Figure 1.1 Layered Security

signal law enforcement if a determined attacker attempts to breach the external walls and windows.

As a thief gets closer to the physical assets, the security safeguards of the bank become more daunting. Even if the crook has disabled the alarm system, a great deal of time and effort will be needed to breach the vault. He will most likely be apprehended long before he ever lays his eyes on the stacks of bills that are his ultimate goal.

At the center of this layered approach are the assets that require protection. Those assets do not have to be cash. It is usually the case that safeguards are required for a multitude of assets including furnishings, computer equipment, inventory, executives, and data. Each asset may, in turn, have its unique layered security system.

Figure 1.2 presents a simple view of an office layout. In the center is a communications control center that is considered a vital asset. The security analyst has implemented layered security to provide more protection for the communications systems in this area. The communications center is positioned completely inside the facility with no connection to external walls or windows. Additional access control devices also are employed.

Another good example of layered security can be found by examining the security plans of the Secret Service. When protecting the president, they establish concentric security rings around the president. Each layer serves its function to screen out potential threats. If an outer ring is breached, another protective layer closer to the subject will be encountered. Ultimately, each bodyguard is trained to physically shield the president from any type of attack or weapon.

Layered security is a key attribute of any comprehensive security program. Neither a single safeguard nor a collection of safeguards can be guaranteed to provide perfect protection. However, layered protection allows the security analyst to orchestrate a wide variety of controls to provide the level of protection necessary for the assets requiring protection. Built-in, layered security protection is a critical element of information systems design too often ignored in the rush to build and field new functionality.

USING MODELS IN SECURITY

Security practitioners have access to a variety of models for analyzing and implementing safeguards. In the examples above, we have described both mathematical and physical models. Other types of models include behavioral, organizational, or information flow models. Depending on the security challenge at hand, different models can be employed to analyze risks

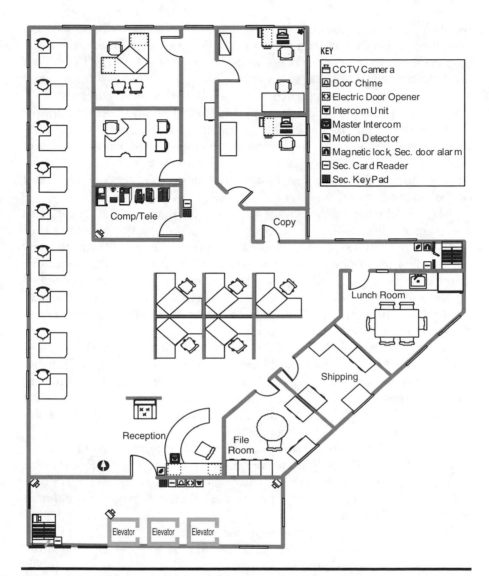

KEY

🖥 CCTV Camera
🔲 Door Chime
🔳 Electric Door Opener
📺 Intercom Unit
🔲 Master Intercom
🔳 Motion Detector
🔐 Magnetic lock, Sec. door alarm
⊟ Sec. Card Reader
🔲 Sec. KeyPad

Comp/Tele

Copy

Lunch Room

Shipping

Reception

File Room

Elevator   Elevator   Elevator

Figure 1.2   Floor Layout for Communications Control Center

and mitigate or eliminate vulnerabilities. To be effective, the selection of the appropriate model is critical.

Physical security problems, such as designing security for a building, are well suited to physical models. It is unusual to see an average homeowner modeling their physical environment to determine the adequacy of their security safeguards. A family home is a relatively simple environment and most of us are comfortable with a visual assessment and gut-instinct risk decisions. In some cases, old-fashioned experience teaches us about such decisions. Perhaps you know someone who has had a shovel or power drill stolen from an outbuilding or shed. This knowledge may encourage you to purchase and use a simple padlock device to limit the risk to your garden tools.

However, anecdotal evidence is not adequate for more complex physical security problems. There is a need for selecting and applying appropriate models. Perhaps the easiest to understand and apply are physical models. Physical security professionals who wish to develop a security plan for a new building will inevitably seek out a physical model to enhance their efforts. The first model they most often choose is a layout of the building itself.

The security analyst will want to assess all the potential threats and use diagrams and blueprints to determine the best way to provide protection to the building and the assets it contains. They will want to view the building in relation to its environment. Developing a comprehensive physical security plan will require the analyst to make recommendations on the site and its environs. A topographical map of the area will help the analyst assess the vulnerabilities of the building site and will dictate the location of fences, gates, and roads.

Security professionals are often called on to make an assessment of someone's trustworthiness. Like physical security problems, these personnel security requirements also dictate the use of models. The ability to assess security requirements for people is no doubt a complex and daunting task. By applying a model, the analyst can more easily make a determination on the relevant attributes.

For personnel security problems, behavioral and functional models are most appropriate. For security purposes, people are a critical element that represents both a safeguard and a major threat. In other words, people are either part of the problem or part of the solution. Separating the threats from the safeguards is critical.

The vetting process demands a comprehensive view of a person's duties as well as the desirable traits and characteristics required. Conversely, a list of undesirable traits or background experiences is generally applied. The holistic elements of a person's experiences and characteristics must then be weighed against the value of the assets they are charged to protect.

Personnel security requirements often dictate periodic reevaluation of an employee's experiences and job requirements. The appropriate behavioral models are then reapplied to account for changes in either the individual or the assets they access or protect. Changes in either the affected assets or the person's characteristics will then require a decision from the vetting authority.

Polygraph testing is actually a simple personnel security model. For all the sensitive technology behind the testing device, it is simply a scientific approach for identifying deceitful communication. The charts obtained from a polygraph test are then used to encourage truthfulness from the person in question. It is a one-dimensional model for one specific, albeit important, aspect of a person's character.

SECURITY MODELS FOR INFORMATION SYSTEMS

Perhaps the most difficult and abstract security challenge is determining how to apply various models to security problems in IT systems. Computers and telecommunications systems do not lend themselves easily to modeling. In fact, numerous security models have been proposed, published, and debated since computers were first introduced. Some are mathematically based, but others are based on the physical components of the system.

It is important to point out the distinction between intracomputer security modeling and intercomputer security modeling. The earliest mathematical and functional models for computer security were developed for intracomputer security. They were designed with the computer system as a disconnected processing device. Data was often brought to the system in hard copy and input using data entry devices like direct-connect keyboards and card readers. After processing, the data was returned to hard copy for distribution and use.

For isolated computer systems, intracomputer security models were sufficient for protecting the confidentiality and integrity of the data undergoing the processing function. Additionally, physical security controls were applied to ensure proper control of the inbound and outbound data, as well as physical protection of the computer equipment. For the first two decades of computer technology, computer security meant physical protection of the isolated computer systems themselves. Information or data security was assigned to protecting the printed output using ages-old techniques for controlling the printed word.

Intercomputer security models became necessary soon after the development of the first primitive computer networks. Initially, intracomputer security policies were developed as extensions to the physical security model. Each computer system was to have its own protections in place and a dedicated circuit connecting these two machines was established as a pipe to share data. Depending on the value of the information being transmitted, encryption could be employed to frustrate those who would seek to intercept the data.

These early intracomputer security models could easily be depicted with physical representation of the connected entities as in Figure 1.3. This boundary protection model is still in widespread use today. The key

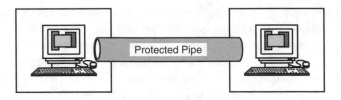

Figure 1.3 Boundary Security Model

to boundary protection models is the definition of what constitutes a boundary. The security boundary can be defined as a single system, a LAN, data systems within an organization, or even an international corporatewide environment. Protection mechanisms at the boundaries are then supposed to enforce security policy by creating separation between those inside the boundary and those outside. Certain security policies can then be enforced by restricting access to IT resources.

As internetworking rapidly advanced, these security models soon proved inadequate. Even robust mathematical models for intercomputer protection were difficult to extend to resources outside the control of the host system. Additionally, the amount and variety of data being exchanged increased exponentially as well. One-dimensional models that simply lumped data into one category that could be shuttled to and fro on protected circuits were no longer adequate. The challenge became one of applying protection models to relationships between users and the data.

Computer security researchers have attacked this problem by endeavoring to abstract the security problem into mediating the relationship between users and data elements. The approach has several advantages over one-dimensional and boundary protection models. The key value is the model's ability to establish security parameters without regard to the limitations of specific technology platforms.

Primarily, the abstraction process can be defined based on attributes of the user similar to functional personnel security models outlined previously. These user attributes are then mapped against discreet data elements. The relationship between the two can then be modeled to determine security requirements. Such models gave rise to mathematical proofs and provable security models.

The elements of abstract models consist of descriptive nomenclature, general mechanisms, and specific solutions. Each element needs to be defined. The goal for an adequate abstract model is a comprehensive list or definition of all the entities to be analyzed.

A descriptive nomenclature defines each entity in the model. For information systems, this is often broken down into two simple categories — subjects and objects. Subjects are active entities. They can perform actions. Examples of subjects include computer users (people) or other computer programs. They are defined by the ability to effect change.

Objects are passive entities in an information system. Examples include data, files, or other entities within the system that are acted on by subjects. They are defined by their inability to effect change. Whether an entity is a subject or an object is delimited within the context of a given role at a given time. Namely, if an entity is active, it is considered a subject. If an entity is passive, it is considered an object.

General mechanisms are processes that define the relationship between subjects and objects. In an information system, there are two simple categories assigned to the general mechanisms — observation and alteration. Observation is defined as the ability to extract (or perceive) data. Alteration is defined as the ability to insert (or modify) data.

The security functionality is defined by the specific solution or set of rules that are codified to establish the allowable relationships between subjects and objects in a system. These relationships also can be called security policies. In the modeling sense, security policies do not conform to our traditional notion of security policy. They simply express the allowable relationships between the subjects and objects within the modeling environment.

An early example of this approach at modeling information systems security is the Bell–LaPadula Model. David Bell and Len LaPadula developed an abstract security model that defined users as subjects and data as objects. Subjects could also be other computer programs or any active component in the systems environment. Objects were the passive elements of the system and were most commonly understood as the data to be protected.

The Bell–LaPadula Model then established four access modes based the two categories of observation and alteration. The effect of the access was described as either extracting information or inserting information. Extracting data was called *observe* and inserting was defined as *alter*. The four access modes are thus:

1. C access — no observe, no alter
2. A access — alter, no observe
3. R access — observe, no alter
4. W access — observe, alter

Security elements could be defined as enforcing the states of information within the system. To have a provable security model using this approach, four components defining the relationship between the subjects and object are required. To make a security decision using the Bell–LaPadula Model, it is necessary to have key pieces of information, known as components. The components are:

1. Current access set:
   a. Describes a current access by a subject to an object
   b. Represented by the triple {subject, object, access-attribute}
2. Structure imposed on the objects:
   a. Describes the objects in relationship to hierarchies
   b. Limits structural relationships between objects
3. Access matrix:
   a. Describes the access attributes that are allowed between subjects and objects
   b. Represented as a two-dimensional matrix
4. Level function:
   a. Composed of three elements:
      i. Maximum security level of a subject
      ii. Security level of the object
      iii. Current security level of the subject
   b. Security level of the subject must dominate the security level of the object
   c. Security level represented by the pair {classification, set of categories}

These four components represent the elements used by the model to make a security decision. In the Bell–LaPadula model, a reference monitor handles these security decisions. This security enforcement mechanism is sometimes called the security kernel or trusted computing base. If these components could be encoded in the system and a protected reference monitor developed, then a mathematically provable security model can be theoretically achieved.

Also included in the Bell–LaPadula model was an understanding of system inputs and outputs. System inputs were considered requests and outputs from the processing function were considered decisions. If a subject attempted any activity with an object, this was a request to be mediated by the security kernel. The outcome of the enforcement of the security functionality and the resultant effect on the data was the decision. The abstract model thus became a sequential process of defining the state, evaluating the request, and making a decision that in turn produced a new state.

There was one significant problem with implementing the Bell–LaPadula model, namely a computer system had to be developed from scratch to provide this level of functionality. The model was ultimately employed in the MULTICS operating system. MULTICS was a mainframe operating system begun in 1965 and used until 2000. However, it was dramatically eclipsed by microcomputers long before it was ready for deployment. The time required to design, analyze, and build this monolithic secure computer system doomed its ultimate acceptance and use. The world had moved on to modular IT systems comprising smaller, more distributed computers connected to routers and switches for quick and easy communication of data.

The main problem with a comprehensive abstract modeling environment like Bell–LaPadula is that once these abstract relationships are defined within the modeling environment, it is extremely difficult to map these requirements back into functional IT systems. An abstract model can be provable and secure, but building one from existing technology components on this premise can be impractical if not impossible.

The Rainbow Series was an attempt to implement the key mechanisms of the Bell–LaPadula model in a collection of requirements (criteria) that would guide the development and evaluation of provably secure systems. The first book to emerge in the series was the *DOD Trusted Computer System Evaluation Criteria*,[1] known as the Orange Book for the color of its cover. While the criteria were under development, they were constantly adjusted in an effort to make them germane in a world of interconnected computer systems. The result was the requirement to develop interpretations of the criteria (model) that could accommodate changes in technology.

These interpretations and explanations were published — each with a unique color cover — to ultimately comprise nearly three shelf-feet of text to describe, interpret, and expound on this model. This colorful collection of books was ultimately relegated to an academic exercise as implementation proved costly and ineffective. Several companies actually completed certification, but navigating the government-sponsored process took years and cost millions of dollars. In the end, the government was unable to enforce the requirement for agencies to purchase the certified products.

Computer security researchers then set off to find a way to model security in a way that was more aligned with the sea of changes in the industry. Subsequent efforts to streamline the criteria have resulted in the Common Criteria. These new criteria have fared slightly better than their predecessors. However, the research and development necessary to interpret and apply the criteria are still overly complex and the security value of Common Criteria compliance remains undocumented.

SHORTCOMINGS OF MODELS IN SECURITY

All models have shortcomings. Road maps are unable to inform a driver of traffic jams and recent construction projects. Blueprints for corporate buildings lack topographical perspective. Small-scale mockups of ships and aircraft cannot provide the scale and perspective for human interaction or ergonomic engineering.

Perhaps the most often cited security objective for IT systems is to have security right out of the box. Government policymakers and even vendors have touted this goal as the Holy Grail of IT security for many years. Quite simply, this is impossible. Not only is it impossible to achieve, the concept itself is foolish. Those who use this phrase really mean they want to have a robust set of security features available in both hardware and software. These controls and safeguards can then be implemented (or turned on) to meet the user's security requirements.

Out-of-the-box security is the assumption that a computer component or, ideally, an entire IT system can automatically configure itself to provide the appropriate level of security for a specified environment. Although there is some theoretical justification for this lofty goal, such a system is impractical if not impossible to design and build. Security in IT systems is a careful balance of safeguards and controls employed to provide the amount of protection necessary for a wide variety of assets and a broad range of environments. There is no foreseeable system that could provide that balance.

We must recognize that all models have their shortcomings and out of the box security is a worthy, yet unrealistic goal. The choice of a security model often predetermines the effectiveness of the security program. An overreliance on a model with significant drawbacks can doom the most technically superior solution.

One such approach is the boundary protection security framework that defines one or more zones designed to separate insiders from outsiders. In its simplest implementation, a boundary protection system would be established to separate a company's internal resources from unlimited access by anyone on the Internet. The most direct and effective solution would be to disallow any connections outside the organization. This physical separation approach is often adopted when security requirements cannot be enforced at the points of connection to outside systems.

If an organization adopts a simple boundary protection security framework, it must necessarily rely on a network topology map as its model (Figure 1.4). Most computer people are familiar with the basic system topology maps that indicate the location and relationships between hardware components in an information processing system. IT administrators and security analysts often use these representational models to determine the location of physical IT assets and the flow of data throughout the organization.

The network topology diagram can be invaluable for many purposes including resource allocation, configuration management, and wiring. The most difficult challenge is keeping such a model current. Most organizations have a complex topology that changes almost daily. How would

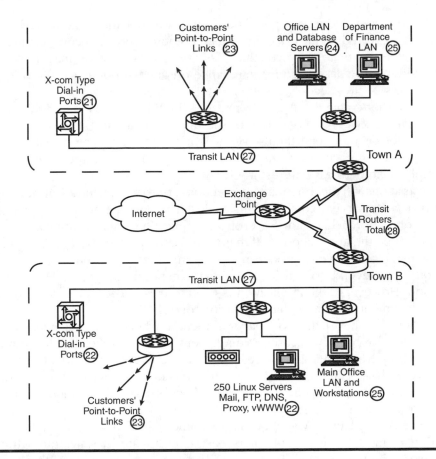

Figure 1.4 Network Topology Diagram

you like to have a road map in your car that does not represent the latest location of roads and intersections?

The network topology map can be useful for a security analyst, but it is vital for those who place undue emphasis on the boundary protection security model. If the entire focus of an information systems security program is simply separating insiders from outsiders, the network topology map becomes the key model. This security approach allocates resources by their relationship to the identified boundary.

The boundary model quickly becomes untenable as security requirements become more refined and functional requirements expand. The logical extension of the boundary security model is to identify ever more zones that must have their boundaries protected. Obviously, there will be overlapping zones and needs to implement security access controls at each boundary. No matter how complex these zones become, the policy implementation is simple: separate insiders from outsiders.

Overlapping boundary protection zones are not the same as layered security. Layered security is defined as the entire array of security controls that interoperate to protect critical assets. Zones may or may not be layered, but the distinction is the reliance on defined boundary and solely an access control security solution.

The shortcomings of this approach should be obvious. Boundary protection models do not allow for the implementation of robust security rules, nor do they lend themselves to easy modification or extensibility. By firewalling each zone, the security analyst tries to define security as simply a large access control problem.

Variations of the boundary protection approach include application and database access control technologies. They are simply extensions of the zone approach. In the case of an application-level security zone, it may not be the application itself that requires the protection. For example, a general office word processing program does not, in itself, require protection beyond normal license management and source code modification. However, if the application is used to create a sensitive document, the document itself must have security controls.

Many aspects of the boundary protection scheme are still necessary, however, for prudent security management. Modern systems still require protection from unlimited access and the concept of insiders versus outsiders has been a security staple for millennia. However, reliance on the network topology map as a model for security implementation is severely limited.

The Bell–LaPadula Model quickly becomes too complex for implementation in modern IT systems. It is based on a state-by-state transaction analysis. Each state must be verified and the steps to achieve the next state must be centrally enforced by the security kernel. Information that travels outside the realm of the kernel must necessarily leave the security policy enforcement arena and control over the information asset must be relinquished.

Models like the Orange Book have their limitations as well. Although the criteria were designed to enforce the security kernel concept, they were based on monolithic computer systems with centralized processing functions. In other words, the criteria were nearly impossible to implement for internetworked systems where data storage and processing takes place at numerous locations in the information systems infrastructure.

The attempt to interpret the criteria for each IT device was also doomed simply because the model was not consistent across disparate components within a network. It was impossible to determine the security assurance obtained when interconnecting these components that each had a different function.

The current Common Criteria will soon suffer the same fate. Although they represent a significant improvement over the Rainbow Series, they still create a technology-dependent model that does not map across other components in a networked information system. For each device or component seeking a security rating, the vendor or system user must provide a protection profile — a statement of the security requirements or needs for the component under review.

According to the criteria, the protection profile needs to be independent of any specific implementation. The stated goal is to establish the ability of the component to meet specific security objectives. The profile is meant to be reusable and to establish a common set of security objectives for the product or application itself that are considered effective in meeting requirements for functionality as well as security assurance.

There is a glaring omission in this approach that guarantees its ultimate failure: the data or information that is to be handled by the component under analysis. At best, such an approach can outline specific security functionality and its ability to implement certain controls. It cannot, in any way, define what is security and what is not. As a minimum, systems security analysts cannot describe the security assurances they obtain when connecting boxes that have been evaluated against different protection profiles. To effectively implement and assess security architecture for an IT system, you must consider security in context.

SECURITY IN CONTEXT

Placing value in context is a critical component of understanding security in IT systems. For many years, security analysts have endeavored to define how secure a system is (or could be) by trying to assess the relative strength of its security features. For example, cryptographers mathematically compute the amount of time and computing power it would require to calculate an encryption key — often a very large prime number. In this case, the key length is the primary factor used to establish this estimate. The longer the key length, the more time and computing power needed to determine the key and decrypt the message.

In this example, it is important to note that the determining issue of security is simply the binary nature of whether or not someone can read the message. To fully understand the value of a security feature such as varying cryptographic key lengths, it is still necessary to understand the perceived value of the information being protected. Touting the benefits of large key lengths to an IT manager charged with protecting logistics communications between warehouses may not be worthwhile. Yet, a federal agency sending sensitive intelligence information around the globe will undoubtedly consider these factors in great detail. That is what understanding security in context means.

Assessing the relative strength of security features in information systems without putting them in an operational context is a difficult and often fruitless pursuit. Government and industry standards bodies are still trying to apply value to security features without putting them into the context of their operational application. In the physical security sense, we can use the example of a bodyguard. A security expert can accurately claim that use of a trained bodyguard provides strong personal security. However, a personal bodyguard would be a wasteful and unmanageable expense for me and yet be completely inadequate protection for the president of the United States.

Understanding security requires us to assign value to the resources we are attempting to protect and to assess safeguards in the context of their application. It is often difficult to precisely determine the value of information, especially in complex, enterprisewide systems. But it is absolutely impossible to make credible assessments of security without an understanding of the value of the information and how it will be transmitted, stored, and processed.

The reason technology companies will never be able to provide a secure system out of the box is not because of faulty products. They can, at best, provide a robust set of security features that can be enabled and monitored by security professionals to provide the appropriate amount of security depending on the value of the information and its application. Security defined outside this context is not security; it is simply a discussion of security features.

Security in context means that it is necessary to understand how much protection is necessary depending on the value of the asset. Equally important is an assessment of the threat environment. One can have a comprehensive analysis of all the security mechanisms in a particular component or set of components, yet without an assessment of all the elements of risk, you are not truly discussing security, but security features.

What does it mean to discuss security in context? The first thing required is an accurate definition of security. The primary definition of security according to the dictionary is freedom from risk or danger. A secondary definition is how you feel about your safety. Because we know there is no complete freedom from risk, we can safely extrapolate that no IT system is free from risk either. Because we are never fully free of risk, any evaluation of security must be based on a risk management process. The risk management process is composed of four elements — threat, vulnerability, asset, and safeguard. Assets have already been defined earlier in the chapter, so we should now consider the other aspects of the risk equation.

Threats are those dangers that arise as a result of either the environment or human intervention. Environmental threats to information systems include heat, water, or other external conditions that can disrupt information processes. Environmental threats can prevent data from being processed or transmitted or can be responsible for causing other system faults.

Human threat can come in the form of hostile intruders or even a clumsy system administrator who inadvertently spills the contents of a soft drink container into a server. The classic understanding of a human threat as solely a hostile system attacker is inadequate. Many recent studies have shown that organizational insiders generate a majority of system exploits. Without a comprehensive perspective on all potential human threats, an analysis of risk is necessarily incomplete.

Vulnerabilities are inherent weaknesses in the system, implementation, or process that may be exploited. When evaluating vulnerabilities in information systems, it is critical to cite specific technical vulnerabilities. The statement, "Someone could break into the computer system" is not adequate. A proper definition of a vulnerability would read: Sendmail before 8.12.1, without the RestrictQueueRun option enabled, allows local users to obtain potentially sensitive information about the mail queue by setting debugging flags to enable debug mode. This type of detailed, specific vulnerability description is required for an accurate assessment of the risks in an IT system. Technical vulnerabilities are conveniently catalogued at www.cve.mitre.org.

Safeguards are countermeasures that help to protect, mitigate, or reduce risk or a negative impact on an organization's information assets. Safeguards can be technical, procedural, or even personnel-enforced. Safeguards can mitigate risks by influencing threats, vulnerabilities, or even assets or any combination of the three.

Most analysts are familiar with technical safeguards that are designed to eliminate vulnerabilities in operating systems, protocols, or applications. These include products like firewalls. However, safeguards can include policies such as required minimum password lengths and administrative monitoring. Moving data assets also can be used as a safeguard, such as having sensitive information moved on to a system not connected to the Internet.

Security must be considered in the context of the data requiring protection and its environment. Endeavoring to seek out any potential technical vulnerability and completely eliminate it is a tedious, time-consuming, and ultimately fruitless process. It is still important to acknowledge the complete range of technical vulnerabilities in the system requiring protection. However, security is not an either-or proposition, it is a matter of degree. Security in context means you apply the proper (and most cost-effective) security where and when it is required.

Understanding the use and application of security models is critical to provide effective and efficient protection of information assets. Just as important is an understanding of the inherent weaknesses and shortcomings of each model. Applying the model best suited for the problem can make complex, ill-defined problems like information systems security much easier to tackle.

REFERENCE

1. Department of Defense Directive 5200.28-STD, *DOD Trusted Computer System Evaluation Criteria* (Orange Book), Washington, D.C., December 1985.

2

DEFINING INFORMATION SECURITY

CONFIDENTIALITY, INTEGRITY, AND AVAILABILITY

One of the most critical aspects of any model development is a detailed understanding of the nature of your subject. Just as a good map contains the detailed representation of the routes and landscape features, any security model must use an appropriate definition of the security environment. For IT and information systems security, a structured decomposition of both security and information is required. This chapter will define the elements of security and how they are applied.

Earlier in the book, we defined the relevance of security in context. We also used that discussion to outline the principal definitions of security. The primary definition of security according to the dictionary is freedom from risk or danger. A secondary definition is how you feel about your safety. So when we speak of security, we are speaking of an ideal state. It is no wonder people quickly become confused when discussing security, even in its IT definition. Our perceptions of what constitutes security may be different from those with whom we communicate.

There is an old story in military circles that highlights the problem of understanding and applying the right definition of security. As the tale goes, an admiral is assigned to a joint command in charge of members of all the military branches. He asks his aide-de-camp, a young Air Force officer, what it would mean to each member of the staff if he were to command, "Secure that building." The young staff officer replies, "Sir, if you tell someone from the Navy to secure that building, he would close all the doors and windows, extinguish the lights, lock the doors, then retire for the evening. If you asked someone from the Army to secure that building, he would station machine gun nests and guards around the building and maintain his vigil until given further orders. If you asked a Marine to secure that building, he would attack the building, destroy it, and guard the rubble with his life."

"I think I am beginning to understand," mused the admiral. "But you are in the U.S. Air Force. What would you do if I asked you to secure that building?" he asked.

"That's an easy one, sir," the young officer quips, "I would get you a three-year convertible lease with an option to buy."

This story never fails to get a laugh among military personnel, but it succinctly points out the problem with defining security. The words may be the same, but our mental image of what security means to us may not be shared with everyone else.

Similar problems exist for any concept that encompasses such a broad spectrum of meaning. Take, for example, love. You may love your spouse, your dog, or your car. You may love all three. If you are like me, you also love egg custard. Although the word love is accurately used in each instance, the specific elements that comprise your love are different for each subject in question. You evince love for your spouse though your caring and attention, as well as practical support for his or her needs. You express love for your dog by your daily care and also your attention. Love for inanimate objects like your car may take on more pragmatic demands such as mechanical maintenance and activities to improve its physical appearance. In these cases, the way you show love may be completely different, although the expansive concept of love is accurately applied to each object.

If security is freedom from risk or danger, the perception of security exists only when we experience freedom from risk or danger. This inexact definition is easy to misinterpret and misapply, especially in the context of security for information assets. We can best see how the two definitions work in tandem by looking at the case of former football coach John Madden.

I do not know anyone who claims John Madden is a dummy. He had a stellar career as coach of the Oakland Raiders and he is an entertaining announcer for my favorite fall sport. However, for years he has refused to fly, citing the risks of air travel, specifically an airplane crash. He opts instead to travel to his nationwide appointments in a luxuriously appointed motor coach.

Objectively, the mathematical odds of Madden being killed in an accident with his motor home are far greater than the risk of dying in an airplane crash. It is also obvious that he is far more comfortable traveling by coach than by air. In fact, he runs his professional life around it. For personal reasons, Madden applies the subjective definition of security to his travel requirements. He feels better about his safety when he is on the road than in the faster, safer, and more convenient aircraft.

In this example, the perception of safety trumps the empirical evidence to the contrary. Madden's security model is his own gut instinct of which mode of transportation makes him feel secure. Although the figures argue otherwise, his perception of his security is that an airplane crash is so unfathomable a consequence that he prefers the statistically more dangerous cross-country drive. He certainly mitigates his risks by hiring a well-trained driver, but the time and convenience factors still make the case for air travel.

Our perception of security plays a critical role in our ability to define and apply security requirements. Like John Madden, many people may make this assessment on a gut level or based on perception as opposed to empirical analysis. This distinction is easy to identify when seeing television advertisements for security products and services like home alarm systems. These systems usually comprise both a product (the alarm system itself) and a service (monitoring of the alarm by a security monitoring center).

In a recent advertising campaign, a security alarm service attempted to define an instinctive (or perception) model of security using three different scenarios. First they set the stage from the perspective of a homeowner, a traveling family man with a wife and children. Then they presented you with the perspective of the daughter of an elderly parent living alone; then finally of a single person away on vacation sitting in a canoe.

Each of the three segments shows the person explaining the security value that a home alarm means to them personally. The traveling family man wants to know his family is safe. The daughter with the elderly parent wants the assurance that responsive help is available for her father. The man in the canoe wants to just relax knowing his house is protected from flooding and burglary. Each person expresses what security means to him or her on a strictly personal level. The company paying for the advertisement, in partnership with the advertising firm, did not want to use the limited time available to explain how the system works or even mention the price.

Those aspects would certainly be considered important, but the company paying for the advertising was not trying to compete on cost. Comparatively, if you think of automobile advertising, it is almost always centered on cost. Manufacturers and dealers tout their financing rates, discounts, and low monthly payments, especially for moderately priced vehicles aimed at the average American. However, home security monitoring services are not about cost or technical superiority; they are all about peace of mind. The value case for security, in this instance, is not aimed at an empirical analysis of the likelihood of a house break-in, flood, or family emergency. The value is the peace of mind they provide their customers.

Even when people demand security, they themselves may not understand exactly what elements they require. That is the role of the security analyst. Nothing is more problematic than someone demanding that a building, a document, or an information system be secure. To accurately employ a security model, the nature and degree of the security requirements must be spelled out in unambiguous terms.

These definitional distinctions are far more important to security practitioners than mere academic exercises. The heart of developing and implementing effective security is understanding and codifying precise security policies than can be translated into a complete suite of safeguards encompassing technology, policy, and human factors. A comprehensive methodology that accounts for each of these factors goes a long way in providing a framework to both design and communicate security concepts to everyone in an organization.

In the specific case of IT, analytical accuracy requires that the security definitions be applied to the information, not the technology. The section on security models depicts the problems that result when your security model is focused on the technology and not the information assets themselves. Technology can be considered secure only as far as the physical instantiation of the technology itself is concerned. In other words, if I claim a router is secure, the concept of security can only be applied to the physical piece of hardware itself. If you refer solely to the software within the unit, it is even more difficult to make an assertion about its security, because the software itself is an information asset and subject to threats faced by all digital resources. It is perfectly acceptable to discuss the security features or capabilities of the router as it applies to the data that transits the router, but the concept of a secure router is only meaningful when physical protection of the equipment is the desired security outcome.

INFORMATION ATTRIBUTES

Applying an adequate definition for security of information resources is more complex than the McCumber Cube would suggest. Although the three key elements — confidentiality, integrity, and availability — provide a complete framework for describing or modeling information security, there are certain attributes to information, data, and digital media that require closer inspection. The most significant is the nature of how we ascribe value to information.

When defining the amount of security necessary for a given IT environment, the key is determining the value the information, data, or digital resources have for the organization or people who require security. Information has value and the metrics of that value is the subject of

Chapter 3. However, it is crucial to this analysis to identify some unique characteristics of information as an asset.

Any security model must take into account the value of the assets that require protection. In our household, we only have a two-car garage, but three cars. An outdoor parking pad accommodates the car that must be left out of the garage. Although time of arrival and parental status influence which car gets left outside, the primary factor is the objective value of the vehicle itself. The least valuable vehicle is left outside where it is more vulnerable to theft and weather damage.

Because our model is based on the attributes of the information itself and not the specific technology used to transmit, store, and process that information, models to define the value of the asset must be applied specifically to the information resources. Logically, information moves throughout these IT systems. To make an accurate assessment of the value of information, it will be necessary to perform an analysis of the information in a specific state of transmission, storage, or processing.

When discussing the value attributes of information, it is important to make another distinction and to do so, we must again use definitions to describe exactly what we mean. The first word is *data*. For our use, we must apply the computer science definition: Data is numerical or other information represented in a form suitable for processing by computer. The key concept in this definition is the part about data's form — a form suitable for processing by a computer. By applying this definition, we see that data in many cases has actually little value to us. It can be perceived as a stream of bits transiting a network connection or a large collection of ones and zeroes in a database.

The distinction between raw data and information is critical to applying security attributes. Information is data in context. A close synonym used in some definitions would be knowledge. An example of this key difference could be described by this example of data: 13, 35, 48. These numbers certainly represent data, but do they represent information?

Suppose you found those same three numbers, or data set, written on a small note that you find taped to the underside of a telephone near a safe containing $50,000 in cash. You now have converted data into information and have even been able to help quantify the value of that information. If, in fact, you have discovered the safe's combination, the protection accorded the information while it was attached to the underside of a nearby object was insufficient. Especially if you were prone to apply this knowledge to acquire the assets.

Security policies and procedures should be applied only to information and not to data *per se*. As presented earlier, security expressed outside the context of valuation is not security, but simply an outline of security features or functions. To accurately and cost-effectively apply security to IT systems, security must be defined according to the value of the information as it passes through its transmission, storage, and processing phases.

INTRINSIC VERSUS IMPUTED VALUE

Evaluating asset value for information can be a difficult task. Just as the concept of security encompasses both objective empirical risk avoidance as well as perception, information assets have two significant defining traits. Information has both intrinsic and imputed value.

Intrinsic value refers specifically to the external nature or worth of the information itself. The best way to describe the difference between intrinsic and imputed value is to apply the concept to other assets. Take cash as an example, the bills in your wallet have both intrinsic and imputed value. The intrinsic value of your money is its worth as green slips of paper. You can use them to write notes on or perhaps consider using them as fuel for a small fire. However, the real value of the currency, as you know, is the ability to trade them for goods and services equal to the worth placed on them as a convenient and portable form of trade. This is the imputed value.

The imputed value of currency is the value placed in it by our government as a vehicle for trade and commerce. The different denominations represent varying amounts of value all tied to the base unit of one dollar. The value certainly changes over time, but the imputed value of the currency remains tied to what has become an international standard.

Let us refer back to our example of the three two-digit numbers of our safe combination. The intrinsic value of the three numbers is quite small, but their imputed value as information could be worth up to $50,000 depending on the risks in obtaining and keeping the cash in the safe. To fully express the value of information, it is critical to assess both its intrinsic and imputed values.

All assets have intrinsic as well as imputed values and often these values are wildly disparate. I have an old guitar that was owned and played by my deceased father. Its intrinsic value as a musical instrument is quite small, because it needs repairs to be even marginally playable. However, its value to me as a memento is significantly greater.

You may drive an old car with high mileage. Perhaps it is over ten years old. Its trade-in or retail sale value according to industry sources may be miniscule. However, you may have owned the vehicle since it was new and have taken good care of it. Likely, it has become reliable transportation, and the fact you own it free and clear is also an important aspect of ownership. You know it would be nearly impossible to locate another vehicle as reliable for even twice the book value of this car. In this case, the imputed value and intrinsic value are not the same.

With most assets, however, it is difficult, if not impossible, to separate the intrinsic and imputed values. Again, using currency as an example, to acquire the imputed value of a five-dollar bill, I would have to possess the bill. If I exchange the five-dollar bill for two dollars of goods or services, I would surrender the five dollars and receive currency in the amount of three dollars in return. It is not possible for someone to deduct two dollars of value from the five-dollar note and establish a new imputed value of three dollars. The five-dollar bill is a form of token that contains both intrinsic and imputed values that are closely intertwined.

Most assets have their intrinsic and imputed values tightly conjoined. A jewelry company that wishes to lease retail space in an upscale suburban shopping mall will most likely pay more for that space than the same amount of space in a rural strip mall. The difference is not the intrinsic value of the retail space, but the imputed value of the retail location. The same holds true for residential real estate. A home located in a convenient, highly desirable residential area will cost more than an identical home away from major roads or near a dirty industrial plant. This is an example of intrinsic and imputed values being different. The fact that you would have to pay tens of thousands of dollars to physically move the house from its less desirable location to a better one limits your ability to manipulate the intrinsic and imputed values of homes based on their location.

If we return to our example of currency, we can feature a relatively recent technology that allows us to manipulate the imputed value of a currency token. A debit card makes such transactions possible. If the debit card is has five dollars of value and I purchase two dollars of goods or services, a vendor with the appropriate technology can automatically reestablish a new value of three dollars for the debit card. This feature — the ability to change the imputed value — makes these payment options desirable for many commercial transactions. The debit card is an example of how modern technology can provide more flexibility in ascribing and defining imputed value in financial transactions.

The importance of intrinsic versus imputed value in assessing information assets cannot be overemphasized. Too often, organizations make security decisions without an explicit understanding of the imputed value of the information assets. This subject is so critical to making cost-effective decisions that it will be treated to its own section in the upcoming Chapter 3. However, the concept must be introduced here to provide background for understanding the security-relevant attributes of information.

In the case of currency, counterfeiters try to create imputed value out of tokens that have only intrinsic value. The currency tokens they produce are only worth the paper and artwork they contain. However, by trying to pass their work off as legal tender, they are attempting to create imputed value they can exchange for valuable goods and services.

For legitimate currency, it is technically impossible to separate intrinsic and imputed value. If I want to realize the value of a five-dollar bill, I must obtain physical possession of a legal five-dollar bill. In the case of information assets, simply gaining access to sensitive or valuable information may be all that is necessary to shift part or all of its imputed value from its legitimate owner to someone else.

An important attribute of information value is the understanding that it is relatively easy to manipulate its imputed value. An example here will be instructive. Let us again return to the poorly concealed combination to the safe containing $50,000. Perhaps the untrustworthy person who located this combination waited to open the safe at a less suspicious time. If I am the owner of the safe and realize the implications of leaving the combination so easily exposed, I could change the combination while leaving the note under the telephone intact. When the potential thief comes to open the safe, they will find the combination changed and their insider knowledge worthless.

Information assets often are easily exploited in the same manner. If your company produces breaded chicken using a secret recipe containing eleven herbs and spices, part of the economic value of your company is contained in the recipe. If that exact recipe is surreptitiously copied, either through electronic or physical means, you could be empowering a potential competitor who will possibly take away a significant portion of your business. Although you still have your secret recipe, your business growth is in jeopardy because someone has extracted some of the imputed value of the information. Information assets demand that special attention be paid to both intrinsic and imputed values.

INFORMATION AS AN ASSET

In the earlier section on security models, the importance of identifying and valuing assets was emphasized. Assessing and implementing security — any security — is a process of protecting assets. The key word here is process. Security is a journey, not a destination. Because the concept of security is necessarily a transitory and idyllic state, security practitioners must deploy technology, policies, and procedures in a manner that easily accommodates the requisite dynamism for protection mechanisms to remain current.

Information, as an asset, cannot be fully understood as a static entity. Information has the characteristics of a living organism. Information often begins small and grows. It marries up with other information. It changes, flows, and evolves. The main differentiator between information and life forms is that information does not die, it must be killed off. However, this concept is covered in more detail in Chapter 3, so we will just introduce the idea here.

Any structured security management methodology or model must take into account the dynamic and fluid nature of information and also must be able to ascribe reasonable value estimates to it at each stage of its transmission, storage, and processing. Because security is not an absolute, but a matter of degree, these aspects of any model are crucial to the element of cost-effective security implementation.

One of the major problems with assigning value to information is that it currently does not appear on corporate balance sheets. I use the term currently to specifically point out my belief that information will sometime in the near future appear as a tangible corporate asset. To manage security effectively, it is necessary to measure its efficacy. If you cannot measure the assets you are endeavoring to protect, you cannot have an effective model to define security requirements.

Information may often show up on a balance sheet in the form of intellectual property. Types of intellectual property include copyrights, patents, trademarks, or trade secrets. These assets have certain rights in law depending on the country where the business is located. These rights can be bestowed, rented, sold, and even mortgaged in some countries. This gives a somewhat more tangible valuation to these important intangible resources.

It is critical to understand that the actual rights to the information are considered the property, not the intellectual work itself. For example, a patent is something that can be bought, sold, or traded. The actual invention itself technically does not belong to anyone. In this case, intellectual property represents a government granted monopoly on certain types of business activities. Intellectual property rights are generally divided into two main categories:

1. Those that protect a product or process by granting exclusive rights on only the copying or reproduction (copyright)
2. A more stringent patent protection that also grants additional rights such as the protection from competitors who have no knowledge of the original design

In either case, there is a legal burden on the individual or corporation to identify these assets and file the appropriate legal documents to provide a level of government-enforced protection.

Information is important to all organizations and it is the *raison d'etre* for innumerable businesses, such as clearinghouses, credit scoring companies, and contact providers. In these instances, it is ironic that items such as computer equipment and brick-and-mortar facilities are part of the balance sheet, but information is not. Most information-dependent organizations could recover quickly from a loss of any physical asset, yet would quickly go out of business without the ability to access and sell their information. Even if current accounting practice does not allow for a convenient way to portray the value of information, it is incumbent on people who depend on information to adequately provide for its management and protection.

THE ELEMENTS OF SECURITY

The word security provides us few clues for understanding and modeling requirements for the protection and management of information resources. To model security for information assets, we must define what we mean when we use the term security. The elements of security, as we define them, are confidentiality, integrity, and availability. This triad concept has been around for many years, yet has never been incorporated into a security model.

Over the years, security analysts, policymakers, and researchers have considered expanding this group to include elements such as accountability and nonrepudiation. Although there is a valid argument to be made for expanding the list of security elements, it is not necessary to do so in order to accommodate these attributes. Elements like nonrepudiation are a facet of integrity and accountability also could be included in that category. It makes no sense to make your model overly inclusive at its fundamental level. These are elements that are to be considered within one of the three widely adopted elements.

Confidentiality

Confidentiality is perhaps the most widely recognized and most deeply studied security requirement. Confidentiality is the basis for the science of cryptography that has its documented beginnings in the Roman Empire. The primary consideration of confidentiality is not simply keeping information secret from everyone else; it is making it available only to those people who need it, when they need it, and under the appropriate circumstances.

Perhaps the most significant imperative for confidentiality is not the element of secrecy, but the capability to ensure the appropriate subjects (both people and other processes or systems) have the requisite access when needed. Since the reign of the Caesars, confidentiality has been seen as a contest between those who would protect the content of information transmissions and those who would gain from the disclosure of the same. Evermore complex methodologies have evolved in this ongoing cycle of protect and exploit.

Centuries ago, information transmission speeds were measured in days and even months. Couriers were provided encoded information and the sender lost control over the transmission as soon as the courier disappeared from sight. The duty of courier was most likely assigned to a trusted soldier or confidante as an additional safeguard.

In the Roman Empire, senior civilian leaders and military commanders had a staff of office that also functioned as an encoding and decoding device. The staff contained the entire Roman alphabet and a complete set of numerals. A strip of parchment was wound around the staff starting at a particular letter or numeral that functioned as a key. A message could then be encoded as the actual letter or numeral was compared against its enciphered pair on the parchment. The receiver had only to take an identical staff and parchment strip and start at the same key letter or numeral to decipher the message from its encoded format. This simple encoding algorithm is known as a monoalphabetic substitution cipher and is still practiced by children fortunate enough to find a secret decoder ring in a box of popcorn snacks.

There were many security challenges with these early systems for ensuring the confidentiality of critical information. The geographically dispersed nature of the physical transportation of protected information made it difficult to change both the encoding algorithms and the keys required to decipher the information. Those charged with exploiting these communiqués had to initially intercept the physical communication and then determine both the algorithm and the key used to encode the plaintext data. Analysis, guile, and even brute force were necessary tools to discover these elements.

Modern cryptographic systems have the same properties as their ancient counterparts. There is an algorithm (or process) to encode the data and a key variable to establish the enciphered session.

Keys that are generated randomly and with great frequency prove difficult to break.

In the 19th century, Flemish cryptographer Auguste Kerchoffs enunciated the elemental key principle used by all modern cryptosystems: the security of the systems depends solely on the security of the key, not the algorithm. This is known as Kerchoffs' Law. As early as his published works in 1883, Kerchoffs understood that ultimately, the cryptosystem's algorithm could be captured and analyzed by those seeking to exploit the information the cryptography tried to protect. In modern computer systems, cryptographic algorithms can be deconstructed and analyzed by code crackers. Thus, a complex and regenerated key is the most critical defensive capability of the cryptosystem.

Although they were keenly aware of Kerchoffs' law, the Nazi military in World War II came too late to realize just how devastating the implications of this important principle were. British forces were able to smuggle a German Enigma encryption machine out of Poland with the help of patriotic Polish engineers who were making parts for the mass-produced encryption device. British and American researchers were ultimately able to replicate the complex algorithm within at the secret Bletchley Park compound in England. In 1940, the scientists were finally able to break the Enigma code by converting some test messages into plaintext. This uncovered the key systems that allowed the Allies to read the secret German military communications.

Cryptography represents the most frequently employed technology safeguard for the protection of information. The subject is treated in great detail in numerous other books and studies, so this text will not consider this science in any great detail. We also will not delve into the various strengths and weaknesses of specific cryptosystems. However, it is critical to understand both the strengths and weaknesses of cryptography as a safeguard in information systems.

In referring to the McCumber Cube, it is quickly obvious that cryptography can be applied as a technical safeguard in numerous instances. Cryptography is a highly effective safeguard for information that is being transmitted or stored. In the early days of computer security research, many people felt that cryptography alone could provide a sufficient technical safeguard for protection of information assets in computer systems.

In the era of monolithic computer systems and limited intercomputer communications, cryptography was envisioned as all the protection necessary for information that flowed between protected islands of data processing. In this case, boundary protection of the computer system itself was deemed adequate.

One of the defining principles of modern IT systems, however, is that confidentiality of information can only be provided with cryptography during the information states of transmission and storage. It is axiomatic that you cannot take data in its encrypted form, modify it (or, more accurately, process it), and then have data that can be decoded into plaintext. Though it is possible to keep information encoded until processing, it is not possible to apply the processing function until the data has been converted back to plaintext.

Perhaps the best way to illustrate this important principle is to use the analogy of a protected communications system that used cryptography long before the advent of the computer. The same Roman military commander we discussed earlier received his encoded dispatches and then had to decipher the data into plaintext before it became actual information for him to analyze and use in his decision-making process. There would be no way for him to skip the deciphering step and process the data in its encrypted form. The enciphered data was not in a form that his mind could process.

The same is true of automated processing systems such as modern computer and telecommunications systems. The processing stage of information is roughly analogous to the processing function of the human brain. Any processing function must work with data in its plaintext state.

It can be argued that an application (or other type of software) can be programmed to process enciphered information. Whatever the process for developing and writing a computer program to function in crypto-text, this would be nothing different from actually writing a program in another language — either a human-based linguistic system or computer programming language. However, such an instance would not work outside the confines of this one representational language and would therefore render the system unsuitable to widespread use and adoption. For that and other reasons, we will not consider such a case as meeting the needs of our IT users and it is therefore outside the scope of this work.

There is a saying among computer security researchers that states, "If you think cryptography is the only technical answer, you understand neither cryptography nor the question." Cryptography is a critical technical safeguard that is ideally applied to information in its transmission and storage states, if it is applied at all. The analysis of the McCumber Cube approach will help you determine if it is required and, then, to what degree.

There are numerous cryptosystems in current use and many more under development. The applicability and effectiveness of each is determined by the quality of the algorithm and the strength and adaptability of the key. Such systems are usually paired with a variety of authentication mechanisms. Technical confidentiality controls include not only cryptography, but authentication and intrusion detection technologies as well.

Maintaining the confidentiality of information resources requires not only technical safeguards, but policy and procedures as well. Procedural controls begin by ensuring only authorized persons can put data into the system and only authorized users can view the resultant information. Perhaps the most vital confidentiality policy, however, is the initial determination of who can view what information and under what conditions.

To provide adequate security enforcement, it is always important to ensure you can develop and publish a comprehensive matrix that defines the nature of confidentiality for your environment. Identifying individuals in the organization may accomplish this, but the most common way is to define people by their job title or responsibilities. In this way, access requirements can be succinctly codified for the organization independent of the individuals in it.

Depending on the size of the information systems environment, this policy process can be either relatively simple or amazingly complex. It begins with an inventory of individual roles and responsibilities throughout the organization that is supported by the IT system. Then a comprehensive list of all the available information resources needs to be developed. These lists are then mapped against each other as roles.

This process is often lacking in even the most security-conscious environments. Alone, this exercise can be extremely beneficial for objectively determining who should have access to specific informational resources. When combined with the structured process defined in this text, it becomes a powerful method to strategically assess organization confidentiality policies and a key tool for tactically applying technology to support security requirements.

Confidentiality is a relatively simple concept that, in practice, requires a broad spectrum of technology and procedural enforcement in IT systems. Once you have developed your confidentiality policies and have charted them in the methodology, you will have a basis for determining the requirements for cryptography and other confidentiality safeguards.

Integrity

The integrity element of security is foundational. Inaccurate information can be worse than worthless. It can provide a false understanding of the business environment or even a military battlefield and lead decision makers into taking self-destructive actions. Integrity consists of ensuring the information is accurate, complete, and robust. As with the concept of security itself, integrity represents an ideal. Obviously, there are limits to the ability of security safeguards to provide for complete and robust information resources, but the integrity attribute is a central aspect to security enforcement. Integrity controls also include cryptographic solutions as well as authentication, nonrepudiation, and comparative analysis.

Many current definitions of integrity are woefully inadequate and many are notoriously incorrect. One widely cited definition defines data integrity as the assurance that data can only be accessed or modified by authorized users. Obviously, this definition is wildly deficient. This definition assumes that authorized users will always acquire, maintain, and update information with 100 percent accuracy. It also presumes the user will not make any type of mistake nor undertake any malicious or nonmalicious activity that could jeopardize the integrity of information resources for which they have authorized access. Because both of these scenarios are patently preposterous, we can safely assume we will not make the mistake of employing it as our understanding of information integrity.

For those familiar with database and storage systems use, the concept of data integrity has other meanings. Data integrity means, in the database sense, that you can correctly and consistently navigate and manipulate the tables in the database. According to database usage, there are two basic rules to ensure data integrity — entity integrity and referential integrity.

The *entity integrity* rule states that the value of the primary key can never be a null value (a null value is one that has no value and is not the same as a blank). Because a primary key is used to identify a unique row in a relational table in a database, its value must always be specified and should never be unknown. The integrity rule requires that insert, update, and delete operations maintain the uniqueness and existence of all primary keys.

The *referential integrity* rule states that if a relational table has a foreign key, then every value of the foreign key must either be null or match the values in the relational table in which that foreign key is a primary key. In this way, data is tracked effectively and that data is said to have integrity.

Neither database concept is exactly what is necessary to define information integrity in the sense that a security practitioner needs to understand and apply it. These definitions were initially developed for early database development at a time when the concept of a global information infrastructure replete with both good guys and bad guys was almost inconceivable. The requirements for data integrity were made with several assumptions, including complete accuracy of data input into the database, and the ability of the retrieving application to find and display (or process) the data flawlessly.

Other mechanisms that have been identified for obtaining and maintaining data and information integrity are physical protection of networked workstations, servers, and PCs. The protection of transmission media is another security practice often cited for the assurance of integrity. Although each of these specific mechanisms will aid in the protection of the information resources, these incomplete lists make for a poor way to define and assess information integrity.

Many security texts and systems vendors accurately point out that information and data integrity can be threatened by environmental hazards. Such threats include heat, dust particles, and electrical surges. Each of these has been known to garble data in transmit or storage and can result in lost information. However, for purposes of this methodology, these would be more accurately considered as threats to availability of the information in question as opposed to a loss of integrity.

For our purposes, the definition of data integrity will be a determination of how accurately and robustly the information reflects reality for a given application. In this case, we are not using the term application in the sense of a computer application. We are using the term broadly to define the intended use of the information to meet the needs of its owners.

Integrity is often defined as the need to ensure that the information is robust and accurate, but describing and quantifying those attributes is difficult. Rarely, if ever, can a decision maker claim to have perfect information. However, having accurate and robust information is critical. The integrity attribute of information is simply defined by the accurate and robust state of the information in relation to its intended use.

You will notice that many of the previously discredited definitions included safeguards as a way to define integrity. Although they are a key element for maintaining information integrity, the safeguards have to be accurately categorized as such. Many security safeguards function to help provide the requisite amount and degree of information integrity. We already presented definitions that included several physical and environmental safeguards necessary to help maintain information integrity, although many elements of an IT system are employed for this purpose.

Applications themselves are an important component in protecting information integrity. Safeguards incorporated into the applications themselves tend to be effective because applications are usually the vehicle by which data is converted to information. The application understands (and usually accomplishes) the transition from data into human-readable information. Applications also can enforce data entry and acquisition rules to screen out inaccurate or improperly formatted data elements. They also provide more immediate feedback to authorized users and administrators when policies or rules are violated. If one relies solely on database integrity constraints, an integrity constraint can only notify the user of a bad value after the user has entered all form values and the application has issued the INSERT statement (using a SQL [structured query language] example) to the database. However, you can design your application to verify the integrity of each value as it is entered and notify the user immediately in the event of a bad value.

Information integrity is one of the most demanding and yet the subtlest and least defined of the information attributes to maintain. The great majority of investment in safeguards and protective techniques are targeted at maintaining information integrity. Yet, it is vital to ensure that integrity is assessed and enforced even at the acquisition of the data or the information's introduction into your systems.

Availability

If information is needed for a decision or for any other purpose and it is not there, it is simply not available. If integrity represents the accuracy and robustness of data, then availability is the timeliness factor. The availability element of security is often relegated as an afterthought, or at best, a control left for a simple demand for redundancy and uptime requirements. In practice, availability is often the single most critical assurance for critical IT systems.

For example, the fact that a profit-making enterprise has a database of all its current customers makes the intrinsic value of the data important. If that information is deleted, the company may lose business from those customers as a result of its inability to meet the demand of access to its business information. Availability is the cornerstone security requirement and one that requires protection.

Historically, information availability has been relegated to the study and application of disparate disciplines and safeguards such as redundancy, backup systems, storage management, disaster recovery, and business continuity. Each of these represents an important aspect of the availability attribute, but none on its own or even in concert with others constitutes a robust and accurate definition. Availability is really quite simple to define and understand: It is the ability of stored, transmitted, or processed information to be used for its intended purposes when required.

Availability is a security constraint that must be considered on an equal footing with the more commonly cited attributes of confidentiality and integrity. The concepts of timeliness and accessibility are aspects just as important as accuracy and protection from unauthorized use. Security parameters must answer the question: Will I have my information when I need it?

There are nominally two main components to ensuring availability of data and managing the risk to information by entrusting it to valuable technology resources. These ensure that systems operate to deliver data as needed and back up data to guard against system failure or data loss. As with any security-relevant requirement, it helps to be able to quantify what constitutes acceptable availability and how much you are willing to pay to achieve that goal.

Redundancy is an important aspect of providing appropriate information availability. In many cases, having redundant databases, networks, and even workstations is necessary to ensure uninterrupted access to vital information resources. The costs of hardware, configuration, and maintenance can be high, but these must be weighed against the consequences of delay. The decision is made by the measurement of risk that is discussed in Appendix B.

Backup and recovery are other safeguards that must be considered to ensure availability. A backup is simply a copy of the data. This copy can, in addition to the data, include important parts of the database such as the control file and data files. A backup is a safeguard against unexpected data loss and application errors. If you lose the original data resource, a backup allows you to reconstruct it.

Backups can be subdivided into physical backups and logical backups. Physical backups are the primary concern in a backup and recovery strategy. They are represented as copies of physical database files. In contrast, logical backups contain logical data (for example, data tables and the associated stored procedures) extracted with a utility and stored in a binary file. Logical backups are most often used to supplement physical backups.

Recovery systems work hand in hand with backup technology to ensure information can be restored to its primary function in the event it is required. A key element of this process is once again a risk management decision. Solutions that provide near-immediate fail over and recovery are, as a rule, significantly more expensive than solutions that demand extensive manual recovery techniques.

Availability also employs a variety of other safeguards and counter-measures to ensure that information resources are available when they are needed for the decision makers.

SECURITY IS SECURITY ONLY IN CONTEXT

Understanding the nature of security requires the practitioner to ensure that security is applied to the information resources in the context of their environment. Security is a moot concept unless it is fully analyzed with the elements of information valuation threats as safeguards. This methodology is designed to help you assess these critical elements.

3

INFORMATION AS AN ASSET

INTRODUCTION

The art and science of security requires a complete understanding of the value of the assets requiring protection. The asset under scrutiny is primarily the information transmitted, stored, and processed by the organization. Secondarily, the computer and telecommunications resources themselves require protection; a significant component of that can and will be addressed by applying of the McCumber Cube approach.

One of the simplest ways to understand what an organization values and how it then labels its information resources is to look at an example used for decades, the U.S. military. In government parlance, information value is defined by broad categories such as unclassified, sensitive, secret, and top secret. There are published definitions of these terms that have been used and adapted since the terms were first coined to describe the amount of value placed on the information. You can search out these definitions in Federal Standard 1037C[1] and the DOD Dictionary of Military and Associated Terms.[2]

These terms will usually dictate how that information is controlled and used. A military person who meets the criteria of an appropriate clearance level and need-to-know usually can gain access to the information. But the tiered security system is a crude way to ascribe value to information resources.

Throughout this book, we will also apply broad categories of asset valuation similar to the military model. However, the McCumber Cube methodology can be tailored to accommodate a more descriptive and refined gauge for measuring the asset valuation of information resources. Within the process itself, you can substitute the overly broad categories for any hierarchical metric you choose. The one you ultimately use should be based specifically on your environment and level of granularity required.

The value of this structured methodology is that you can substitute the best metric to suit your valuation method. A military system can use the traditional confidential, secret, and top secret classifications for a system that controls multiple types of classified information. This is referred to as collateral national security information by the U.S. government. However, even the military has found it necessary to refine its simplistic three-tier classification system.

On top of these levels are additional categories that define more stringent levels of protection. These categorization systems include the Department of Energy Special Access Program, the Department of Defense Special Access Program, and the Director of Central Intelligence Sensitive Compartmented Information Programs. There are a variety of other specialized access lists and caveats that can be added as well. Dissemination controls and other restrictive markings can include notations to further refine its distribution and use. Code words also are employed as a way to describe sources and methods used in the collection of the information.

Models that focus either primarily or exclusively on the IT infrastructure itself rather than on the information resources do not have the flexibility to be mapped to different environments. In other words, an IT environment that provides adequate security for a manufacturing concern will most likely not be adequate for the Central Intelligence Agency. The reason is simple: each organization places widely different values on their information assets. Although information resources are critical to both, each organization will have to evaluate the likelihood of possible negative consequences for not protecting the information.

The primary issues of asset valuation a security analyst needs to consider are the consequences of *not* protecting the information. There are four primary categories for these consequences that cover the possible outcomes. I call them the Four Ds:

■ Destruction
■ Delay
■ Disclosure
■ Distortion

Every possible negative security outcome can be assigned to one of the Four D categories.

Destruction covers any type of access denial against legitimate users. It includes actual destruction of the information through such attacks as physical destruction of data media. Disks can be physically damaged, data can be deleted from databases, and both explosives and natural events (such as hurricanes and tornadoes) can destroy computer centers and their systems.

Delay defines any type of temporary denial of access or data use. The numerous denial of service attacks of recent memory dramatically demonstrate the insidious nature of simple delay. If a decision maker cannot gain access to vital information when needed, the consequences can be severe. Delay is, in many cases, an easier exploit to conduct than outright destruction; its effects can usually be just as damaging.

In the last several years, many attackers are finding that simply degrading the capabilities of IT systems is sufficient to meet their malfeasant goals. In some cases, they can simply use automated security safeguards to help cripple a system's capabilities. As safeguards used in modern information systems are adapted to automatically detect and respond to attacks, certain simple exploits can be used to trigger the safeguard mechanisms. Many of these protective responses include isolating affected systems and blocking ports and services to external sources. An uncomplicated command that is associated with an exploit could be used to force the system to automatically invoke a response that degrades the system's capabilities.

Disclosure and distortion are perhaps the most insidious consequences to consider. Disclosure is defined as unauthorized access to information resources. The reason disclosure is so insidious is that this exploit may not be exposed until it is too late or never at all. Many security safeguards are designed solely to enforce an insiders versus outsiders perspective of enforcement. The assumption is that the insiders can be trusted, but outsiders cannot. However, an effective security program must be able to enforce security policies that mandate the proper access to and use of all information resources.

An ages-old physical security maxim is: Prevent what you cannot detect; detect what you cannot prevent. If an attacker or other type of threat obtains unauthorized access to your resources, security analysts will at least require evidence to determine that the exploitation took place. In the physical security realm, a cut fence, a broken window, or a severed lock will bear forensic witness to the method of attack. By following this physical evidence trail, a security specialist or law enforcement person can determine how the attack or theft was perpetrated. It also aids in assessing the damages or losses incurred. However, with information resources, such a forensic trail may be hidden deeply or perhaps be nonexistent.

Disclosure could be the consequence for someone whose password is compromised. If you are one of the millions of people that hide your computer password under your keyboard, someone can use your password to look at sensitive corporate data or even confidential personal information. The ultimate loss for such a security breach using this ill-gotten knowledge will be determined by how the disclosed information is used.

The information thief may provide this sensitive internal information to a competitor for personal gain; or they may simply retain the information for potential use sometime in the future. If you do not have a system that notifies you of the last authorized login time and date, you may never even know the information was disclosed to an unauthorized party. Unlike obvious evidence of broken glass, the disclosure of a password and unauthorized use of the system may go completely undetected.

Distortion can be a consequence with all the same problems associated with the loss of imputed value. If an unauthorized or unintended alteration is made to the information, decisions can be made that are ultimately detrimental to the organization that maintains the information resources. One of the most difficult security challenges is ensuring that information is not maliciously or accidentally distorted. Acting on inaccurate information can result in more severe consequences than not having the information at all.

DETERMINING VALUE

Information is a strategic asset to an organization. Many have used IT to transform business practices and achieve significant competitive advantage. Those who have been most successful have focused on the information itself rather than the technology as the basis for gaining an advantage. Technology is the means of delivering the information; the underlying asset itself is the key resource. Information is stored in operational databases or decision support databases.

To assess how or why information is valuable, it is useful to define information as an asset. As an asset, information has the potential for future benefit. Whether for national security or economic gain, it provides the capability for making effective decisions. The information asset provides strategic benefit if it is controlled by the organization. If information belongs to one organization exclusively, it becomes a commodity that can be used, sold, or shared to its advantage. Once control over the information has been obtained through purchase, discovery, or development from within, the cost for said data has been expended, making the information an intangible asset to an organization.

Being unique from tangible assets, information can be shared among many people without any depreciation of its value. Unlike finances, equipment, or staff that need to be proportioned among users, information's value remains equal to all users. In most cases, there is no increase in cost or reduction in value from sharing data. In fact, there can be a multiplicity in the value of the asset if more people can use it and more gain can come of its dissemination in an organization. Unlike other commodities that depreciate with usage, information retains its original value.

Different types of information have different values. A home telephone number may have limited value in a transient society, although a cell phone number can be invaluable. The more accurate information is, the more useful and valuable it becomes. For some data, accuracy of 100 percent is required, although for other data, 75 percent may be good enough. In the second case, increasing the accuracy further actually reduces the value of the asset. In the first case, if the information falls below a specific level, it is useless and cannot be trusted. A case in point is the banking industry. Accurate records of financial data and transactions must be precise. If financial decision makers cannot trust the accuracy of their data, they will not use it.

It is important at this point to distinguish between data and information. Data is not the same concept as information. Information is data placed in context, analyzed, and processed into a consumable resource or asset. In many cases, a small amount of information can have more value than a large amount of data. It is important to recognize the difference. The McCumber Cube methodology is based on information valuation and analysis, not data valuation.

Information has different values to different users depending on their resources, intentions, or market position (Figure 3.1). It receives little financial recognition relative to its value as an asset. It uses organizational resources in terms of data capture, processing, storage, and maintenance, but is largely ignored as a value from a business perspective. It is this resource that enables an organization to make decisions, deliver services, or achieve a competitive advantage. The real cost of an information system resides in the information it is storing rather than the software and hardware it uses to store it. IT strategies should be focused on sustaining the value of the information product rather than on the equipment or system used to disseminate, store, or maintain it.

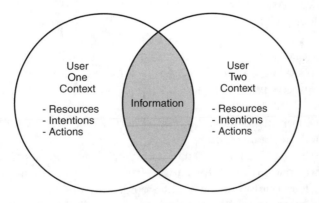

Figure 3.1   User Context

One must define and price a process to acquire or reacquire information should it be lost. Operational assessment includes the value of information to actual, ongoing operations. An example of this is where information is required for consumption as part of a current business practice. If the information is lost or unusable, one or more business processes cannot continue until the information is replaced. This valuation is heavily dependent on user needs.

A market-based valuation process assesses the resale value of information. Information is developed and provided to meet the needs of a customer. Examples of market-based scenarios include the news media or real estate firms that are purveyors of information to the public. Market value of information takes into account the development costs as well as how badly the consumer of the information needs it and whether or not there are alternative sources of the information available. This method uses comparisons with actual experiences and depends on supply and demand forces that are functions of location and time.

The collection of information, as with other collectibles, considers the perceived value to the user as distinct from the explicit developmental, operational, or documented market value. Information is often generally perceived to have value without a clear or direct purpose other than its possession. The question is raised as to whether or not this information has value.

Developmental valuation takes into account the efforts and resources required to develop or reconstruct information independent of other considerations. This involves defining and pricing a process to acquire or reacquire the information should it be lost. The bases of valuation are:

- Development basis
- Operational basis
- Market basis
- Collection basis

The consolidation of information increases its value (Figure 3.2). Proper integration becomes a factor in operational systems. The lack thereof becomes a major impediment to efficient use of the information asset. Although total integration may be unrealistic, identifiers that enable the linking of information and coding schemes for aggregating data are beneficial to an organization.

Many modern database management systems are being designed to capture and manipulate information from all operational areas of an enterprise. The comprehensive data environments are both a strategic corporate advantage and a significant vulnerability for security practitioners. The centralized information storage architecture translates into many

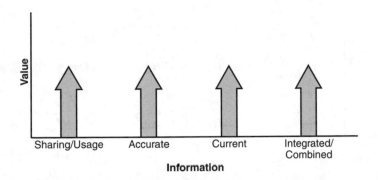

Figure 3.2 Information Value Increases

access points to populate the databases. Additionally, the complex nature of the software that manipulates the information means that security practitioners have a difficult time identifying and isolating events that may violate the organization's security requirements.

Many information resources are depleted over time. Information is one resource that does not follow that pattern. New or derived information is created as a result of analyzing or combining information. The original remains and the derived is added in a self-generating cycle. It is for this reason that information is often abundant and difficult to manage.

Most information changes value depending on its age (Figure 3.3). It must be updated and current to be most useful to an organization. If unused, information can become a significant liability because of the costs incurred from acquiring, storing, and maintaining it. A major problem typical to most organizations is not the lack of information, but the abundance thereof leading to information overload and reduction in decision-making performance. Effective use of information requires proper access. Information has a low value if it cannot be found or accessed. Proper cataloging increases the value of the data. People need to know where the information is and how to access it.

The value of an asset can be measured from its use or exchange. The cost of acquisition of the asset approximates the value of said asset at the time of its purchase. Using this idea, the asset is valued based on how much other people or organizations are prepared to pay for it. The same can be said of the value of information. Information sold on a usage basis or as a product is a widely traded commodity on the Internet. Information can be sold over and over again without losing value. It also retains its original value to the organization. The exception to this is when a group sells its exclusive rights to the information.

Valuing information is a difficult task because it does not follow the same rules that apply to other assets. The cost of collecting information

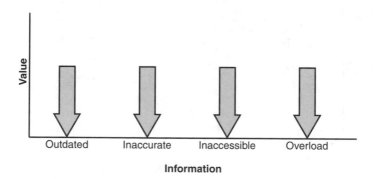

Figure 3.3   Information Value Decreases

can be used as a measurement of its value if it is operational data. Management data can be valued based on the cost used to extract it from operating systems. Unused, redundant information has negative value. Many users who have access to information multiply its value. Current information is more valuable than older information. Acceptably accurate information is valuable in its proper context.

In most cases, information's value lies not in its contribution to revenues or products, but as a catalyst for decision making and gaining a competitive advantage. The valuation of information could have huge implications for the IT industry. Determining how and why to value information must be useful and relevant. Organizations must be aware of information as an asset. Managing the cost of data collection, storage, maintenance, and analysis increases accountability and reduces waste. Valuation of information provides a better approach to measuring the effectiveness of IT by measuring the value of the information rather than the hardware.

Information valuation may have many benefits for organizations. Companies, in creating and maintaining information assets, make a long-term investment in resources, systems, and people. To determine the importance of information it is useful to follow a logical process. First, identify information as an asset and list the attributes of the information that single it out as important. For example, if a company is consumer related, then customer-related information is highly valuable. It is necessary to develop methods for valuing the information. Include information on the accounting balance sheet as an asset. This will lead to better management of information assets. Once information is identified, valued, and recorded as an asset, then the potential to successfully exploit it for financial or strategic gain is greatly enhanced.

Applying a method used by accounting practices is an attempt to measure the value of information by attaching a number to it. This method seeks to ascertain market value of intangible assets. Unfortunately, information does not follow all the economic principles of tangible assets. The value of an information asset must take into account an active market where frequent buying and selling of that asset takes place if you are to apply accounting methodology to information valuation. The problem is that this market is currently limited, for example, to the sale of information lists. To fulfill the strict accounting standards of asset valuation, information would never be as valuable as when it is first obtained. This is certainly not the case. Following the same line of reasoning, more information would always be better than less, and information collected twice would be worth twice as much.

Another obstacle to achieving a valuation of information in a traditional sense is the identification of information assets and their attributes. A group should document their information assets as a preliminary step to identifying or assessing them at an organizational level. Without this first step, a valuation is extremely difficult. Other problems with placing a valuation on information assets include the fact that information may or may not hold its value over time. Information value depends on constant updating; information degrades quickly, making its value dynamic. The value of information for problem solving is time critical; only the right information at the right time helps in decision making.

Companies put an enormous value on information, without thinking on the whole about capitalizing it, putting it on the balance sheet, valuing it, or insuring it. These issues remain relevant and as business becomes more information based, its value is taking on greater prominence. Users of information often cannot perceive why it should be managed. They see information as a problem that should be dealt with by those in the IT department. However, once information overload is accepted as a problem, people are motivated to find a solution.

There is a growing location-independent workforce, which means that information collection and access is dispersed, leading to challenges of trust building and ownership of information assets. Digital commerce, for example, has the challenge of securing and protecting intellectual property rights. Personally identifiable information may become the new-world currency, with growing concerns among consumers. Business partnerships must demonstrate that information collected will only be used for specifically intended purposes.

The quantity of information has increased for a number of reasons. There is a general increase in business communication, within a company and with customers or suppliers. Trends such as globalization and deregulation increase competition and organizations are downsizing, therefore having fewer employees to manage the information. Outsourcing of work means a wider range of other groups with which it is necessary to communicate. There are also more ways to communicate: by fax, voice mail, e-mail, Internet and online conferencing, in addition to the more traditional methods, telephone, face-to-face meetings, and mail.

MANAGING INFORMATION RESOURCES

Many organizations cannot adequately cope with the volume of information they receive. Managers often feel the need to collect information to back up their decisions or keep up with competitors. An evolving professional understands how to leverage information for organizational benefit, viewing the organization as a whole rather than as individual groups or functions. Effective managers will identify what information should be created or captured and how it can be leveraged in making strategic decisions. They will determine who should or should not have access to the information and when it should be destroyed.

There is a cost for not managing information properly. Time is wasted as people look for information. Factors such as the holding of files in different software formats and the speed of the Internet at critical times of day contribute to this. Decisions can be delayed by the existence of too much information. Information collection can distract employees from their main responsibilities. It is necessary to develop strategies for dealing with the information retrieved, and interesting to imagine the potential increase in productivity if proper valuation were to be achieved.

Managing information assets can be broken down into various components. Leveraging information involves data mining, managing knowledge, workflow, content, and relationships. Valuation involves assigning a rank to the intellectual property and managing the risk to that asset. It is crucial to protect the privacy, security, and ownership of intellectual property. There is a need to prospectively forecast infrastructure based on the information. Management must monitor the information through auditing, compliance, and performance measurement and maintain the information by properly storing, preserving, retrieving, and disposing of it when necessary.

Information, when seen as a valuable corporate resource, defines an organization's effectiveness as well as its assets. A well-developed information resource defines the current state of the organization, supports effective decision making, and provides a means of monitoring the organization's performance. Inadequate information assets result in poor and destructive decisions, missed opportunities, wasted resources, and ineffective use of technology. Fundamental challenges exist in the need to better manage information flow and to determine of the link between organizational strategy and the use of information.

An organization's interests lie in increasing the value of group-centered information, decreasing the cost of maintaining the group's information,

Table 3.1 Favorable Situations

	Value of Group-Centered Information	Cost of Maintaining Information	Value of Other Information	Cost of Other Information
Favorable Situation	High	Low	High	Low

increasing the number and value of useful interfaces to other groups, and decreasing the cost of maintaining access to intergroup information (Table 3.1).

It should be noted that the information value to a corporation cannot be computed directly as the sum of each group's information value because of redundancy and conflicting values between groups. For example, the information valued by Group C may be inconsistent, out of date, or erroneous from the perspective of Group B. Using a large university medical center's scheduling dilemma as an example may illustrate this concept.

The medical center contains a number of outpatient clinics, each with its own staff and scheduling procedures (Table 3.2). Management decides to automate patient visit scheduling hospitalwide. Two situations are being considered:

1. Situation 1 — allows each clinic to implement the scheduling system as a stand-alone application.
2. Situation 2 — requires a high degree of integration with shared viewing access to patient and schedule information and the ability to book appointments across departments.

Table 3.2 University Medical Center Considerations for a New Scheduling System

	Value of Information	Cost of Maintaining Information	Value of Other Information	Cost of Other Information
Current (paper books)	High	Medium	Medium	High
Situation 1 (stand-alone)	High	Low	Medium	High
Situation 2 (integration)	Medium	Medium	High	Low

In Situation 1 (stand-alone), the information about patients located within each individual clinic is of high value and low cost. The stand-alone situation lowers the cost of maintaining the information by automating existing paper scheduling books. If information from a different clinic is needed, a phone call or e-mail message will be used. Situation 2 (integrated) lowers the importance of local information by moving it to a shared database and makes costs higher in order to implement and maintain the information. Increased costs include the equipment and added training needed to schedule across departments and to standardize scheduling.

Objects of information are real assets that are enhanced or reduced in value by the way they are organized and managed by the organization. The value of an information system consequently is not measured as a sum of the value attributed to it by each group, but rather by its probable contribution to the corporation's information assets. In the above example, the most important information asset in the medical center is the collection of data about its patients. The asset's contribution to the success of the medical center and the cost of managing that asset is the most important factor to be considered in the selection of which scheduling scheme to implement.

To establish a useful method of valuing information assets it is necessary to know whether information is available when and where it is needed and if the cost of accessing the information is acceptable. Once accessed, is the information reliable and accurate and does corporate policy maximize the information's benefit to the success of the organization?

At the university medical center, the decision to proceed with Situation 1 (stand-alone) or Situation 2 (integration) should begin with an assessment of the current state of the information asset. They know that patient information is not available because information about a particular patient is physically stored in various clinics without easy and reliable access. Patient information is not accurate because all information about the patient from the various clinics is not available. The medical center has a great deal of information that could be used in the care of the patient, but the current system keeps the information fragmented.

When analyzed from the perspective of the medical center's information assets, the automated scheduling situations appear differently from the above situation. The proposal for local scheduling systems does not add to the medical center's information assets' value.

The cost component from the perspective of the medical center's information assets changes the situation selection criteria. Decision makers must understand the total cost of managing the information asset. Specifically, they need to know how much it costs the medical center to record

Table 3.3 Medical Center's Information Assets Considerations

Patient Information	Value			Costs	
	Availability	Accuracy	Policy	Record	Coordinate
Current (paper books)	Low	Medium	Low	Medium	High
Situation 1 (stand-alone)	Low	Medium	Medium	Low	High
Situation 2 (integration)	High	High	High	Low	Low

the patient information asset and how much it costs to coordinate access to the information.

Each individual clinic expends resources to keep records of a patient's schedule (Table 3.3). When information must be shared between clinics, resources are expended to request and gather patient data. Errors and omissions must be tracked and distributed from one clinic to the next, adding to the cost of managing the patient information asset. If the medical center decides on Situation 1 (stand-alone), the cost to individual clinics of maintaining their own patient information may be reduced. The cost of coordinating information among clinics remains high. Even if the cost of Situation 1 is reasonable, its modest benefits make it difficult to justify. Situation 2 (integration) is likely to lower the cost of recording patient information, but the cost to coordinate and share information should be significantly lower.

The method for using the medical center's information assets as a basis for the selection of the patient scheduling situation works by identifying the information assets affected by each situation and for each asset, evaluating its current value and the cost for managing the information. For Situation 1 and Situation 2, it is necessary to assess the probable change in the information's value and the cost of managing the information asset. If the asset's medical-centerwide values increase and the total cost of managing the asset decreases, the proposed situation would result in an increase in the asset's contribution to the medical center. The situation with the greatest projected increase in information assets contribution should be the one to be approved and funded.

An organization-centered view of information's value alters the perceived benefits and costs of decision making. The concept of information being a corporate asset is key to maximizing the return on its collection and use. Strategic planning or project justification should be based on the project's potential for enhancing the contribution information makes to the success of the organization and its mission.

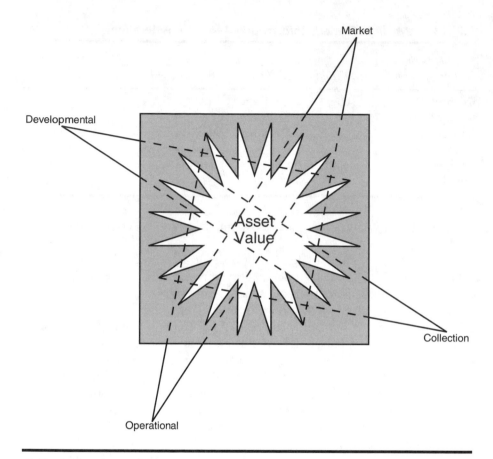

Figure 3.4 Asset Valuation Models

There are benefits to the valuation of information. It raises awareness of the importance of information and increases accountability for the management and effective use of the information asset (Figure 3.4). Valuation of the true asset will change the focus from the technology surrounding it to the information itself.

The behavior of information as an asset is not well understood and therefore applying historic accounting practices to information does not meet the need. The valuation method of choice would need to take into account the unique properties of information assets. When we apply these metrics to the McCumber Cube, we use the simplistic high, medium, and low labels. Although this may seem grossly inadequate, consider the military's classification system that is based on a similar tiered system with categories for unclassified, confidential, secret, and top secret. There are numerous other caveats and compartments layered on and between these rudimentary classifications, but the basic system has been employed for decades. As we evolve toward a better understanding of information resources and information-centric security, it will be necessary to develop a more in-depth and granular valuation system for information in all its forms.

REFERENCES

1. National Communications System Technology & Standards Division, *Federal Standard 1037C — Telecommunications: Glossary of Telecommunication Terms,* Washington, D.C.: General Services Administration Information Technology Service, 1996 [updated 2000; available at www.its.bldrgoc.gov].
2. Department of Defense, DOD Dictionary of Military and Associated Terms [online database available at www.dtic.mil/doctrine/index].

4

UNDERSTANDING THREAT AND ITS RELATION TO VULNERABILITIES

INTRODUCTION

Threats, along with assets, vulnerabilities, and safeguards, are the essential elements of risk management in an information system. Threat represents one of the four major elements of the risk assessment process. Understanding and considering the full spectrum of both human and environmental threat is pivotal to effectively implementing and managing a cost-effective security program for information resources. Too often, analysts employ simplistic anecdotal threat concepts or merely use broad, ill-defined labels such as "hackers" to define the threat environment. Either approach will negatively impact the effectiveness of a security program.

The anecdotal method for assessing threat is to attempt to identify and stay current of the threat through news articles, stories, or casual observations. This unstructured approach assumes the security analyst has an omniscient perspective and the stories and examples used to justify the security requirements are fully representative of the holistic threat environment. Even if these circumstances were achievable, this security approach is condemned to being purely retrospective and thus reactionary. Assuming you can obtain a comprehensive report about attacks and exploits, you must mitigate the risks in your systems only after learning about them from others. If your information resources are the first to be exploited, your peers will be praying they can quickly learn from you how to thwart the attack before their information resources are affected.

Applying labels to threats and then attempting to anticipate their tactics is another time-honored approach that has proven ineffective. The most popular technique is to start by assuming that your information resources are the target of external, hostile attackers with significant computer systems experience —often called the hacker. There is an entire chapter that could be written on the evolution of this word and it application, but it would not be instructive here.

Using this stereotyped attacker as a model, the analyst seeks to simulate, or at least anticipate, the actions of a person with the motivation, intent, and skills of this phantom menace. The analyst then seeks to assess the security safeguards of the system under review by tools and techniques designed to emulate the activities of the assumed assailant. When vulnerabilities are identified, safeguards to mitigate the risk are assessed and implemented. This is the most prevalent form of penetration-and-patch security as discussed in another chapter, so suffice it to say that relying on this approach for a security program denies the larger realities of the threat environment. To accurately define and manage security in an operational environment, a structured methodology to categorize and assess threat is required.

THREAT DEFINED

Threat is any person, event, or circumstance with the potential to cause harm to an asset. Threats take advantage of system vulnerabilities, that is, a weakness in a component that could be exploited to violate the system's security policy. Threats have an unacceptable impact that can be severe enough to degrade an essential mission capability or system causing an unacceptable result. The security environment attempts to deter threats by employing processes, practices, procedures, safeguards, or consequences for actions to discourage a person who intends to exploit an organizational asset.

Threats are either environmental, that is, created by a potential natural disaster such as a tornado, or man-made (Figure 4.1). Within the second category, there are internal or external threats. Agents that are not directly employed by the target organization create external threats, although agents within the organization are the cause of internal threats. Man-made internal threats fall into two categories — hostile or nonhostile. Hostile threats are malicious and are intentionally perpetrated to do harm to the organization. They may be either structured or nonstructured in nature. Nonhostile threats from agents of the organization may be structured or nonstructured as well. Mistakes or errors of omission are examples of nonhostile threats.

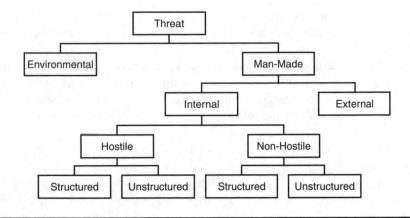

Figure 4.1   Threat Categories

Threat factors are a product of historical data and trend projections. Statistical and expert analysis can be used to provide default threat factor ratings. The ultimate purpose in threat determination is to identify and rank those threats that apply specifically to the assets of an organization. To develop this material, it is vital to gather historical and statistical data to be able to accurately quantify the predictive models.

Threat measurement is a relative calculation of the magnitude of a threat. Considerations must be taken into account for system connectivity, motivation, and capability of the threat and the occurrence determination for a class of threat. These threat measurement factors create a threat profile that is a measurement of the relative motivation and capability of a threat. Threat motivation is the degree a threat wants to cause harm to the organization. Capability measures the knowledge about the use of the information infrastructure and systems of an organization that a threat has.

A novice attacker is not the only threat. In general terms, computer and information systems attackers can be grouped into broad categories based on their location, intent, and skills. The most focused is often identified as the foreign intelligence service operative. These are skilled, aggressive adversaries who attempt to exploit the information infrastructure for intelligence purposes. They seek to identify members, evaluate their level of access to information of intelligence value, and even recruit their services, all in cyberspace. There are significant advantages to doing business this way, such as easily concealing one's identity and gaining information rapidly. The cyber-terrorist attack goes beyond computer intrusions, denials of service, or defacing of Web pages to ultimately target actual destruction of data or systems.

Use of the Internet and other information systems gives terrorist groups a global command and control communications capability. Such groups have limited resources and electronic intrusion can help them achieve their objectives at minimal cost, so it is expected that cyber-terrorism will continue to be a threat.

Organized crime also is used to represent a major threat whose goal is to target computer systems to commit fraud, acquire and exploit proprietary information, and steal funds. Criminal organizations like those in the former Soviet Union use electronic intrusion to hinder police investigations, collect intelligence, destroy or alter data on investigations, and monitor the activities of informants. As these groups develop and acquire more capabilities, the threat stands as one of the most likely to see growth in the coming decade. Organized crime attacks are likely to exploit information for financial gain or to obtain access to sensitive information that is useful in the conduct of criminal enterprise. Critical infrastructure attacks do not fall within the operational purview of organized crime; however, the potential for organized crime entities to act as domestic proxies for terrorists or rogue nation states is a possibility to consider.

Historically, hackers and those seeking opportunities out of curiosity were motivated primarily by learning the intricacies of computer systems and network operations. In most cases, they were unlikely to engage in serious criminal activities. In contrast, today's hackers appear to be motivated by greed, revenge, or politics and their actions have become more malicious. They are more likely to aim their attacks not just at individuals, but also at enterprise information systems.

The malicious insider, who has legitimate access to proprietary information and mission-critical systems, poses a significant threat because of having trusted status and familiarity with security practices. When an insider betrays his trust, he has a much greater opportunity and ability to do harm than someone on the outside. Moreover, he is less likely to be detected. The malicious insider, motivated by greed, revenge, or even political ideology, can act alone or with outsiders.

Although the insider threat is problematic, a sound security program will implement capabilities to identify behaviors and activities that represent possible insider exploitation of information resources. The activities of malicious insiders can often be identified through the analysis of access control and log files. They can also be detected through the correlation of both digital and physical evidence. In any event, insiders must be considered and assessed at least on par with the potential outsider threat. It is not safe to assume insiders are inherently more trustworthy than outsiders.

When attempting to analyze and measure threat, one should consider access. Access is the amount of physical, logical, or electronic presence a threat could have to the organization. Another factor to consider when measuring threat is the probability of occurrence. This takes into account

Table 4.1   Various Technical Vulnerabilities

- **CVE-2000-0844** — some functions that implement the local subsystem on Unix do not properly cleanse user-injected format strings, which allows local attackers to execute arbitrary commands via functions such as gettext and catopen.

- **CVE-2000-0825** — Ipswitch™ Imail™ 6.0 allows remote attackers to cause a denial of service via a large number of connections in which a long Host: header is sent, which causes a thread to crash.

- **CVE-2000-0816** — Linux® tmpwatch — fuser option allows local users to execute arbitrary commands by creating files whose names contain shell metacharacters.

- **CVE-2000-0829** — the tmpwatch utility in Red Hat® Linux forks a new process for each directory level, which allows local users to cause a denial of service by creating deeply nested directories in /tmp or /var/tmp/.

- **CVE-2000-0888** — named in BIND 8.2 through 8.2.2-P6, allows remote attackers to cause a denial of service by sending an SRV record to the server, aka the "srv bug."

- **CVE-2001-0155** — format string vulnerability in VShell™ SSH gateway 1.0.1 and earlier allows remote attackers to execute arbitrary commands via a user name that contains format string specifiers.

- **CVE-2001-0353** — buffer overflow in the line printer daemon (in.lpd) for Solaris™ 8 and earlier allows local and remote attackers to gain root privileges via a "transfer job" routine.

- **CVE-2001-0440** — buffer overflow in logging functions of licq before 1.0.3 allows remote attackers to cause a denial of service and possibly execute arbitrary commands.

the number of incidents attributable to the threat classes and the population size of the sample. Threat measurement is the second component of risk, after asset valuation, and is equal to access, threat profile, and occurrence measurement.

Vulnerabilities are those specific weaknesses that can be exploited by these threats to impact an asset (Table 4.1). System and network hardware, operating systems, applications, protocols, connectivity, physical environment, and current safeguards are all potential vulnerabilities.

Exposure determines whether a vulnerability may be exploited via physical or electronic exposure to the vulnerability. Physical exposure is a binary value that determines if the vulnerability can be exploited via physical access to the system. Electronic exposure is a binary value that determines if the vulnerability can be exploited via electronic access to the system.

A vulnerability subcomponent is a measurement of the severity of the vulnerability by measuring potential damage caused by exploitation, relative age as a measurement of when the vulnerability was discovered, and area of impact to operations, which is binary values used to determine the operational concerns impacted by the vulnerability.

Vulnerability is the third component of risk and is equal to exposure, vulnerability ranking, and subcomponent. Risk to an organization is the combination of a threat exploiting a vulnerability, which could negatively impact an asset. It is based on threat, vulnerability, and asset measurements (Figure 4.2). Risk analysis must determine which threats can exploit which vulnerabilities against specific assets. For the risk management analysis to be accurate, threats must be juxtaposed against specific vulnerabilities they can exploit. The mapping of threat and vulnerability is often called

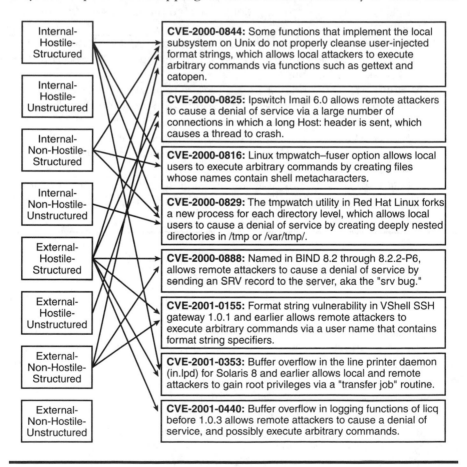

Figure 4.2 Threat–Vulnerability Pairing

threat–vulnerability pairing and is an important part of the risk management process.

Although progress is being made to secure wireless networks, rushing to deploy wireless systems poses a major threat of information theft. In addition, the ongoing underground movement to tap into hotspots, including those maintained by businesses, opens up the potential for service and bandwidth shoplifting.

Security systems are evolving from after-the-fact detection software into platforms that focus on prevention of intrusions before they occur. Companies should consider deploying console software that correlates data across all parts of the network so they can determine if an attack against one part of the infrastructure is related to a problem on another.

Instant messaging and other peer-to-peer programs create vulnerabilities in the network's defenses, particularly because many users are deploying the instant messaging software on their own. Securing instant messaging by at least setting usage policies is a practical first step. Protecting information assets, whether proprietary data or patents, should be a security priority for all organizations in order to prevent corporate espionage. Business and accounting scandals are indicative that every organization should improve the trustworthiness of its transactions and provide audit trails.

ANALYZING THREAT

A vital component of a proactive security plan is an analysis and understanding of the threats facing an organization. Unfortunately, the dialogue regarding IT threats is riddled with invocations of security clearance requirements, sound-byte rhetoric, and the lack of common threat categorization. As a result, the private sector is expected to make risk management decisions in the absence of a valid threat context. Threat assessments must be conducted to complement vulnerability assessments and enable organizations to make educated decisions to guide their security programs and spending. The threat of a large-scale critical infrastructure attack in today's environment can be characterized as those with the intent lack the capability and those with the capability lack the intent, both of which are subject to change.

To make responsible risk management decisions, it is important to avoid overreaction and also important not to systematically disregard the full spectrum of threats for lack of empirical evidence.

Any organization is likely to encounter a subset of threat agents responsible for nearly all the attempted or successful intrusions against the organization's infrastructures. These threat agents include insiders, industrial espionage, organized crime, and structured and unstructured hackers. The insider threat remains one of the most pervasive in the modern IT environment. Insider activity may be missed as organizations devote attention to monitoring their external environment and insiders become more adept at hiding their activities. There is also the concern about the use of insider placement as a penetration tactic. Organized threat agents, unable to penetrate external security mechanisms may seek to place individuals within the organization as temporary workers, employees, or even as system administrators. It is important that a security program implements safeguards to protect against insider threat. Such safeguards would include background checks for employees with access to critical systems, a recurring training and awareness program to help employees identify and report potential insider incidents, and implementation of internal security controls and network monitoring.

Much has been written regarding the threat of industrial espionage conducted by both competitors and state-sponsored intelligence organizations. Although industrial espionage is a continuing threat, it is one that many companies are familiar with and most attacks impact the confidentiality, not the availability, of the information. The sensitivity of business information will drive the safeguards required to protect its confidentiality. These elements are defined within the risk management function and the resultant decisions must be based on empirical data gathered when analyzing threat potential.

Routinely, organizations are most likely to face threats from both structured and unstructured attackers. Scanning and probing of networks occurs routinely against specifically targeted and random systems.

The demonstration of appropriate due diligence provides protection against the emerging threat of legal liability associated with IT security policy. Courts are taking actions to shut down IT infrastructures or hold organizations liable for their information security negligence. One way to validate efforts is through the use of independent threat and vulnerability assessment that documents a security profile and establishes recommendations for mitigating vulnerabilities or safeguarding from threats common to a particular industry.

ASSESSING PHYSICAL THREATS

The reality of physical threats has been driven home by the events of September 11, 2001. When evaluating threats to an IT environment, it is important to recognize the viability of the physical threat and to evaluate the impact that a physical event would have on the continuity of business operations. Physical threats may manifest themselves in the wide range of attacks, from bomb threats, causing the evacuation of a key facility, to large conventional truck bombs. Physical attacks may be launched with the intention of impacting the infrastructure as well as the general population.

In today's threat environment, a threat assessment methodology is a vital component of an organization's security program. This methodology should account for a wide variety of threats, including physical threats, and should be based on realistic threat information projecting future threats while also accounting for previous experiences, incidents, and documented attacks within an organization's peer group. Threat assessments should contain a description of the threat agent, probability of that agent conducting an attack against the target, tools the agent could use to attack the target, level of access the threat agent could obtain to use the tool against the target, and potential impact an attack would have on operations. The methodology also should identify potential safeguards and the reduction in exposure achieved through the implementation of the safeguard. Every attempt should be made to quantify the results of the threat assessment. Items emerge from threat assessments that quantify exposure, especially in terms of cost, so management can immediately relate to the potential exposure and the benefits of implementing a proposed safeguard.

As businesses venture into electronic commerce, the need for secure networks is greater than ever before. Whole sectors of society such as banking and telecommunications depend on the availability of reliable and secure networks. Awareness of the importance of information security continues to grow with new threats from hackers, organized crime, and terrorists exploiting information for their own intent. Many organizations have suffered significant losses as a result of the threat. Reflecting this fact is the increasing size of the computer security marketplace and the importance governments are beginning to place on protecting information infrastructures.

Connectivity is increasing at a rate often beyond the capacity to implement security controls. Market pressures on hardware and software vendors reduce the introduction of security features and testing prior to product release. Retrofitting security into existing systems and applications is difficult and expensive, with serious impact on operations.

A fundamental problem exists in the implementation of security controls in that very few organizations invest in proper threat assessment before implementing controls. Organizations need to qualify specific threats to evaluate risks accurately. Some threats may be overlooked while resources are applied to threats that have minimal impact. Security is the identification and management of risk, yet technology is changing faster than traditional risk assessment models can adapt. Organizations are increasing the size of their networks by adding more systems and system complexity. Suppliers, contractors, clients, and customers are increasingly integrated into a seamless network. The inherently insecure Internet and telecommunications infrastructure is the common means of providing connections.

These information architectures create information infrastructures that cross both organizational and national boundaries where no single entity has control or responsibility for security. Information infrastructures include telecommunications, healthcare, finance, government and defense, oil and gas, power generation, transportation, and the Internet.

Identification and evaluation of threats is still a complicated process. It involves the analysis of methods, access, skill levels, and costs used to exploit a given weakness within a system. Threats to information assets are not limited to technology alone. Physical controls, business and operational processes, telecommunications, and employee awareness all play vital roles in protecting from threat. Threats include accidents, errors of omission, and environmental factors such as natural disasters. Threats may be either malicious, in that someone purposely attacks a system, or not malicious, as in the case of a tornado destroying an organization's information hardware.

INFRASTRUCTURE THREAT ISSUES

In large networks, there are continuous changes in the number and type of systems, connections, and software. Information and physical assets, potential safeguards, and business requirements are always evolving. System vulnerabilities and the threats to them must be understood before policy and risk management decisions can be implemented. Threat assessments attempt to determine what threats exist, their likelihood, and the consequences or potential loss resulting from an attack.

Infrastructures are basic structural foundations for a country. Critical infrastructures include commerce, national security, telecommunications, the Internet, transportation, emergency services, oil and gas, power generation and distribution, healthcare, and finance. Each of these infrastructures has an information component that uses and is reliant on computers and networks to provide services (Figure 4.3). The information component of this infrastructure encompasses many systems connected in different networks owned by government agencies, commercial organizations, and financial institutions. Because of the highly connected nature of networks, unrelated networks, endpoints, and systems have potential access points into the systems within these infrastructures, opening them up to threat.

Infrastructures are ultimately interdependent. The generation of electrical power is dependent on the availability of oil and gas and a transport system thereof. Emergency response systems rely heavily on telecommunications. The size, complexity, distribution, and rate of change in the

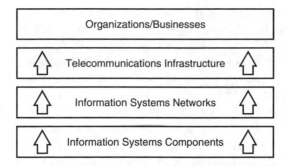

Figure 4.3 Relationship between Networks and Infrastructure

information infrastructures create security vulnerabilities that can lead to threats. Vulnerabilities at a lower functional level of a system undermine safeguards at higher levels. Basic password controls at the application level can be undermined within the network protocol or operating system. Encryption schemes in the network protocols can be attacked at the operating system level and in a widely distributed network may expose information or controls in other computer systems to the possibility of threats.

A critical challenge in securing systems is the ability to identify emerging threats. The speed at which new technology is introduced creates a rapidly moving target for threat assessments. Each new technology requires high-level technical expertise to analyze. By the time threat vulnerabilities are identified, technology has changed again. Confidentiality, fear of publicity, or incomplete information makes analysis difficult. An accurate prediction of exactly when, how, and by whom a potential threat will manifest itself is difficult. However, a structured assessment of the threat as outlined here provides a concise way to map the threat to specific categories for analysis and assessment.

Historically, information security threats have targeted individual systems. The motives for these attacks varied, but the methods and goals were limited to the computer system as the primary target. A fundamental change is occurring in information security with increasing automation and globalization of information. Attacks against infrastructure are of special importance because of the ramifications that result from the inability of that infrastructure to perform its function. The interdependence of these critical infrastructures multiplies the threat potential. When considering infrastructure vulnerabilities, threats to individual systems and the infrastructure itself must be accounted for. Infrastructure attacks typically require a more coordinated effort and provide better data points for indicator and warning analysis.

There are two major types of targeted attacks in threat assessments. The systems attack is an attack targeted against individual systems or control centers that are not usually detrimental to the overall operation of a whole infrastructure or organization. An infrastructure attack, on the other hand, is designed to significantly compromise the function of an entire infrastructure rather than individual components.

A threat assessment looks at the potential and actual damage from an attack. A successful system attack is an intrusion in which the basic integrity of a system is compromised. This compromise may lead to the loss of confidentiality, data integrity, or system resource availability. This attack does not target the infrastructure in which the computer operates.

A successful infrastructure attack is capable of sustaining compromise over a longer period of time. This attack usually targets recovery systems as well. Due to the interdependence of various infrastructures, an attack on one infrastructure may cascade into failures within other infrastructures. This threat could easily result in a national security emergency.

A limited infrastructure attack is an attack against an infrastructure that causes significant damage and cost, but is recovered without major disruption and does not affect other infrastructures. A limited infrastructure attack would mimic a major natural disaster such as a power outage caused by a hurricane.

Infrastructure attacks require precise targeting and successful, coordinated attacks against multiple system and control points. Attacks may also require the compromise of many levels within the infrastructure architecture such as protocols, software applications, and hardware itself, along with recovery systems. Successful attacks are not easy to accomplish. The success of an attack depends on multiple enabling events, significant planning, and technical capability. Despite the difficulty of an infrastructure attack, it is within the realm of possibility of those groups whose mission is to wreak economic havoc or promulgate terror.

Isolated attacks or accidents can be extremely costly to an organization. In the case of an infrastructure attack, losses can be on the magnitude of national significance. Implementing safeguards within networks and systems is essential to reduce vulnerability to threat. Threat detection will reduce the number of potential attacks. Threat assessments identify threats based on feasibility and indicators of vulnerability. Predicting, detecting, and monitoring potential threats to business and national security are critical.

Four elements are required for a threat to exist — agent, intent, target, and mechanism. There must be an agent with intent to carry out an attack. There must also be a target and mechanism whereby the agent can exploit vulnerability within a system. When these elements are present, there is a strong feasibility of attack.

The feasibility for a threat to exist is based on current technology, methodology, and skill of the attacking agent. Extensible technologies have enabled threat feasibility involving denial-of-service, spoofing, or covert channel attacks. Methodology is a technique, such as the use of password guessing algorithms, used to perpetrate a threat. Technical skill and knowledge of systems, processes, and practices is required to carry out the threat.

Identifying threat feasibility is the first step in threat assessment. Application of this process yields a significant number of potential threats, many of which will never be exploited. Therefore, further analysis is required to refine the likelihood of a threat actually occurring. More critical analysis is required in order that valuable counterattack resources are used most effectively and efficiently.

In threat assessment, feasibility is refined to detect the presence of specific indicators of potential threat. A prerequisite of indicators is intent by the agent of the threat. Intent helps to qualify the potential effort, skill, and expense the attacker is willing to invest in exploiting system vulnerability. Indicators are specific actions on the part of individuals or groups. An example of a threat indicator is the communication of specific threats in an affinity group that meets in cyberspace. The methodology used to exploit vulnerabilities could be published on a Web site. If security analysts note these indicators, they create a higher potential that the feasibility will be exploited and therefore additional safeguards may be needed.

When there are indications of targeting against an information asset, threats that have not actually occurred are potential threats and those demonstrated to be feasible are active threats. When implementing security measures, considering the efficient expenditure of security resources, the threats that are directly applicable to the vulnerable information asset should receive the highest priority.

As the world society becomes more dependent on data processing, information generation, and communication, the potential for significant loss increases if these systems are interrupted. With the increasing complexity of technology and connectivity, new threats are appearing that pose risks to information infrastructures. This extended threat model is designed to help identify potential threats in a more structured manner. Furthermore, these threats are prioritized based on specific information about the effort required to exploit them and indicators of the likelihood that they will be exploited.

The design and application of a threat assessment model requires thoughtful consideration of threat, risk, and vulnerability, taking into account the agent, intent, potential target, and mechanism of attack. Threat must be recognized as a continual process that requires ongoing data collection and analysis to identify new and changing threats effectively.

5

ASSESSING RISK VARIABLES: THE RISK ASSESSMENT PROCESS

INTRODUCTION

The nature of IT security has evolved rapidly in the relatively short life span of computer technology. Initially, security analysts and IT managers assumed they could simply eliminate security vulnerabilities in their computer and telecommunication systems and eliminate any chance of either intentional or unintentional exploitation of their information resources. This approach is more popularly known as risk avoidance. The risk avoidance strategy is a rather simplistic perspective that requires all vulnerabilities to be eliminated when they are identified. In theory, a risk avoidance approach would appear both logical and necessary to eliminate all potential risks to the assets in question. However, experience quickly taught both researchers and IT system managers that risk avoidance was simply untenable.

Risk avoidance can best be explained with basic examples from daily life. Any time you get behind the wheel of your car to drive on a public road, you take significant risks — dangers are everywhere. Most people take prudent precautions to minimize their risks. It is wise to use a seat belt and a car seat for infant passengers. Additionally, you want to limit and preferably eliminate external distractions such as cell phone calls, changing a CD, or applying makeup. Good defensive drivers also use their turn signals and turn their head around before changing lanes. Each of these safeguards helps reduce the risk of your everyday commute. However, most of us know at least one person who was involved in an accident through no negligence on their part. Hopefully, the result was only bent metal, but far too often, physical injury or even death may be the result. In this case, you can never claim it is possible to completely avoid risk, but each of us takes precautions to the degree we feel comfortable.

For some, unrealized risks either become too abstract or are simply ignored. There are always those who are willing to defy the risks or simply use poor judgment. This is the common it-will-not-happen-to-me attitude that can cause tragic loss for the one making the poor decisions or innocent parties who can be adversely affected. One's personal risk tolerance should always be considered in relation to others, especially others who may not share the same level of risk acceptance.

Humans do not make risk decisions according to the dictates of mathematics in their normal day-to-day lives. People do not sit to calculate probabilities and the expected value of the outcome and then attempt to maximize the end result. People do not base their judgment on safety solely on probability and consequence; they also include moral and ethical values and usually factor in concepts as trust and degree of uncertainty. Thus, humans perceive risk as a complex, multidimensional analysis that includes social and cultural factors and even has a basis on gut instinct.

It quickly becomes obvious in the case of automobile travel that all risk cannot be avoided. Prudent drivers take precautions and use safeguards to limit their level of risk. However, the risk tolerance of others may still impact the likelihood of a negative consequence. Ultimately, the issue of understanding risk in these situations is one of risk management, not of risk avoidance. The same concept is true for IT systems. Avoiding risk is impossible, thus risk management must be the mantra.

When a risk decision appears similar to our previous experiences, it can also introduce errors such as the assumption that representative data accurately portrays changes in probability. The other major concern is that those elements that do reflect changes in the probability of an outcome are ultimately given less weight than those considered as representative. These important factors can adversely affect risk decisions. Even a trained risk analyst would have an undue confidence in their risk decisions based on relatively small sample data.

For most of our daily experiences that involve risk (like driving a car), the way we understand the dangers and strive to mitigate them is based simply on gut instinct. Most of us do not use actuarial tables or transportation statistics to determine the ideal route to take to our job or school. We may be aware of a particularly dangerous intersection or stretch of highway and endeavor to drive slower or be more alert when we are there. A lack of awareness of the assumptions on which our judgments are based can result in overconfidence and a failure to appreciate what we do not know. However, the precise mathematical odds are not normally a factor in our daily driving decisions.

The same has been true for most IT security decisions. Even when the IT industry embraced the concept of risk management over risk avoidance, most security practitioners and researchers continued to base their implementation trade-offs on gut instinct arising from their experience and education. In the absence of a credible formula for assessing risk, this is not necessarily wrong. We could logically anticipate that someone with a strong technical background and many years of targeted experience would best optimize our security posture.

For most of the last decade, security management has been practiced thusly. The most successful security practitioners have been technical experts with deep experience. Unfortunately, most have not applied a consistent and accurate model for evaluating and mitigating risks in IT systems. There is a coming transition from technical security implementation to empirical corporate systems risk management.

To return to our driving example, we may wish to examine the elements of personal risk management and our risk management strategies. One of the ways most drivers manage their personal risk is through insurance coverage. In fact, it has evolved as a state legal requirement throughout the United States. Drivers are required to carry insurance to protect others and have several options for mitigating risk for themselves and their family members. If you finance a car, the institution that lends the money will usually require additional insurance to protect their financial interest in the vehicle as well. The insurance product you buy, therefore, is designed for your situation to mitigate risk to you, your lender, and your fellow drivers.

The insurance companies that provide these risk mitigation policies do not rely on the gut instinct of their managers and employees. They use risk management models such as actuarial tables to make almost every company decision. They charge higher insurance rates for customers who have young or inexperienced drivers on the policy. People who frequently drive great distances or have a record of traffic infractions also have higher premiums. There is also a statistical table that assesses where you live and drive most frequently. Statistical models that mathematically calculate the amount of risk each customer represents to the insurer ultimately define the rates a customer pays.

Insurance companies are always under pressure to ensure these analyses are as accurate as possible. If they are not, the insurance company will lose customers to competitors if the rates are too high and will definitely risk profits and shareholder value if the rates are too low. These built-in incentives ultimately keep the entire automobile insurance system in balance. Of course, these same constraints are at play in every type of insurance situation including homeowners insurance and most other insurance products.

There are numerous reasons to explain why this type of sensible, empirical analysis has not been as quickly adopted by the IT industry. The primary impediment to adoption of mathematical models has been the lack of quantifiable data regarding the value of the assets and the resultant costs associated with its exploitation. We have already reviewed the challenges of assigning monetary value to data and information resources; however, this does not preclude us from adapting the valuable lessons of the insurance industry to IT security.

Defining risk management for IT systems then is the process of designing, developing, sustaining, and modifying operational processes and systems in consideration of applicable risks to information asset confidentiality, integrity, and availability. Applicable risks are defined as those reasonably (or better, mathematically) expected to be realized and to cause an unacceptable impact. These unacceptable impacts are best assessed by the use of information valuation metrics.

Risk management for IT systems incorporates an analytical systems approach to the entire operational and support cycle. It provides not only the security practitioner, but also the corporate management and executive decision makers a reliable, accurate, and repeatable process for security analysis, implementation, and enforcement. If you cannot measure your security program, you ultimately cannot manage it. This structured risk management process, therefore, will necessarily evolve to become the cornerstone for all effective security implementations.

The structured risk management process must meet several empirical objectives. The first is the obvious requirement for cost-effectiveness. No responsible organization wants to overspend on their security program. It is a common complaint among security practitioners that they do not receive adequate support, monetary and otherwise, for their security programs. It is important to understand that no one invests in security simply to be more secure. A security program is basically a type of insurance — a process whereby valuable information assets are accorded the amount of protection required but no more. When security practitioners make the claim that they do not have the necessary resources, it normally follows that they have been unsuccessful in accurately quantifying the risk management process for the key decision makers. If each party is making claims based simply on experience or gut instinct, it is nearly impossible to reach an agreement on the resources necessary to implement a cost-effective program.

Any and all attempts to reduce the amount of risk in an IT system are counterbalanced by various expenses and other types of security overhead. It is critical to consider all the possible expenses related to the security safeguard under consideration. These expenses can include acquisition costs, monitoring, maintenance, and even performance degradation within the system. Each and every safeguard will require some type of investment.

There is a myth in the ranks of IT professionals of the availability of transparent security tools and procedures. In fact, many organizations claim to require security that is completely transparent, at least to end users. If such a product or procedure exists, I have yet to find it. All security has some overhead, even if it is only a marginal increase in bandwidth requirements.

The performance impact of security technology and procedures cannot be ignored in a risk management process. The time it takes to type a password, the latency requirements for link encryption, and even end-user training must be factored. Then there are the ongoing life-cycle costs to operate, maintain, upgrade, and manage the products and processes that enforce security requirements.

As risks are mitigated, costs necessarily increase and system performance is degraded by the overhead of running security products and processes. To effectively manage the trade-offs involved, a risk management process must be used to optimize the value of the entire security program. There is a zone where risk mitigation and its associated costs are best for a particular organization, as depicted in a notional diagram in Figure 5.1.

Where an organization ultimately ends up within this zone is wholly dependent on the value of their information resources and the nature of the missions the information supports. Perhaps the information system under consideration is a simple informational Web site where basic availability is the key security requirement. Such a security program would be

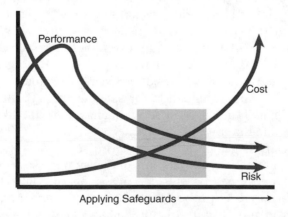

Figure 5.1   Risk Management Payoffs

positioned to the far left-hand side of the zone. An intelligence system that supports military combat troops would necessarily be located toward the extreme right-hand side of the zone where greater costs are incurred given the value of the information and the organization's reliance for protecting lives.

Irrespective of the IT system itself, the investment of time and effort in developing a risk management process will quickly pay for itself in optimizing the cost-effectiveness of any security program. As with any security-relevant decision, the value of the information will ultimately dictate the amount of effort required for risk management analysis. Any IT environment that processes information of even minimal value will benefit from a structured risk analysis.

To create accurate actuarial models that make the individual companies competitive yet successful, the automobile insurance industry had to determine the key elements of risk for their risk analysis process. These elements include the age of the driver, their driving record, the value of the car, repair costs of the vehicle, installed security devices, the driving environment, and numerous other factors. If we wish to make similar assessments of risk to information resources, we must evaluate the corollary features of information and of the IT systems that transmit, store, and process it.

LEARNING TO ASK THE RIGHT QUESTIONS ABOUT RISK

When an organization first begins to wrestle with the security and privacy issues of their IT systems, senior leadership usually asks if bad things could happen to their systems. This natural concern sometimes arises as a result of stories and articles in the press or trade publications. Because even the most junior IT security practitioner knows it *could* happen, the people who must make the resource decisions now want to know the likelihood that it *will* happen. And even the most senior IT security practitioner would, at best, cite statistics gathered by organizations like the Gartner Group and the Computer Security Institute. These answers are not exactly the best foundation for spending significant portions of a corporation's limited capital. Most senior managers would like a little more data before making a larger investment.

The next step to gathering this data is a series of tests to determine the degree of vulnerability the systems in question possess. In many cases, these tests are performed by outside consultants or contractors. The tests usually will be used to probe for unmonitored entry points and other vulnerabilities in the IT infrastructure. Once the testing is complete, a report is generated that usually explains in great technical detail the location and nature of the vulnerabilities that were exploited. These reports also can be used to alert management and IT staff to the ease with which information resources can be exploited.

At this point, many people feel they have enough data to present to management to make a case for expenditures on security safeguards. They have shown how they can exploit corporate information and have identified some vulnerabilities that can most likely be eliminated with straight-forward preventive measures. Everyone involved in the project now gathers their data and presents the findings in a management meeting. In some cases, the conversation may go like this:

Security Team: We've finished our testing and found that our systems are fairly easy to exploit. In fact, many of our employees have written their passwords down where we were able to find them. Using this information allowed us to see their files. The technical IT security consultants we hired were also able to shut down our Internet firewall because of the way we had it configured. It took the IT department nearly two hours to get it back up and running.

Management: That sounds like a valuable exercise. What do we need to do to fix these problems?

ST: I guess we need to start by cracking down on our employees who write down their passwords. We could send out a memo and then perform checks to make sure they are following the guidelines. The IT security consultants will also give us a report describing the scripts they used crash the firewall.

M: Before we go too much further, some of us may have to come clean. I have a list of passwords I keep here in my wallet; I'm sure many others have the same. I currently have six different passwords just for our office systems. Then I have my home Internet account, bank card PIN, credit card PIN, and even an access code to check my frequent flyer account on the Net. Surely, you can't expect everyone to commit all that to memory — especially since your security team requires us to use computer-generated passwords that change every three months. A password like "grghebw1k" is not easy to remember. You said at the last meeting that this password policy was necessary to enhance security. It seems to me your plans are having unintended side effects, which actually may degrade our security.

ST: We can revisit our password policy if you feel it is necessary. But how about the firewall problems? Do you want to talk about the techniques the consultants used to hack the firewall.

M: I thought the term you used originally was "crash." Is that correct?

ST: Yes. They used an exploit they found on a hacker's Web page that can be used to crash the type of firewall we have installed. It renders the system temporarily inoperable and the firewall has to be manually restarted. It was the same exploit used by some ethnic Albanians to crash a firewall used by the Yugoslavian government during the Kosovo crisis. I'm happy to report we located a security patch from the vendor and have already updated the firewall software so this won't happen again.

M: I'm glad to hear it. Do you think our company could face the same kind of problem? We are not a high-profile target. I doubt we need to protect ourselves like the Pentagon. What else did the consultants find? Do they think we need to do anything else to improve our IT security?

ST: While they were here, they gave us a presentation on the latest encryption and intrusion detection technologies. These guys are sharp. If you'd like, I'll set up a time for you to get the same presentation.

M: Before we go that far, perhaps your team can help put some of this into perspective. I know what encryption is and I can guess what intrusion detection technology involves. They both sound expensive. Do we really need this high-tech stuff? I find it hard to believe we need all this state-of-the-art equipment for one Class C network and a handful of remote users. As I said before, we aren't the Pentagon. In any case, it sounds like you have already solved our firewall problem with a no-cost security patch.

ST: That's true, but we can use some of these new technologies to improve security. With intrusion detection, we can see if someone is trying to hack our system.

M: I'm not sure I understand who would want to hack our systems. And before I waste more time on this discussion, I want to look at the specific issues at hand. It seems like the two big concerns out of your security review were password exposure and a technical firewall problem we have already resolved with a system patch. Just send out a memo reminding everyone to protect their passwords and to avoid writing them down on a paper they leave lying around the office. Meeting adjourned.

In the exchange above the security team was focused on the vulnerabilities they found and where they were located. They were there to answer the What and Where questions of security. During the same meeting, management was focused on the Why, How much, and Who of security. There was only one meeting, but several different agendas.

The security team was primed to explain the security technicalities to management and to use this occasion to promote new security safeguard technology. Management (understandably) wanted to know if they truly needed these enhancements, and if so, how much they were going to cost. Neither group ultimately met the other's expectations. In the end, management usually adopts a cautious course based on the exposed vulnerabilities and the security team leaves with no commitment for further upgrades.

The IT security professional must ensure they are answering the questions that are being asked no matter who is asking. And it is vital to make sure you structure any test or analysis to develop the proper answers. When these questions are written down, the job is much easier. Once agreement is reached on the questions to answer, the nature of the work to be performed is more easily deduced.

Here are some questions you can write down:

- How easy would it be for someone to steal our corporate information?
- How easy would it be for someone to crash our network?
- What vulnerabilities exist at our Internet connection?
- What is likelihood that we will be hacked by someone?
- What damage could they do?
- What could one of our employees do with unauthorized access privileges?
- How easy is to circumvent these access controls?
- Is it easier for insiders than someone trying to come in from the Internet?
- How much should we spend on our IT security program?
- Who is responsible for protecting our IT and informational resources?

There are innumerable possibilities and the broader the question the more work required to arrive at the answer. This process also can be used in meetings to ensure everyone's expectations are properly established and fulfilled. The technique of accurately defining the questions greatly improves the quality of the results.

The IT security professional is often the victim of miscommunication. Writers and journalists like to create hype surrounding hackers and government misuse of information. Vendors tout their hardware and software as a total network security solution. Consultants may offer to evaluate an entire network security program by a low-cost penetration exercise. For a security program to be effective, it is vital to gather the data to answer the questions you are asked. Major problems are often the result of drawing improper conclusions from the data that is available. Providing the answers to what and where will not help someone looking to be taken to the why.

After I retired from the military, I took a job with one of those DC-area consulting companies that are collectively known as Beltway Bandits. As a newly minted security consultant, I worked on a variety of projects for Department of Defense clients. One of the most memorable was an assignment to develop certification and accreditation documentation for the computer systems deployed aboard the *USS Blue Ridge* — the command ship for the U.S. Seventh Fleet. The contract called for me and another consultant to perform our analyses and testing while the ship was underway somewhere in the admiral's area of responsibility. That was pretty much anywhere in the Pacific Ocean.

After completing the appropriate proposal and contract paperwork, I was told to stand by for instructions on where to meet the ship. Because its exact movements and destinations are kept closely guarded, the Navy could only give me a specific time and date for meeting the ship on short notice. Two weeks later, an international satellite call to my Washington, D.C., office one Thursday morning directed my small team to meet the ship in Hong Kong by Saturday.

After a wild and eventful trip, I finally found the ship docked across the harbor in Kowloon. I reported aboard and promptly fell asleep in my assigned bunk for 12 solid hours. A day later, I was called to give an in-brief to the senior naval officer in charge of the fleet's communications and computer systems. This particular captain was a grizzled veteran whose career had taken him around the world several times. He was also extremely competent with technology and was a hands-on computer authority. During my presentation, he stopped me after listening intently for several minutes.

"That is all well and good," he snapped. "But when you disembark in two weeks, I want to be assured all my systems are secure." His comment brought silence to the cramped room just off the admiral's bridge. I had to pause for several seconds before responding.

"With all due respect, I really cannot do that, sir," I replied with appropriate deference acquired from years of military service. I noticed I was not quick enough to clarify my statement before a dark look came over his face.

"I thought you guys were the computer security experts," he snarled. "What are you doing here if you cannot secure my computers?"

"Sir, we are the right people for this job. We will be analyzing and testing your systems. We will look for vulnerabilities and for compliance with Navy and Department of Defense requirements. We will search for unauthorized connections, software, and other potential problems. When we have completed this work, we will provide you a written report and a presentation outlining our findings. You will have a complete view of your systems' configuration and the risks associated with them. You and your subordinates will then use that report to make decisions on risk mitigation and you will ultimately accredit the systems for operation."

"That sounds exactly like the task we hired you to do. Why is that any different from what I said?" he responded sternly.

"It is only different in that I never even used the word security. In human terms, security is a state of mind, not a verifiable state of being. The only way I could assure you that these computers were secure is if I disconnected them from all their external connections and threw them into the sea. Even then, there is a chance a potential enemy could dredge them up and analyze the hard drives for sensitive information."

"Point taken," he replied. "Now get started so we have this project done by the time we dock in Korea. If you have not completed your work by that rendezvous, you may be at sea with us for a couple more months."

In IT security, almost all the enforcement technology we currently have available is based on process —the How. Firewalls, encryption, access control, and even security administration are all built around telling the information systems how to implement a convoluted process that is supposed to enforce the dictums of the security policy. Currently, most of these technologies and point solutions are designed to simply prevent certain activities from taking place. For example, a firewall is designed to keep unauthorized users and data from entering an organization's network. The firewall administrator must then go through a detailed and difficult process of defining specifically which processes and data are authorized and then programming the firewall to keep everything else out.

Every comprehensive review of IT security describes the importance of having a security policy. Computer security consultants worth their salt patiently explain to their clients why they need this policy to accurately determine the efficacy of their security program. The policy forms the basis of all the discussions of What. Unfortunately, the consultant then must determine the degree to which the many components of security that make up the process (the How) effectively implement the policy (the What). This difficult game of abstraction is how the best consultants earn their high fees.

By now you might be asking yourself, "Why not opt for products and tools that let you apply the What instead of expending all the effort to implement the How?" Unfortunately, most IT security technologies are designed to be another link in the security process chain. These tools cannot enforce the What because they simply cannot implement an information-centric security policy. They can only implement binary technology-based security policies.

Let us look at an example: your medical records. There are policies or rules regarding the use of this sensitive information that may be as simple as this:

■ The patient may request and be allowed access to all information in his or her file at any time.
■ The Records Department must document all access requests and use of these records. It must keep these records accurate.
■ The hospital Finance Department may see and update charges, payments, insurance information, and other relevant fields, but must not have access to sensitive medical information.
■ An authorized physician can gain access to your record (and may do so without your approval if you are incapacitated), but may not have access to your financial data.
■ The medical insurance company may gain access with your approval for doctors' diagnoses and other relevant data. If you refuse to grant this access, you may be denied reimbursement of your medical fees.

Now, think about all the IT security technologies you may be aware of and try to imagine enforcing these five simple rules with complex network technologies like firewalls, public key encryption, access control systems, operating system tools, and application security products. After a few moments of reflection, it is easy to see the difficulties of defining security technology processes for even a few simple security policy requirements in a limited systems environment. The requirement for a structured information-based methodology is evidenced by the problems of abstraction by endeavoring to define the security policy through an assessment of individual technology components.

Defining the What of security policies becomes a possibility only when we can develop the ability to apply these policies directly to the information assets themselves. In the example above, we would need to be able to assign these policies to the medical record itself. This is not only the most efficient way to translate information management requirements to functional implementation, it is also the most effective way to secure the information or data assets. If the security and management policies were thus tightly coupled with the record itself, then a centrally managed policy enforcement controller would be able to mediate any attempts by a person or other program to effect that asset.

Current access control and network-based security technology is already proving unable to adapt to the demands of the digital marketplace. Valuable information and digital assets such as music recordings and art are most effectively used when they can be shared with others. However, companies, copyright owners, inventors, artists, musicians, designers, and others must be the ones to set the rules to enforce their digital rights. These new information-based security technologies will finally allow us to realize the profits and cost savings promised by a worldwide Internet.

Information-based policy enforcement technologies like the one described here are just emerging. These new capabilities will open up completely new ways to share information and data, collaborate with others, and organize the cacophony of information that has become the World Wide Web. Effective security policy enforcement will allow decision makers to find more effective ways to employ their information resources. These networks and systems must have the ability to enforce exactly how each bit of data is used regardless of where it is being transmitted, stored, or processed.

Most creative and intelligent workers prefer the freedom that comes from defining the What as opposed to enforcing the How. Slavish adherence to processes over results is the domain of bureaucrats and assembly lines. Modern digital IT systems are required to share valuable information and data assets while ensuring they continue to enforce security policy requirements their owners have defined.

THE BASIC ELEMENTS OF RISK IN IT SYSTEMS

Just as an automobile insurance company must employ more than one simple actuarial table, information security practitioners must evaluate several key elements of the risk management formula. These elements are information asset values, threats, vulnerabilities, and safeguards. Each of these elements is critical to assessing and implementing a cost-effective security program.

INFORMATION AS AN ASSET

The first major element of risk analysis is certainly the value of the information itself. Information assets are the heart of the risk assessment process. As with the McCumber Cube methodology, an accurate risk assessment process is also information-centric. This means that the assets evaluation function of the risk assessment process is ultimately a matter of determining the value of the information resources you are protecting.

Because there is an entire chapter dedicated to this analysis, we will not go into repetitive detail. However, it should be obvious that any security analysis must include a detailed inventory and empirical assessment of the value of the information resources. It is possible to make a detailed assessment of security functionality of specific IT components without considering the value of the data it transmits, stores, and processes, but it is impossible to define security for a system without this critical element.

As part of the information valuation process, it is important to make a discerning assessment of information value. If an organization goes to the trouble of collecting, maintaining, and using data, it is illogical to say that some (or all) of this data has no value. Certain data sets and information resources may require low levels of security protection, but to claim than any data or information has no value would argue that the assets should not be maintained in the system under any circumstances. That is the reason the McCumber Cube methodology does not account for information resources with no value.

In the McCumber Cube methodology, we will assign a simple ranking of high, medium, or low to use as the textbook example. Obviously, this simplistic ranking is by no means fully adequate to accurately evaluate anything but a relatively small IT system managing on a meager amount of data. However, the guidelines in the information valuation chapter can be used to expand your analysis to more discreetly calculate the impact to your organization if the assets are destroyed, disclosed, delayed, or distorted.

DEFINING THREAT FOR RISK MANAGEMENT

Once you have accurately determined the value of your information resources, the real work begins. One of the most difficult aspects of any empirical risk analysis is defining the threats to information and IT resources. For many people, the threat to information transmitted, stored, and processed in modern computer and telecommunications systems involves one overexposed concept — the hacker. When the perception of the external, malicious (and often teenaged) hacker is espoused, far too many people assume it is the most significant, if not only, threat faced by modern IT systems.

In numerous organizations, the miniscule resources that had been earmarked for IT security programs are spent solely in assessing and deploying a small array of antihacker technologies. After purchasing the ubiquitous firewalls, implementing a basic network DMZ (demilitarized zone — a network security euphemism), these organizations are satisfied performing a quick, inexpensive penetration test to infrequently assess the efficacy of these technologies. These solutions are usually able to discourage most external threats that could be classified as hackers; some were even able to block certain types of e-mail abuse. However, no controls are in place to mediate, manage, and audit the activities of authorized users. Although they could enforce a few binary conditions at their network boundaries, they could not determine if the actions of their own employees were being performed in conformance to their written policies. This approach ultimately results in an ineffective penetration-and-patch security program that will be discussed in the vulnerability section below.

Threats fall into two major categories — environmental and human. Environmental threats consist of a broad spectrum of nonhuman phenomena that can cause disclosure, delay, denial, or distortion of information resources. Included in environmental threats are the obvious natural disasters such as fire, flood, or even an unsound office environment for PCs and servers. Most often, environmental threats affect the availability of information and data resources. However, it is important to identify all possible scenarios as an integral part of a structured security program.

Too often, environmental threats are left to the purview of disaster recovery procedures alone. It is vital to ensure a corporate disaster recovery program includes IT resources, but it must never be assumed that redundancy and backup controls alone are sufficient when managing this threat. Environmental threats need to be factored into all aspects of the security methodology and are considered as integral to the methodology as human threats. This important distinction is a critical aspect of a structured security implementation methodology.

The human threat is assuredly the most insidious and dynamic. Engineers are fond of saying that any system engineered by a human can be reverse engineered by another human. This principle holds true for security technology as well as security programs. The human threat represents the most complex and ultimately the most significant security problem.

Whether you prefer to believe the statistics promulgated by the FBI or the Computer Security Institute, the picture is still the same: anywhere between 60 percent and 80 percent of data exploitation takes place by insiders and authorized system users. If your risk management analysis considers solely those threats that constitute network security breaches perpetrated by hostile outsiders, you are only managing a small minority of technical and procedural vulnerabilities.

One of the most important aspects of the structured risk management approach is the eye-opening realization of the entire human threat spectrum. Potential human threats obviously exist outside the organization. However, they also exist within the organization and must include an authorized system user. The elements of human threat are based on the characteristics of the humans involved. They can be generally described by these traits:

- People inside the systems environment
- People outside the systems environment
- People with malicious intent

- People with nonmalicious intent
- People with in-depth computer skills
- People without in-depth computer skills

It is vital to recognize that these are broad categories and there are understandably wide variations between these general characteristics. However, they give us a way to parse and decompose the human threat in order to grasp the entire spectrum of human threat. Because we covered this topic in Chapter 4, we will move to the next key element of the risk assessment process.

DEFINING VULNERABILITIES FOR RISK MANAGEMENT

Many organizations have launched their IT security programs with penetration studies. These efforts are usually performed with the intent of developing a recognized baseline of the vulnerabilities within their IT systems. Almost inevitably, however, an initial penetration study begins the spiraling cycle of penetration-and-patch security. The real problems arise over time as the people charged with IT security play a losing game of catch-up. As new corporate IT systems and electronic services are deployed, these individuals struggle to find the vulnerabilities in the new systems while the process of developing and fielding even newer capabilities proceeds unabated. The vulnerability gap just keeps getting wider.

Two venerable security practitioners — Dan Farmer and Wietse Venema — wrote one of the landmark papers espousing this technique. Their names are most frequently associated with their now-legendary software program SATAN (System Administrator Tool for Analyzing Networks). Two years before making their tool publicly available to great fanfare, the two researchers published on Usenet a classic paper in December 1993 titled, "Improving the security of your site by breaking into it." They then set about writing the code to automate the penetration process. Ultimately, the concept of a network penetration tool that could be downloaded and used by anyone with access to the Internet caused quite a stir in the technology community and Dan was summarily fired from his job at Sun Microsystems after he made his product publicly available.

Much has changed in the intervening years. More and more security products are available. Commercial products have largely replaced freeware and shareware security tools such as SATAN. Even though these new tools require a larger investment in both acquisition costs and training, they tend to be more stable and more accurate because a company trying to make a profit backs them. They also provide more complete documentation and most come with technical support.

What has not changed, however, is many people's idea of what these tools are for and how they are best employed. Envisioning other security-relevant analogies to the penetration-and-patch model for IT systems can prove amusing:

■ Improving your fire safety awareness by setting your house on fire
■ Improving your executive protection program by shooting at your CEO
■ Improving your defensive driving techniques by crashing your car

These may seem overstated, but I think the underlying principle is important. IT security is the sole remaining security discipline that often has the penetration-and-patch model at its core.

The penetration-and-patch security model actually sounds like it makes a great deal of sense when practitioners are first exposed to it. Basically, this method of evaluating IT systems security calls for the security practitioner to attempt to break into their system from an outsider's perspective (penetration), then fix any and all holes found during the exercise (patch). In this way, as the logic of it implies, the security practitioner can eliminate the vulnerabilities malicious intruders would use to exploit the systems and its vital information resources. This repeated exercise then becomes the foundation for the entire IT security program.

Ultimately, the penetration-and-patch model leads to failure. It is logical to assume that the penetration team will overlook a number of vulnerabilities that were not considered or were unknown at the time of the test. Each subsequent iteration will continue to overlook a number of vulnerabilities until a significant number exist through negligence of the lack of an appropriate security countermeasure. Figure 5.2 is a notional diagram of the problem that arises from an overreliance on penetration-and-patch security. As the growth in vulnerabilities grows through both system evolution and oversight of the penetration testers, security erodes dramatically over time.

Ensuring you have a comprehensive analysis of the threat environment is the best way to avoid this overreliance on the penetration-and-patch security process. Organizations that rely on the perspective that the threat is almost solely from network savvy, external entities with malicious intent will necessarily misappropriate their limited security resources. The penetration-and-patch approach can provide valuable data regarding existing vulnerabilities and security compliance. Penetration testing should be an integral part of an overall security program life cycle. However, it must be employed and evaluated as just one aspect of the greater security management process.

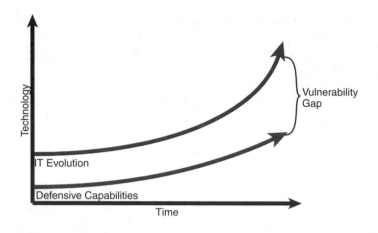

Figure 5.2   Penetration-and-Patch

At the heart of this issue is the phenomenon of vulnerability centrism in IT systems security. Vulnerability centrism is the concept that exposure to risk is a result of the presence or absence of vulnerabilities and is a corollary to the hacker-centric security program. Once a vulnerability is detected, the associated risk is best mitigated by eliminating the identified vulnerability. Then the search for more vulnerabilities is conducted until another one is found. This then becomes the next problem to solve by finding a specific point solution to eliminate the vulnerability. The process is thus repeated.

Vulnerability centrism is popular not just because it initially seems logical, but because it is simple to implement and easy to defend if the organization experiences a loss. Someone practicing this type of security needs only a couple common vulnerability probing tools to search for vulnerabilities. Once the vulnerabilities are exposed, system patches and targeted countermeasures are recommended. If the system is then rendered useless by a relatively simple denial of service problem during a peak processing period, the security staff may claim they did not account for that specific vulnerability. In other words, because no one from the outside actually broke in to inflict the damage, they are blameless.

Using an automated probing tool to look for vulnerabilities can also alleviate the operator from doing any actual analysis, because vulnerability centrism ignores some of the basic elements necessary to create risk. For an organization to have risk, they must account for the threats and value of the assets as well as the current safeguards already in place. It is ironic that many probing tools produce reports that identify levels of risk based solely on the presence of a specific vulnerability. These are often in the form of red, yellow, and green lights or low, medium, and high identifiers.

However, without a complete analysis of the elements of risk, these ratings are all but worthless.

None of this is meant to imply there is not any value in probing your systems for vulnerabilities. The SATAN tool certainly raised security awareness among the computing community; many systems administrators still use the tool or one of its commercial variants to help them assess weaknesses in their systems' configurations. However, these tools are most effectively employed when you are comparing the number of potential vulnerabilities against the ones that are actually present at various network access points. In other words, system penetration and hacking studies are best performed as a security compliance function as opposed to a foundation for a security program.

Many security practitioners look to begin their IT security program with a penetration study. If they do not have a documented security policy or system configuration baseline with which to compare and analyze the results, the study can be a nearly worthless exercise. If they do not have the necessary policy and compliance requirements in writing, then there is usually a significant amount of groundwork necessary before the actual penetration exercises can begin. Although this can be a time-consuming process, undertaking the policy and standards development effort at this point can save the organization enormous amounts of money and human resources spent in knee-jerk point solutions and uncoordinated security programs.

Applying purely offensive testing to develop a defensive capability implies that you can test for all potential threats. Even with sophisticated hardware and software tools, nothing can yet replace sound analysis of test results as compared to the organization's security needs and the existing and planned IT environment.

Vulnerabilities need to be defined specifically. That means there is a unique technical definition for each vulnerability as it is identified. Sometimes the term *exposure* is used to define a category of vulnerability. Because of their technical nature, vulnerabilities evolve over time. To employ them in the risk assessment process, they must be uniquely identified and tied directly to your information systems environment to be included as part of the risk assessment process. Because a comprehensive and dynamic library of vulnerabilities and exposures already exists, this is included in Section III as a reference.

DEFINING SAFEGUARDS FOR RISK MANAGEMENT

The McCumber Cube methodology is aimed at assessing and defining the complete range of safeguards needed for adequate security policy enforcement. The safeguards are synonymous with the security measures stratum of the McCumber Cube. Safeguards may be technical, procedural, or based on some element of human intervention. I often refer to them as the three Ps — products, processes, and people.

Detailed safeguards assessments are performed to match safeguards with applicable vulnerabilities and threats to determine the effectiveness of alternative individual and complementary safeguards. Safeguards can be technical (e.g., encryption, firewalls, and mandatory access controls), procedural (certain information assets are not allowed on certain systems), or administrative (e.g., media control and training procedures). In many networks, simply addressing the safeguards of appropriate systems administration and training can mitigate much risk. Safeguard evaluation must be tied to the safeguard's ability to mitigate some or all of the risk associated with a threat–vulnerability pair.

A structured risk assessment methodology emphasizes business value for safeguard investment. The process provides a traceable, reliable decision support process that encourages necessary and sufficient protection. The resulting safeguard implementations will best mitigate aggregate risks for the information system infrastructure for the cost. Based on the risk determinations, recommendations will be made advising the safeguards that should be applied to best reduce the risk. As safeguards are applied, risk can be recalculated to determine the risk reduction achieved as a result of the safeguard.

THE RISK ASSESSMENT PROCESS

Once you gather this information you have the basic elements of the risk assessment process. Follow this process to make decisions on how much should be invested in the information systems security program. A more detailed outline of the entire risk assessment process is shown in Table 5.1.

Table 5.1   Detailed Outline of the Risk Assessment Process

1. Identify business process:
a. The risk methodology determines risk for a particular business process. It is the business processes that are the foundation of the company's business and therefore risk should be defined in regard to these processes.
b. This methodology will tie the business processes to the assets they rely on, to the architecture that supports the assets, and to the vulnerabilities of the architecture. Together this will lead to a determination of the risks of the business process.
2. Determine operational concerns:
a. There are three operational concerns to be considered:
i. Confidentiality — the privacy and protection of data from unauthorized access or exposure.
ii. Integrity — the accuracy of the data or systems used by your organization.
iii. Availability — the accessibility of an asset for its intended use at a given point in time.
b. These operational concerns apply to the business process, not to each individual asset. The operational concerns are defined with regard to the output of the business process.
3. Identify or define assets:
a. Each business process relies on multiple assets — identify the assets and data items that are part of this business process.
b. Although the majority of assets that will be identified will be informational, an asset can be of the following types:
i. Informational — most assets that are defined will be informational; they will be data objects.
ii. Functional — for example, an Internet connection can be a functional asset.
iii. Physical — any physical component or equipment can be an asset.
4. For each asset determine:
• Business role.
• Logical data flow.
• User population.
• Access rights and controls:
i. Physical access.
ii. Logical access.
a. Supporting architecture:
i. System and network hardware.
ii. System and network operating systems.
iii. System and network applications.

(Continued)

Table 5.1   Detailed Outline of the Risk Assessment Process (Continued)

	iv.			Network protocol
	v.			System connectivity.
	vi.			Physical environment.
5.	Assign asset measurements:			
	a.			Each asset will be rated for sensitivity and criticality with regard to the critical process in question.
	b.			The two asset measurements will be rated on a scale of 1 to 5 (1 — not important, 5 — extremely important):
		i.		Sensitivity — the relative measurement of damage to the business process if the asset was disclosed to unauthorized users, such as competitors.
		ii.		Criticality — the relative measurement of how crucial the asset is to the accomplishment of the business process.
6.	Determine importance:			
	a.			Importance is a subjective rating of high, medium, low, or none assigned to each asset.
	b.			This rating determines the importance of the asset to the business process.
	c.			The importance rating is determined from the asset measurements assigned in the previous step and a subjective analysis of those values.
		i.		Although the value assigned to each asset measurement will be independent of the operational concerns of the business process, the importance rating will have to consider the operational concerns.
			A.	For example, an asset with a sensitivity value of 4 and a criticality value of 1 may have an importance rating of *high,* if sensitivity is more of a concern to the process than criticality. On the other hand, if sensitivity is of low concern and criticality is of higher concern, then the importance rating will be *low.*
			B.	There is no mathematical way to determine the importance rating; the factors above have to be combined with an awareness of the organization's business and operations to determine the rating that makes the most sense.
7.	Identify vulnerabilities:			
	a.			Based on the supporting architecture vulnerabilities can be determined.
	b.			Vulnerabilities can be determined in several ways:
		i.		Combination of tools and information gathering techniques:
			A.	Scanner — host/network scanning tool.

(Continued)

Table 5.1   Detailed Outline of the Risk Assessment Process (Continued)

	B.	Vulnerability advisories — review CERT (www.cert.org), CIAC (www.ciac.org/ciac/index), or other organization advisories for vulnerability information.
	C.	Vendor support — contact the vendors of each network component to determine known vulnerabilities of that component.
ii.		Use of risk assessment tool containing vulnerability library and systems components.
8.		Determine significant vulnerabilities using the following factors:
a.		Risk contribution — each vulnerability will contribute to the total risk of the system.
i.		Assets/components affected by the vulnerability — certain vulnerabilities may only affect one asset, others may affect multiple assets. Certain vulnerabilities may affect assets that are critical to the process, although another may affect assets that are not critical. The risk contribution will depend on the number importance of the assets affected.
ii.		Associated operational concerns — each vulnerability will have an impact on one or more of the operational concerns. The risk contribution will depend on the operational concerns affected as well as the rating of those concerns.
9.		Identify threat categories:
a.		Define the three general types of threats:
i.		Internal versus external threats.
ii.		Hostile versus nonhostile threats.
iii.		Structured versus unstructured threats.
b.		These threats can be group into eight threat categories (see Chapter 4):
i.		Internal hostile structured.
ii.		Internal hostile unstructured.
iii.		Internal nonhostile structured.
iv.		Internal nonhostile unstructured.
v.		External hostile structured.
vi.		External hostile unstructured.
vii.		External nonhostile structured.
viii.		External nonhostile unstructured.

(Continued)

Table 5.1 Detailed Outline of the Risk Assessment Process (Continued)

c.	Depending on those threat types that are of concern to the organization a subset of threat categories will be selected. (E.g., if only internal threats are of concern, then the four external threat categories will be eliminated from the assessment process.)
d.	The remaining threat categories will be ranked based on threat measurement factors:
i.	Physical and electronic access — does the threat category have physical or electronic access to the system?
ii.	Capability — the level of capability required for the threat to exploit any vulnerabilities in the system.
iii.	Motivation — the level of motivation of a threat category.
iv.	Occurrence measurement — the probability that a threat category will exploit the system.
10.	Identify current safeguards:
a.	Determine the safeguards that are currently in place. This determination will be used to determine the baseline risk.
11.	Determine mitigated vulnerabilities:
a.	A subset of vulnerabilities will be eliminated several reasons:
i.	No threat to exploit the vulnerability.
ii.	Current safeguards mitigate the vulnerability.
iii.	The vulnerability does not apply to a particular component because the service or software that creates that vulnerability is not present in this particular component.
12.	Determine impact:
a.	Impact is a subjective rating of high, medium, or low assigned to each vulnerability.
b.	This rating determines the impact of the vulnerability on the business process.
c.	The impact rating is determined from a subjective analysis of the importance of the asset affected, the operational concerns to which the vulnerability applies, and the relative rating of the applicable operational concerns.
13.	Safeguard recommendations:
a.	For each vulnerability, a set of safeguards will be identified that will either reduce or mitigate the vulnerability.
b.	Each safeguard will have an associated cost that can either be a dollar amount or a relative cost of high, medium, or low.
14.	Determine residual impact:
a.	Each safeguard will either reduce or mitigate the impact of the vulnerability.

(Continued)

Table 5.1   Detailed Outline of the Risk Assessment Process (Continued)

b.	Each safeguard will be analyzed to determine the impact remaining if or when the safeguard is applied — this will be the residual impact.
c.	The residual impact and cost of each safeguard together with business and operational priorities will be considered by the asset and process owners in determining those safeguards that will be applied to reduce the impact to an acceptable level.

15. Establish risk:

a.	Risk is a binary value based on the residual impact ratings remaining after all safeguards have been identified.
b.	If there are any vulnerabilities with a high impact the risk will be high.

II

THE McCUMBER CUBE METHODOLOGY

6

THE McCUMBER CUBE

INTRODUCTION

The McCumber Cube is shorthand for a paper published as "Information Systems Security: A Comprehensive Model,"[1] in October 1991. The model itself was also used by the National Security Telecommunications and Information Systems Security Committee (NSTISSC) and published in National Security Telecommunications and Information Systems Security Instruction's (NSTISSI) *National Information Systems Security (INFOSEC) Glossary.*[2]

The McCumber Cube was developed as a response to the attempts in the late 1980s and early 1990s to define the relationship between the communications and computer security disciplines. As the advent of the Internet age dawned, it was clear the distinction made little sense. However, no one was able to adequately portray the systemic interrelation of the components of each.

The development of the McCumber Cube was necessary to define an accurate model not constrained by organizational or technical changes. As with all models, the value lies in its ability to adapt to the information environment irrespective of the specific technologies involved. The model is necessarily three-dimensional to capture the true nature of the interplay of the elements in information systems security. The model is depicted as Figure 6.1.

For many the years, the U.S. government separated the disciplines of communications and computer security. The fundamental reason for this was the preexistence of the communications security infrastructure. Although the need for communications security has existed since the emergence of interpersonal communications, the modern era of technical communications security was the result of offensive and defensive operations in World War II. The well-documented evolution of technical

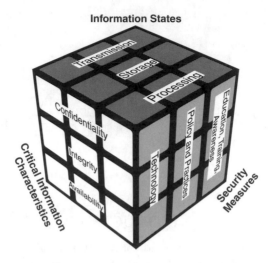

Figure 6.1   McCumber Cube Model

cryptography and the exploitation of encrypted communications spawned an extensive and technically complex environment of policies and products championed by the NSA.

One of the vital insights of World War II cryptography was that reliance on the cryptographic algorithm itself for protecting sensitive or classified communications was inadequate. By analyzing a captured German Enigma encryption machine from a sunken U-boat, British and U.S. researchers were able to ultimately determine the encryption key and decrypt highly sensitive German military message traffic. The lesson was not lost on the Allies. From that time on, the cryptographic key became the focus for protecting our own communications system.

As computers and other computational resources evolved into critical defense technologies in the 1950s and 1960s, it became obvious that security for these new machines was critical. They were used to calculate weapons systems data, atomic and nuclear specifications, and geographic information used by military planners and weapons systems developers. At first, it was adequate to shield the stand-alone systems themselves for their classified computational missions. These early systems were also used for computationally intensive cryptographic calculations to either help reinforce our own cryptosystems or crack the codes of other nation-states.

Soon, however, access to computer systems was exploding as universities, research firms, and private industry all demanded automated processing of large amounts of data. As these capabilities moved outside the confines of sensitive military and government organizations, they became powerful tools for a quickly expanding industrial base as well. The lessons of World War II cryptography told us not to place our security emphasis on the machines, but on the key that unlocks access to the information itself.

The U.S. government endeavored to address computer security as a discipline distinct from the existing communications security infrastructure. Many people involved in the early development of computer security policy and practice felt there was a significant distinction between the two disciplines and skills were not easily shared among the various research and deployment teams. So for many years, computer security researchers toiled in facilities and organizations separate from the communications security environment.

With the early advance of intercomputer communications, it became apparent to everyone in government circles that the two disciplines had to be integrated. Computers communicate. Communication systems compute. The evolution of technology has long since eliminated any arbitrary distinction between a computer and its communication components or a communications network and its computing system. The same is true for the security disciplines. Merely combining the COMSEC and COMPUSEC disciplines under an umbrella of common management is unacceptable.

Even if we address the other, albeit less technical, aspects of information systems security such as policy, administration, and personnel security, we still fail to develop a comprehensive view of this evolving technology. The reason for this becomes clear when we are reminded it is the information that is the cornerstone of information systems security. In this sense, any paradigm that emphasizes the technology at the expense of information will be lacking.

THE NATURE OF INFORMATION

The key element of the McCumber Cube is its reliance on an information-centric model. Both communications and computer systems are developed for some functions of information management. Defining the nature of information could be a tedious task. To some it represents the free-flowing evolution of knowledge; to others, it is intelligence to be guarded. Add to this the innumerable media through which information is perceived and we have a confusing array of contradictions. How can we present a study of information that has universal application?

It may be best to develop a simple analogy. The chemical compound H_2O means many things to all of us. In its liquid state, water means life-giving sustenance to a desert-dwelling Bedouin; to a drowning victim, it is the vehicle of death. The same steam we use to prepare vegetables can scald an unwary cook. Ice can impede river-borne commerce on the

Mississippi River or make a drink more palatable. Science, therefore, does not deal with the perception of the compound, but with its state.

As the compound H_2O can be water, ice, or steam, information has three basic states; at any given moment, information is being transmitted, stored, or processed. The three states exist irrespective of the media in which information resides. This subtle distinction ultimately allows us to encompass all information systems technology in our model.

It is possible to look at the three states in microcosm and say that processing is simply specialized state combinations of storage and transfer; so, in fact, there are only two possible states. By delving to this level of abstraction, however, we go beyond the scope and purpose of the model. The distinction between the three states is fundamental and necessary to accurately apply the model. For example, cryptography can be used to protect information while it is transferred through a computer network and even while it is stored in magnetic media. However, the information must be available in plaintext (at least to the processor) for the computer to perform the processing function. The processing function is a fundamental state that requires specific security controls.

When this information is needed to make a decision, the end user may not be aware of the number of state changes effected. The primary concern will be certain characteristics of the information. These characteristics are intrinsic and define the security-relevant qualities of the information. As such, they are the next major building block of our information systems security model.

CRITICAL INFORMATION CHARACTERISTICS

Information systems security concerns itself with the maintenance of three critical characteristics of information — confidentiality (Pfleeger's secrecy), integrity, and availability.[3] These attributes of information represent the full spectrum of security concerns in an automated environment. They are applicable for any organization irrespective of its philosophical outlook on sharing information.

CONFIDENTIALITY

Confidentiality is the heart of any security policy for an information system. A security policy is the set of rules that, given identified subjects and objects, determines whether a given subject can gain access to a specific object.[4] In the case of discretionary access controls, selected users (or groups) are controlled as to which data they may access. Confidentiality is then the assurance that access controls are enforced. The reason I prefer the term confidentiality to secrecy is merely to avoid unwarranted implications that this is solely the domain of armies and governments. As we will see, it is a desirable attribute for information in any organization.

All organizations have a requirement to protect certain information. Even owners of a clearinghouse operation or Web site need the ability to prevent unwanted access to supervisory functions within their systems. It is also important to note that the definition of data that must be protected with confidentiality controls is broadening throughout government.[5] Actual information labeling and need-to-know imperatives are aspects of the system security policy that are enforced to meet confidentiality objectives. The issue of military versus civilian security controls is one that need not impact the development of a comprehensive representation of information systems security principles.

INTEGRITY

Integrity is perhaps the most complex and misunderstood characteristic of information. Government seems to have a better foundation in the development of confidentiality controls than those that ensure data integrity. Some texts define integrity as "assets (which) can only be modified by authorized parties."[3] Such a definition unnecessarily confines the concept to one of access control.

I propose a much broader definition. Data integrity is a matter of degree (as is the concept of *trust* as applied to trusted systems), which has to be defined as a quality of the information and not as who does or does not have access to it. Integrity is that quality of information that identifies how closely the data represents reality. How closely does your resume reflect *you*? Does a credit report accurately reflect an individual's historical record of financial transactions? The definition of integrity must include the broad scope of accuracy, relevancy, and completeness.

Data integrity calls for a comprehensive set of functions to promote accuracy and completeness as well as security. This is not to say that too much information cannot be a problem. Data redundancy and unnecessary records present a variety of challenges to system implementers and administrators. The users must define their needs in terms of the information necessary to perform certain functions. Information systems security functions help ensure this information is robust and (to the degree necessary) reflects the reality it is meant to represent.

AVAILABILITY

Availability is a coequal characteristic with confidentiality and integrity. This vital aspect of security ensures the information is provided to authorized users when it is requested or needed. Often it is viewed as a less technical requirement that is satisfied by redundancies within the information system such as backup power, spare data channels, and parallel databases. This perception, however, ignores one of the most valuable aspects of our model that this characteristic provides. Availability is the check-and-balance constraint on our model. Because security and utility often conflict, the science of information systems security is also a study of subtle compromises.

As well as ensuring system reliability, availability acts as a metric for determining the extent of information system security breaches. Ultimately, when information systems security preventive measures fail, remedial action may be necessary. This remedial activity normally involves support from law enforcement or legal departments. To pursue formal action against people who abuse information systems resources, the ability to prove an adverse impact often hinges on the issue of denying someone the availability of information resources. Although violations of information confidentiality and integrity can be potentially more disastrous, denial of service criteria tend to be easier to quantify and thus create a tangible foundation for taking action against violators.

The triad of critical information characteristics covers all aspects of security-relevant activity within the information system. By building a matrix with the information states positioned along the horizontal axis and the critical information characteristics aligned down the vertical, we have the foundation for the model.

SECURITY MEASURES

We have now outlined a matrix that provides us with the theoretical basis for our model. What it lacks is a view of the measures we employ to ensure the critical information characteristics are maintained while information resides in or moves between states. It is possible, at this point, to perceive the chart as a checklist. At a high level of abstraction, one could assess the security posture of a system by using this approach. By viewing the interstices of the matrix as representing system vulnerabilities, you can attempt to determine the security aspects of an information system as categorized by the nine intersection areas. For example, you may single out information confidentiality during transmission or any intersection area for scrutiny.

The two-dimensional matrix also has another less obvious utility. We can map various security technologies into the nine interstices. Using our example from above, we note that it is necessary to protect the confidentiality of the information during its transmission state. We can then determine which security technologies help ensure confidentiality during transmission of the information.

In this case, cryptography would be considered a primary security technology. We can then place various cryptographic techniques and products within a subset in this category. Then we repeat the process with other major types of technology that can be placed within this interstice. The procedure is repeated for all nine blocks on our grid. Thus we form the first of three layers that will become the third dimension of our model-security measures.

TECHNOLOGY

The technology layer will be the primary focus of the third dimension. We will see that it provides the basis for the other two layers. For our purposes, we can define technology as any physical device or technique implemented in physical form that is specifically used to ensure that the critical information characteristics are maintained through any of the information states. Technology can be implemented in hardware, firmware, or software. It could be a biometric device, cryptographic module, or security-enhanced operating system. When we think of a thing that could be used to protect the critical characteristics of information, we are thinking of technology.

Usually, organizations are built around functional responsibilities. The advent of computer technology created the perception that a group needed to be established to accommodate the new machines that would process, store, and transmit much of our vital information. In other words, the organization was adapted to suit the evolving technology. Is this wrong? Not necessarily; however, it is possible to create the impression that technology exists for technology's sake.

Telecommunications and computer systems are simply media for information. The media need to be adapted to preserve certain critical characteristics with the adaptation and use of the information media (technology). Adaptation is a design problem, but use and application concerns bring us to the next layer.

POLICY AND PRACTICE

The second layer of the third dimension is that of policy and practice. It is the recognition of the fact that information systems security is not just a product that will be available at some future date. Because of our technology focus, it is easy to begin to think of security solutions as devices or add-on packages for existing information systems. We are often guilty of waiting for technology to solve a problem that is not solely a technological problem. An enforceable (and enforced) policy can aid immeasurably in protecting information.

A study has shown that 75 percent of federal agencies do not have a policy for the protection of information on PC-based information systems.[5] Why, if it is so effective, is policy such a neglected security measure? It may be due in part to the evolving social and moral ethic with regard to our use of information systems. The proliferation of unauthorized software duplication is just another symptom of this problem. Even though software companies have policies and licensing caveats on their products, sanctions and remedies allowed by law are difficult if not impossible to enforce. No major lawsuit involving an individual violator has come before our courts and it appears many people do not see the harm or loss involved. Although there are limits established by law, it seems we as society accept a less stringent standard.

Closely associated with the matter of policy is that of practice. A practice is a procedure we employ to enhance our security posture. For example, we may have a policy that states that passwords must be kept confidential and may only be used by the uniquely authenticated user. A practice that helps ensure this policy is followed would be committing the password to memory rather than writing it somewhere.

The first two layers of the third dimension represent the design and application of a security-enhanced information system. The last building block of our model represents the understanding necessary to protect information. Although an integral aspect of the preceding two layers, it must be considered individually because it is capable of standing alone as a significant security measure.

EDUCATION, TRAINING, AND AWARENESS (HUMAN FACTORS)

The final layer of our third dimension is that of education, training, and awareness. (I have recently settled on the term human factors to more accurately capture this safeguard category.) As you will see, were the model laid on its back like a box, the whole model would rest on this layer. This phenomenon is intentional. Education, training, and awareness may be our most prominent security measures; for only by understanding the threats and vulnerabilities associated with our proliferating use of automated information systems can we begin to attempt to deal effectively with other control measures.

Technology and policy must rely heavily on education, training, and awareness from numerous perspectives. Our upcoming engineers and scientists must understand the principles of information security if we expect them to consider the protection of information in the systems they design. Currently, nearly all university graduates in computer science have no formal introduction to information security as part of their education.

Those who are responsible for promulgating policy and regulatory guidance must place bounds on the dissemination of information. They must ensure information resources are distributed selectively and securely. The issue is ultimately one of awareness. Ultimate responsibility for its protection rests with those individuals and groups that create and use this information; those who use it to make critical decisions must rely on its confidentiality, integrity, and availability. Education, training, and awareness promise to be the most effective security measures in the near term.

Which information requires protection is often debated in government circles. One historic problem is the clash of society's right to know and an individual's right to privacy. It is important to realize that these are not bipolar concepts. There is a long continuum that runs between the beliefs that information is a free flowing exchange of knowledge and that it is intelligence that must be kept secret. From a governmental or business perspective, it must be assumed that all information is intelligence. The question is not should information be protected, but how do we intend to protect the confidentiality, integrity, and availability of it within legal and moral constraints?

THE MODEL

Overview

The completed model appears below. There are nine distinct interstices, each three layers deep. All aspects of information systems security can be viewed within the framework of the model. For example, we may cite a cryptographic module as technology that protects information in its transmission state. What many information system developers fail to appreciate is that for every technology control there is a policy (sometimes referred to as doctrine) that dictates the constraints on the application of that technology. It may also specify parameters that delimit the control's use and may even cite degrees of effectiveness for different applications. Doctrine (policy) is an integral yet distinct aspect of the technology. The third layer — education, training, and awareness — then functions as the catalyst for proper application and use of the technology based on the policy (practice) application.

Not every security measure begins with a specific technology. A simple policy or practice often provides sufficient protection of information assets. This policy or practice is then affected by communicating it to end users through the education, training, and awareness level alone. This last layer is ultimately involved in all aspects of the information systems security model. It may also be solely an educational, training, or awareness security control. The model helps us understand the comprehensive nature of information security that a COMSEC or COMPUSEC perspective cannot define.

Use of the Model

The model has several significant applications. Initially, the two-dimensional matrix can be used to identify information states and system vulnerabilities. Then, the three layers of security measures can be employed to minimize these vulnerabilities based on knowledge of the threat to the information asset. Let us take a brief look at these applications.

A developer would begin using the model by defining the various information states within the system. When an information state is identified, one then works down the vertical path to address all three critical information characteristics. Once vulnerabilities are noted in this fashion, it becomes a simple matter of working down through the three layers of security measures.

If a specific technology is available, the designer knows that policy and practice as well as education, training, and awareness will be logical follow on aspects of that control. If a technology cannot be identified, then policy or practice must be viewed as the next likely avenue. (Again, the last layer will be used to support the policy or practice.) If neither of the first two layers can satisfactorily counter the vulnerability, then, as a minimum, an awareness of the weakness becomes important and fulfills the dictates of the model at the third layer.

Another important application is realized when the model is used as an evaluation tool. As in the design and development application, the evaluator first identifies the different information states within the system. These states can be identified separately from any specific technology. A valuable aspect of the model is that the designer need not consider the medium.

After identifying all the states, an evaluator or auditor can perform a comprehensive review much the same way the systems designer used the model during the development phase. For each vulnerability discovered, the same model is used to determine appropriate security measures. The third dimension of the model ensures the security measures are considered in their fullest sense.

It is important to note that a vulnerability may be left unsecured (at an awareness level in the third layer) if the designer or evaluator determines that no threat to that vulnerability exists. Although no security practitioner should be satisfied with glaring vulnerabilities, a careful study of potential threats to the information may disclose that the cost of the security measure is more than the loss should the vulnerability be exploited. This is one of the subtle compromises alluded to earlier.

The model also can be used to develop comprehensive information systems security policy and guidance required by an organization. With an accurate understanding of the relation of policy to technology and education, training, and awareness, one can ensure that regulations address the entire spectrum of information security. It is of particular importance that corporate and government regulations not be bound by technology. Use of this model allows management to structure its policy outside the technology arena.

The model also functions well in determining requirements for education, training, and awareness. Because this is the last layer, it plays a vital role in the application of all the security measures. Even if a designer, evaluator, or user determines to ignore a vulnerability (perhaps because of a lack of threat), then the simple acknowledgment of this vulnerability resides in the last layer as awareness. Ultimately, all technology, policies, and practices must be translated to the appropriate audience through education, training, and awareness. This translation is the vehicle that makes all security measures effective.

The 27 individual cubes created by the model can be extracted and examined individually. This key aspect can be useful in categorizing and analyzing countermeasures. It is also a tool for defining organizational responsibility for information security. By considering all 27 such cubes, the analyst is assured of a complete perspective of all available security measures. Unlike other computer security standards and criteria, this model connotes a true systems viewpoint.

The information systems security model acknowledges information, not technology, as the basis for our security efforts. The actual medium is transparent in the model. This eliminates unnecessary distinctions between COMSEC, COMPUSEC, TECHSEC, and other technology-defined security sciences. As a result, we can model the security relevant processes of information throughout entire information systems — automated or not. This important aspect of the model eliminates significant gaps in currently used security architecture guidance for information systems.

I developed this model to respond to the need for a theoretical foundation for modeling the information systems security sciences. The organizational realignments that have recognized the interdependence of several complementary technologies will need refinement in the near future. We can begin that process now by acknowledging the central element in all our efforts information. Only when we build on this foundation will we accurately address the needs of information systems security in the next decade and beyond.

REFERENCES

1. McCumber, John, Information Systems Security: A Comprehensive Model, *Proceedings of the 14th National Computer Security Conference,* Washington, D.C., October 1991; reprinted in the *Proceedings of the 4th Annual Canadian Computer Security Conference,* Ottawa, Ontario, May 1992; reprinted in *DataPro Reports on Information Security,* Delran, NJ: McGraw-Hill, October 1992.

2. National Security Telecommunications and Information Systems Security Instruction (NSTISSI) Number 4009, *National Information Systems Security (INFOSEC) Glossary,* Washington, D.C., June 1992.

3. Pfleeger, Charles P., *Security in Computing*, 1st Ed., Upper Saddle River, NJ: Prentice Hall, 1989.

4. Department of Defense Directive 5200.28-STD, *DOD Trusted Computer System Evaluation Criteria* (Orange Book), Washington, D.C., December 1985.

5. Office of Technology Assessment, United States Congress, *Defending Secrets, Sharing Data: New Locks and Keys for Electronic Data*, Washington, D.C., October 1987 .

7

DETERMINING INFORMATION STATES AND MAPPING INFORMATION FLOW

INTRODUCTION

One of the key attributes of the McCumber Cube approach is the requirement to extrapolate and analyze information flow characteristics. The concept of information flow is a unique aspect of this methodology and is superior to a technology-based approach. In technology-based methodologies, security safeguards are applied to specific IT products, media, or subsystems. In other words, safeguards are defined by the current capabilities and vulnerabilities of the particular technology products and protocols employed in the network infrastructure. This means that every time a system component is replaced, upgraded, or modified, the security attributes of the system need to be completely reassessed and in many cases, adapted to the new technology. Although the McCumber Cube methodology will not preclude the necessity for adapting technical controls to changes in technology, it ensures consistency of security policy and safeguards enforcement requirements.

Information flow analysis within the McCumber Cube methodology requires the security practitioner to decompose the elements of the IT system in one of the three primary information states — transmission, storage, or processing. These information states can be assigned to information regardless of its location in the IT system. In most cases, information will exist simply as data — ones and zeroes — within the system.

However, the distinction between data and information is not important for information flow analysis. To determine information flow, one needs to determine the information state and location within the system.

At any point in time, information exists in one of three states. Information can be in a state of transmission, storage, or processing. There are no other options. Examples of the three states abound and are often intuitively obvious. Several researchers and security pundits have proposed additional information states such as display. Just like those who propose additional security attributes such as nonrepudiation, display easily fits into the state of storage. This is most likely simply an issue of semantics.

Although the data in display mode would not be considered in storage in the traditional sense of being stored away, it exists as postprocessing product that is now stored within the display function. As these displays change with new information, they simply transition between storage functions of different data sets. The model is consistent and the parsing of either state or security attributes into evermore refined subcategories does not always suit the needs of a security practitioner.

One of the major problems with attempting to expand on these categories arises when you cannot determine if you have accounted for all potential possibilities. The need to create these subcategories can create an unwieldy model that fails to account for certain information states. By applying the three primary states to each information resource as it moves through the system, you can develop a complete security model for any environment.

INFORMATION STATES: A BRIEF HISTORICAL PERSPECTIVE

The three information states have existed since the dawn of human information exchange. Early humans developed language to facilitate the transmission of concepts and ideas between themselves. Information or ideas deemed important were often committed to paintings or drawings rendered on cave walls. Processing was a state almost solely applied to the human brain. As early man perceived the information transmitted to him, he adapted that information to suit his survival needs.

As the history of information rapidly evolved, man developed more effective ways to transmit, store, and process information. There is little wonder that more advanced ways of managing information were vital. I am certain early hunters eagerly exchanged information with other hunters about their experiences. By knowing the historical location of prey and the anecdotal stories of others, a hunter could position himself better to increase his chances of success. He could capitalize on the purely providential discoveries of others and avoid problems experienced by the unfortunate. By processing this information properly, he could enhance his chances for survival.

As the ages passed, the ability to effectively gather, store, and process information became a strategic and tactical advantage for individual people and larger societal systems like nation-states. Those individuals and groups who best gathered and managed information would prosper over those who were less effective. In this way, superior information management capabilities established a Darwinian process that evolves in favor of those who possess information superiority.

Nowhere is information superiority so dramatically displayed as in warfare. For millennia, quality information has been recognized for its vital role in winning — and losing — in these high stakes games for survival. Often, military historians and planners refer to this information as intelligence. Though specific definitions are still being debated, superior knowledge of one's enemies and the battlefield are central to success in life and death situations.

It is not surprising, then, that innumerable advances in information management and technology were brought about by those engaged in war. Some of the earliest forms of cryptography still in use today are known as Caesarian ciphers. They were developed under the Roman caesars to securely obtain battlefield information and to safely transmit command and control information to military commanders in the field.

For most of human advances, information management was confined to finding more effective ways to capture, store, and transmit information in physical media like animal hides and eventually the more efficient and compact paper medium. The development and widespread adoption of electronic communication capabilities began in the 19th century with the telegraph. Until this watershed advance, even Guttenberg's printing press was simply a more efficient way to manage the physical storage and transmission of the paper medium.

Electronic transmission of data created great opportunities as well as new vulnerabilities. In paper-based media, it was necessary to gain physical access to process the stored information contained therein. Basically, you had to obtain access to the paper-based information in some manner to exploit the information. In an electronic system, it became possible to intercept the transmission at some point and translate the electronic data pulses into readable information. In many cases, the sender and intended recipient would have no indication the information had been compromised.

Ultimately, it became vital to develop and employ new security safeguards that could protect information during its electronic transmission state. Cryptographers had developed and employed evermore complicated encoding schemes as information exploiters became adept at decoding intercepted information. The science of cryptography needed to evolve its paper-based capabilities into the electronic coding of sensitive information.

At the beginning of World War II, cryptographers assigned a level of trust to their encoding schemes that was most often tied to the complexity of the algorithm used to encipher the data. It was necessarily assumed that the more complex the encoding algorithm, the more secure the data during the transmission state. However, Polish, English, and ultimately American researchers and mathematicians ushered in a significant advance in the science of cryptography when the Allies captured a German Enigma encoding machine.

Through the use of an early computational device, researchers were able to crack both the algorithm and the changeable key used by the Germans to encode their most sensitive military data. This landmark scientific breakthrough became one of the most closely held Allied secrets of the war. Nazi and other Axis information intercepted and decoded played a decisive role in winning the war in Europe.

Since World War II, the science of cryptography has focused on the generation of more computationally complex keys. Although complex encoding algorithms are a key security attribute of any cryptographic system, the actual trust in the system is now primarily vested in unique keys that would require an enemy to invest years to crack. After World War II, entire governmental organizations were chartered and funded by many countries to maintain the superiority of these electronic cryptographic systems for the protection of information primarily in its transmission state.

As advances in information management rapidly progressed with the introduction of electronic transmission capabilities, information security was focused almost solely on the states of storage and transmission. To protect stored information resources, security practitioners relied almost exclusively on physical security safeguards. These included safes, protective covers, and even the physical location of these paper-based information assets. In some cases, information was stored in an encoded state to be decoded by the intended recipient when it was needed for a decision-making process.

Little historical precedent was available with the development and rapid adoption of computers. Security practitioners were caught off guard as machines were developed to automatically process information. All the research and development of information security systems had been focused on the adaptation of old paper-based media storage and more complex encoding schemes. The widespread adoption of computing technology introduced the ability to remotely process information and tie this new function inextricably with the electronic transmission of data.

It is historically significant that computers have ushered in daunting new information security requirements. Until the advent of modern memory-based computer systems, the processing functions of information were never accomplished in an automated fashion. For most of human evolution, it was tacitly assumed that the processing function was the sole realm of the human brain. The computer's ability to take in information or data and create new information has changed the landscape of information management in dramatic ways we are just now coming to realize.

AUTOMATED PROCESSING: WHY CRYPTOGRAPHY IS NOT SUFFICIENT

One of the key attributes of the computer system is that it automatically processes information. By the use of programs, information is brought in to the computing environment, manipulated by these programs (which are simply complex algorithms), and new information is created. It can be theoretically argued that within the basic processor, the processing function is simply the rapid change of transmission and storage states. However, for purposes of our methodology, the broader and more generally accepted interpretation and application of the three primary information states is the most effective.

When computers were first introduced, security researchers and cryptographers erroneously assumed security requirements could be enforced in this new environment by the adaptation of cryptographic solutions. However, in practical application, they soon learned that the science of cryptography was insufficient. One of the key principles of the information processing function is that you cannot process encrypted information, decrypt it, and produce the requisite new information. For computer programs to function properly, they had to work with information in plaintext. If a program were to be coded in such a way as to work with encoded text, this new enciphered text would simply become a new language (and a new form of plaintext), because it would be nearly impossible to apply a variable key to maintain the security attributes of the encryption algorithm.

This may all sound a bit too theoretical, so suffice it to say that information in its processing state needs to be in a form of plaintext. For many software programs, the programming language dictates the processing algorithm and the representational data may not become information again until it is transmitted out of the processing or storage function as either electronic, digital, or hard-copy output. This makes it necessary to closely evaluate the information state changes within your IT environment.

There is a saying currently in vogue with IT researchers: If you think cryptography is the solution to the problem [of information systems security], you understand neither cryptography nor the problem. This saying has evolved from the understanding that cryptography has an important role in safeguarding information in its transmission and storage states, but it is not adequate in and of itself. That is another vote for a structured, information-based methodology like the McCumber Cube.

One of the keys to the methodology is the identification and mapping of information states with an IT system. It is also the least understood. The reason information state analysis is so little used is that, until now, almost every security analysis methodology or security enforcement process was based on a technology-centric model. In fact, many recommended methods are nothing more than a vulnerability checklist that needs constant updating as technology changes. As we have discovered, however, those processes based on the point-counterpoint of vulnerability and safeguard challenges ultimately leave the organization unable to determine the overall state of its security plan and lacking the information necessary to make cost or benefit tradeoffs for an effective risk management program.

The key to the McCumber Cube methodology is the application of state analysis. In the following sections, we will give examples and provide guidelines for determining system boundaries and identifying and mapping state evolution in modern IT systems. At this point, it will not be necessary to include a comprehensive outline of all vulnerabilities or identify all potential threats.

SIMPLE STATE ANALYSIS

State analysis is a critical aspect of our structured methodology. The attributes of information states will indicate where security safeguard requirements need to be defined. We will discuss these processes in Chapter 11, but we need to first understand how to identify the information states and information flows in our technology environment. The first step is to define the boundaries of our system.

Someone leaving a telephone message represents an example of a complete albeit simple information system. Information flowing through a virtual telephone connection is obviously in transmission. A voice mail recording of the call can contain the same information in a state of storage. When the intended recipient retrieves the voice mail and listens to the stored message, their brain processes this same information. The transmission and processing functions are thus ephemeral states that exist for a specific element of information (the message) at certain points in the information system. The storage function is static for the life of that element of information. If the recipient erases the message, once the technology components physically remove the representative digital data from a memory or storage medium, the information will cease to exist.

A key element to mapping information flow is defining the boundaries of the system in question. Establishing boundaries for an IT system can be more difficult than it first appears. Some systems are defined solely by a specific processing function or software application. This could be the case for a dedicated device to gather limited weather data and transmit it to a base station. You may have such a system in your home today. The entire system could be defined as the sensors, the transmission medium, and the main processor, storage, and display unit. This system is depicted in Figure 7.1.

We can quickly and easily identify the various information states by parsing the system into its three primary components — a remote unit with sensors, a wire to connect the sensor to the base station, and the base station itself. In each of these components, we must now determine which information states are present.

In this simple example of an information system, no data is processed or retained by the sensor — it is simply a device to obtain data and transmit it back to the main processing and display unit as it is acquired. The sensors on the remote unit include a barometer, an anemometer, and a temperature gauge. These three sensors send real-time data back to the base station through the wire that connects the two. The sensors in this case neither process nor retain any data. They simply send the raw feed to the base station.

The wire connecting the remote sensor unit to the base station will represent the transmission of the raw data. Simplistically, the transmission function begins where the wire is connected to the sensor and ends when it is connected to the base station. It is at these points that state changes exist.

Figure 7.1 Weather Reporting System

The base station in our example has both a digital memory and a visual display unit. The operator can maintain a record of daily high and low temperatures, maximum wind velocity, and a daily barometric historical trend. These rather simple functions are reset every 24 hours. The base station takes the raw data feeds and translates them into information that we, in turn, can reprocess in our brains to help us control our comfort by predicting the weather and adapting either our behaviors or environment in relation to the information we are provided by the base station.

Within this base station are both a processing state and limited storage states for the barometric trends and daily temperature extremes. With this simple IT system, we have now identified the transmission, storage, and processing functions. The information flow is one way from the remote sensor, through the wire, and into the base station for processing and storage. We now have the state analysis aspect of a security review accomplished.

A simple state analysis like this works effectively for all types of dedicated information systems as well as those that are application specific. In these cases, the information is normally of one type for security purposes even if it is a robust collection of data. To accurately identify the states, the analyst must track the data from its acquisition through its use, maintenance, and ultimate disposition.

It becomes easier to see the implications of state analysis changes in technology by using the telephone system as an example. The original telephone system was a relatively simple environment where temporary communications sessions were established. For each session, an operator would create a dedicated circuit between callers to establish a dedicated wire-based connection session. After the link was created, information could be exchanged between the telephone units at each end. The processing and storage functions were left to the capabilities of the minds of the humans on each end.

The security attributes for such a system were routinely confined to the characteristic of system availability. The telephone system operators worked to provide consistent service for their customers who needed to know they could make a call in the event of an emergency or simply for their own convenience. Central operators, who could listen in on the connections they created, easily violated confidentiality, however, those outside the connection environment had to obtain and employ highly specialized tools to conduct wiretaps or exploit other confidentiality vulnerabilities. The integrity attributes of the information were left to the veracity of the participants. Once the participants in one of these calls hung up the connection, the virtual transmission capabilities ceased and no information was retained nor was it possible to manipulate any of the information exchanged after the fact.

The introduction of modern processing (computer) technology into the relatively simple telephone system has changed the entire security environment for telephony. Tiny processors in current telephone systems and after-market devices now allow us to use our telephones to record conversations, capture images, store large quantities of data, and manipulate the information before, during, and after we send it. Within the telephone infrastructure are computer systems and technology to manage all three states. All aspects of transmission, storage, and processing are now incorporated into these interconnected global systems. Someone responsible for evaluating or implementing security technology for this environment will now need to critically define all possible information states in each affected component.

The basic change has come from the recognition that all information, whether it be images, music, or books, can be rendered as data in computer systems. Color, perspective, and sound can be captured and replayed throughout a collection of processors, wires, radio waves, light waves, magnetic pulses, and optical media. Regardless of the medium, any security analysis must consider the three primary states of the information in order to begin a structured methodology to make intelligent choices for its protection and safeguarding.

INFORMATION STATES IN HETEROGENEOUS SYSTEMS

Obviously, many large-scale IT systems can be used for a multitude of functions. Multipurpose computer systems can host a nearly endless variety of applications that include voice, data, and imagery. A LAN in even a small office environment will contain numerous instantiations of transmission, storage, and processing functions. These states will exist in a variety of applications and functions. Identifying the primary information states across a variety of applications and system components is necessary.

In heterogeneous environments such as a LAN, it becomes necessary to examine information state changes for each application within the environment. To determine what information states exist, you can either approach the state analysis by introspection of each component or by the various applications supported by these components. In either case, you should end up with the same results.

If you approach the problem by system component, you need to answer the following questions:

- What function does this component perform?
- What applications are supported by this component?
- Does this component perform multiple functions for different applications?

- Which states of transmission, storage, and processing exist within this component?
- Did I perform a complete inventory of information assets that are affected or managed by this component?

If you approach the state analysis by application (the employment of information and data), you simply apply the same questions, but you begin by looking at the various uses of information throughout the system. You need to determine:

- What information does this application use?
- Where does this come from?
- Where does this information travel within the system?
- What state changes does this information make?
- Did I perform a complete inventory of all state changes and every possible information flow?

In each case you should be able to diagram and define the various information state changes for each application and for each component within the system. Boundary definition in either case is critical. Although information may flow between various systems, infrastructures, and components, it is vital that you can account for the accuracy and timeliness of the information when it enters your defined boundaries and that you can ensure the appropriate confidentiality, integrity, and availability attributes of the information as it passes out of the control of your system.

Heterogeneous system boundaries also can apply to regional, national, or even multinational networks. As the breadth and functionality of the system expands, the challenge in applying the model is to determine the expectations of the system users and the role of security safeguards in the environment under study. A defense-in-depth view I often apply when analyzing ever-broadening system boundaries is to look at what type of enforcement control and protection the system operator can realistically enforce.

At the individual component level, an application of the McCumber Cube methodology normally defines the security functionality of the component itself. In other words, the methodology is used to determine a set of security-relevant functions the specific component could provide for any type of information, regardless of the type of information or the external threat environment. This type of analysis was originally envisioned by governments for ascribing security criteria to computer components. Examples include the blah, blah criteria (also known as the Orange Book), the Common Criteria, and the CTCPEC. Each of these standards represented an attempt to define security for products without consideration for the value of the information transmitted, stored, or processed by them or for the threat environment the system operated within.

At the organizational systems boundary level, the McCumber Cube methodology is most effective because it is employed to define security safeguards for systems under someone's span of control. Additionally, the process also identifies and includes in the assessment the value of the information resources transmitted, stored, and processed by the system. The methodology then enables the analyst to refine and optimize the security requirements based on that criterion. Finally, a system perspective also considers the threat environment the system operates within. With these parameters considered, it becomes possible to make informed tradeoffs and employ cost-effective security controls. On an even larger scale, the McCumber Cube methodology can help assess a security environment (Figure 7.2). For information, components, and media outside the security analyst's control, the methodology still provides a way to assess the effectiveness of the various security functions employed and the likelihood of information exploitation. By identifying information states and data flows, it becomes significantly easier to identify potential vulnerabilities and external risks.

In the following chapters, we will explain the decomposition process for each of these three levels of IT systems to apply the McCumber Cube methodology. The IT systems environment and the goals of the security

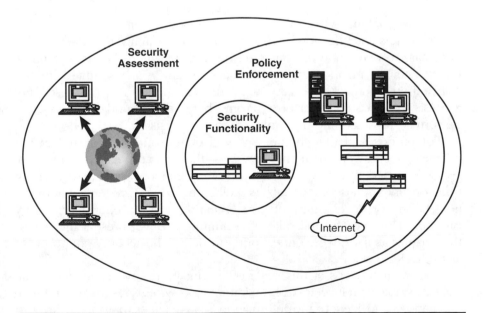

Figure 7.2   Layered Security Analysis I

analysis will dictate the level of detail and specific analysis techniques employed. Before those areas are developed, we must first discuss how decomposition of information states is practiced.

BOUNDARY DEFINITION

One of the key advantages of a structured security methodology that is information-based (or asset based) is its application across the entire spectrum of current technologies as well as future products and systems. To adequately apply this methodology, it is critical to define the system boundaries by accurately defining and mapping them. Another aspect of this boundary analysis is a determination to what level of decomposition is this analysis most valuable.

DECOMPOSITION OF INFORMATION STATES

Within many IT systems components are entire information systems within the component itself. A desktop system, for example, is composed of numerous information state changes within the computer system itself. The system's memory is a storage device as well as the hard drive. There are processing functions most obviously employed within the processor, but also contained within the video accelerator card and even the modem. Each of these system subcomponents can then be decomposed into more minute state changes that take place on the chip itself.

To understand the boundaries of the security analysis required, it is necessary to determine the outcome desired. In Figure 7.3, the tiered IT environment is mapped against the security analysis best suited for the selected environment. The first step is to determine the type of security analysis you wish to perform. From there, the boundary analysis is performed to determine the limits of your analysis.

For purposes of this chapter, we will define our level of abstraction as one of security enforcement analysis — the LAN and related topologies. We will also define how this methodology can be applied to security functionality within components as well as broader IT systems where the goal is one of developing and implementing a comprehensive security program. However, for the sake of continuity, we will present the rest of this chapter as if we were endeavoring to define the security environment at the LAN level.

The required steps at this stage of the methodology are to define the boundary, make an inventory of the information systems resources, and then decompose and identify the information states at the appropriate level of abstraction. Each of these steps can be accomplished and documented rather quickly and provide the basis for the security analysis to come.

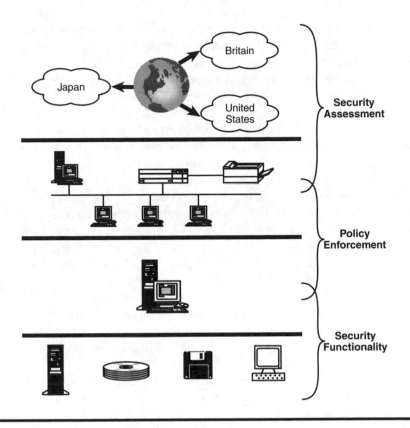

Figure 7.3   Layered Security Analysis II

Step 1: Defining the Boundary

The McCumber Cube methodology is not founded on an educated guess of attacker profiles and then a test to simulate their possible attack scenarios. As we have discussed, such processes are flawed. All sound security analysis is based not on attacker profiles, but around understanding and protecting the assets requiring protection to the appropriate degree. Attacker profiles may change and new attackers with novel approaches are a consistent reality. The only way to ensure you are prepared to deal with any new threat is to ensure you have accommodated the requirements of confidentiality, integrity, and availability of the resource in each of its states of transmission, storage, and processing.

It is important to point out that determining the security boundary does not in any way mean that a security practitioner should rely on boundary protection techniques alone. The boundary security technique is an approach whereby a systems boundary is developed and all (or most) security functions are enforced at the boundary. In such a scenario, there is an assumption that the boundary will remain relatively static and that the only threat comes from unauthorized outsiders — those outside the defined boundary. The point of defining the boundary for use of the McCumber Cube methodology is to simply define the location of information resources and the systems components that are used to transmit, store, and process that information.

There are several guidelines available to help make the determination of which systems comprise the IT systems existing within your boundary (Table 7.1). You can employ an organizational approach whereby all information used by an organization must be accounted for and mapped to specific systems components. In this case, it is also useful to have an inventory (Table 7.2) of the various system components owned by the organization. However, it is important to ensure all components that handle data within the identified boundary are accounted for. A thorough physical inventory is highly recommended. It is not unusual to identify several components or systems that were not included in the inventory for a variety of reasons. Systems may have been purchased with funds not tracked by the inventory system, leased components may be installed, and vendor demonstration units and components belonging to outside organizations also may be present and should be included within the scope of a security analysis.

Again, the challenge is one of actually defining the boundaries. This boundary definition problem is identical to the challenges faced by any type of security analysis or certification process. This is summed up nicely by the National Institute of Standards and Technology's approach for

Table 7.1 Boundary Checklist

☐	Organizational Chart
☐	Network Systems Topology Map
☐	Location Charts or Diagrams
☐	Blueprints

Table 7.2 Inventory Checklist

☐	Network Systems Topology Map
☐	Inventory Lists
☐	Equipment Lists
☐	Thorough Walkthrough
☐	Other Documentation

security accreditation in their *Guide for the Security Certification and Accreditation of Federal Information Systems* (second public draft):[1]

> One of the most difficult and challenging problems for agencies has been identifying appropriate security accreditation boundaries for their information systems. Security accreditation boundaries for agency information systems need to be established during the initial assessment of risk and development of security plans. Boundaries that are too expansive make the security certification and accreditation process extremely unwieldy and complex. Boundaries that are too limited increase the number of security certifications and accreditations that must be conducted and thus, drive up the total security costs for the agency. Although there are no specific rules for determining security accreditation boundaries for information systems, there are, however, some guidelines and considerations … that may be helpful … in making boundary decisions tasks more manageable.
>
> … In general, if a set of information resources is identified as an information system, the resources should meet the following criteria: (i) be under the same direct management control; (ii) have the same function or mission objective; (iii) have essentially the same operating characteristics and security needs, and (iv) reside in the same general operating environment (or in the case of a distributed information systems, reside in various locations with similar operating environments). The application of the criteria results in the assignment of a security accreditation boundary to a single information system. There are certain situations when management span of control and information system boundaries can be used to streamline the security certification and accreditation process, and thus increase it overall cost effectiveness.

Once you have defined the boundary for your security analysis based on these criteria, you are ready to proceed to the next step of the process, making an inventory of IT resources.

Step 2: Make an Inventory of All IT Resources

Once you have identified the extent of your network parameters, you need to work within its confines to identify the various technology resources and components that transmit, store, and process the data. Even though we are employing an information based security model, it is necessary to account for not only the information resources, but also the equipment, systems, and components used. This inventory will be used as a basis for determining the nature and location of information states within the security enforcement environment.

Step 3: Decompose and Identify Information States

The problem becomes one of determining to what level you should decompose information states in order to define and implement the appropriate safeguards. One of the guidelines I recommend to make this assessment is to review a comprehensive list of known security vulnerabilities for the types of components in the information system under review. A sound overview of these known security problems will give you an effective idea of just how minutely your information states need to be defined. For most system components, assigning the appropriate information states will be straightforward, as most of the technology building blocks of these heterogeneous systems have clearly defined roles.

In the example of an organizational information system, information states can be readily identified. A component or system, such as a workstation, PC, router processor, or mainframe, is involved in the processing function. Recall that these automated processing functions require information to be in plaintext (unencrypted). The processing function is identified at any stage where information is updated, modified, appended, or otherwise manipulated. Basically, it is anything that is not storage or transmission.

The transmission function is similarly easy to identify. Transmission can encompass movement of information from one location to another. The medium will be important for understanding vulnerabilities and safeguards, but is irrelevant for this stage of the methodology. It can be a wire-based transmission or wireless. It can be any of a number of protocols. At this point in the process, it is important simply to note that information is being moved.

The storage function can be any mode for storing information resources. It can be a database, a compact disk, or any other type of media. The distinction here is that the information is static. It is important to recognize the wide variety of storage states. It does not need to be a centralized database or even a popular database application. Anywhere data rests is a storage function.

There have been claims from some researchers that a separate function should be identified for display of information. There is no need. Information being displayed is simply a form of storage — usually with associated access from those within eyesight of the display function. Even real-time data displays should be considered storage functions as they

Wireless
Access Card

Transmission

Processing

Storage

Figure 7.4   Personal Computer Information States

refresh their images with information that is retrieved from the processing function through a transmission medium.

It should therefore be obvious that most workstations and PCs comprise all three basic information states and should be identified as possessing such (Figure 7.4). Security assessment and implementation activities must account for the fact that almost all of these systems have the ability to transmit, store, and process information resources. If a PC on a network has the capability to modify corporate information, it must be considered as having as much of a processing function as a mainframe computer or network server.

All information states and states changes need to be identified completely in the environment within the predefined boundaries.

DEVELOPING AN INFORMATION STATE MAP

Once this state identification process has been completed for all aspects of the information systems environment, you should have all the pieces necessary to develop an information state map. An information state map is not the same as a network topology map. It represents the flow of information through the system under review. Some people prefer to overlay the information state map to a network topology diagram, but it should be possible to divorce the information state map to perform the upcoming security analysis of the structured methodology.

The information state map will identify the various state changes of the information through storage, transmission, and processing. Aspects of the map that require greater detail are those where several functions and states are identified within the context of a set of components or subsystems. For example, workstations or PCs attached to the network need to be identified as supporting all three information states. Vulnerabilities exist for all three states in the type of environment, so it is vital to identify and deal with the security ramifications for each of these systems. The same icon can represent systems that are identically configured, but the security elements need to be identified for all three state functions in each unit.

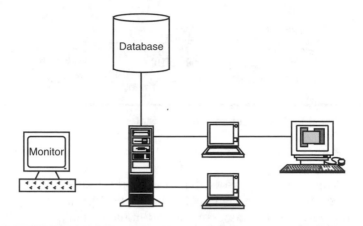

Figure 7.5 Simple IT System State Map

I have included a simple technology map (Figure 7.5) for a small LAN. It represents an environment for a simple application in which the boundaries have already been defined. This diagram is technology-based in that the model represents the various technology components that make up the information systems infrastructure. Once we have mapped this system, we need to decompose the components and overlay the information states and state changes to the map.

In Figure 7.6, we have overlaid the information state changes on top of the technology infrastructure. It is important to accurately reflect information state evolution by actually tracking the information resources as they flow through and between the various technology components. Although it is possible to create an accurate information flow map based solely on technology components using a simple system, a more complex infrastructure would require the analyst to actually define and follow the flow of information resources as opposed to relying simply on identifying physical system components.

Figure 7.6 represents the first phase of the structured methodology — mapping information flow. It is a critical step because this is an information-centric model and not a technology-based approach. The actual operating system, protocols, and various media that are employed can and will change, yet information flow through the system should be mapped and managed at a level of abstraction above the physical medium. In other words, security assessments need to be implemented and managed based on information states, not based on the whims of changing technology.

The information flow maps you create will certainly change and evolve just as the technology infrastructure that supports the organizational information resources. There is no security implementation that can remain

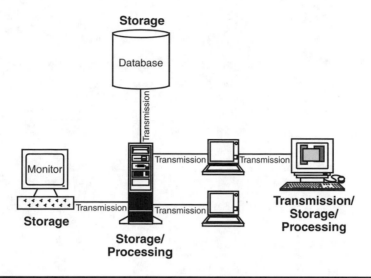

Figure 7.6   Simple IT System State Map with Information State Overlay

static in the face of evolving resource requirements and changes in technology. However, it is vital to develop information flow maps and maintain them in order to continually track the effectiveness of an information security environment. Now that you have mapped the information flow for your environment, it is time to apply the McCumber Cube in assessing and implementing your security requirements.

REFERENCE

1. National Institute of Standards and Technology, NIST Special Publication 800-37 — *Guide for the Security Certification and Accreditation of Federal Information Systems,* 2nd public draft, June 2003 [available at www.csrc.nist.gov/sec-cert].

8

DECOMPOSING THE CUBE FOR SECURITY ENFORCEMENT

INTRODUCTION

The McCumber Cube methodology is a structured process that examines security in the context of information states. This construct is central to the approach. Information is the asset, so security requirements that are defined as simply responses to threat–vulnerability pairs are not sufficient for the assessment and implementation of information security requirements. Vulnerabilities are technical security-relevant issues or exposures (see Chapter 4) that may or may not be problems with the technology system or component. Obviously, because vulnerabilities by definition are technical in nature, they will change with the technology. Some will be noted as programming errors or unnecessary features and will be repaired with a patch, update, or subsystem modification. The McCumber Cube approach allows the analyst to define and evaluate the safeguards at a level abstraction just above the technology.

To be clear, the McCumber Cube methodology does not obviate the need for tracking and managing technical vulnerabilities. In fact, mitigating risk in a specific operational environment will always require the analyst or practitioner to consider the entire library of technical vulnerabilities as a critical aspect for implementing and managing their security program. In recognition of this, I have included a compendium of information on the most widely used library of vulnerabilities as defined in MITRE Corporation's Common Vulnerabilities and Exposure library. However, mapping security requirements based solely on these technical vulnerabilities and exposures is not an effective way to assess and implement security. Thus we have the McCumber Cube methodology for analyzing security functionality based on the information assets themselves.

Another important tool to use in the process is a comprehensive library of safeguards, such as patches for operating systems, security appliances, authentication products, auditing techniques, backup and recovery options, and all the others. Such a library does not currently exist. However, you can develop your own based on your current systems environment and planned implementation. When going through the McCumber Cube methodology, actually including them as options when assessing each block as described below would be a valuable exercise. Depending on the depth of the security assessment, it is usually an effective technique to actually list safeguards (existing or planned) in each category.

One of the major advantages of the methodology is the user's ability to evaluate the entire spectrum of security enforcement mechanisms. It also recognizes the interactive nature of all security safeguards and controls. To be able to effectively assess and implement security in complex IT systems, it is critical to consider all possible safeguards including technology, procedural, and human factors. The penetration-and-patch security approach and vulnerability-centric models of security assessment focus almost solely on technical controls and do not provide the appropriate level of consideration for nontechnical controls. Only the McCumber Cube effectively integrates all three categories of safeguards.

This methodology also works on any level of abstraction to provide comprehensive analysis and implementation of security in information systems. However, the majority of security practitioners, policymakers, and analysts are concerned about the proper implementation and enforcement of security at the organizational level. With that in mind, this section will be used as an exemplar to outline each of the steps of the process. This section will define a generic information system environment and walk the user through each step required to perform a comprehensive and effective security assessment using the structured methodology.

There would be no way to create a text that could possibly outline every conceivable safeguard, vulnerability, or instantiation of an information state. This chapter simply walks you through a series of simple examples to show how the structured methodology is employed. To fully assess a full-scale environment, you need to follow the steps outlined for each of the information states you identified in Chapter 7.

This is not to say that you cannot leverage analyses performed for other information states and even completely copy the safeguard values you created for one state to an instantiation of an identical state. It does mean, however, that you have to account for the attributes of confidentiality, integrity, and availability for each state you identified by assessing safeguards in all three categories. This ensures that you have completely captured all elements of the information systems security program for the environment within the boundaries you have identified.

A WORD ABOUT SECURITY POLICY

The McCumber Cube methodology can dramatically aid the security policy development process. Almost every security researcher, practitioner, or implementer has claimed that security policy must drive the security architecture. On its face, this statement is true. However, the problem arises when one is confronted with the requirement to develop such policies. Many people begin by copying the efforts of someone else or perhaps they employ a checklist developed by a security expert. This process usually results in poorly implemented policies.

The definition of what comprises a security policy is not fixed. Sometimes policy requirements are rather vague and are captured with statements such as: All sensitive company information shall be kept confidential and will only be accessed by authorized employees. It is obvious that the actual tools and techniques that will have to be implemented to enforce this well-meaning directive remain inadequately defined.

Other security policies may be captured by a statement such as: All personnel system users must create and employ a password consisting of 12 alphanumeric characters with at least 2 numbers. This rather specific policy may be a good one, but begs the question: Why? It also leaves unspoken the degree to which the password protects the sensitive personnel information. If such a password causes users to write their password on a sticky note and paste it under the keyboard to aid their memory, it may prove less effective than a shorter, more easily remembered password.

By using the McCumber Cube methodology to help develop your security policies, you will have the tools necessary to determine how much protection is necessary given the value of the information resources. You will also be able to make a more definitive assessment of where policies are required and where enforcement technologies or human factor safeguards can either replace or support the policy requirement. The methodology also provides a specific lexicon of security terminology so security administrators, executives, users, and IT personnel can all discuss security-relevant issues using the appropriate risk reduction terms. This feature alone makes using the methodology far superior to hit-and-miss policy development activities.

For example, someone charged with assessing and implementing security in a corporate information system could make the case for investment in additional security technologies by specifically citing the potential loss exposure of information destruction, delay, distortion, and disclosure. Using the methodology allows the security administrator to pinpoint the risks mitigated and the potential loss from not implementing the appropriate controls. Using a structured methodology allows security technology developers and implementers alike to provide quantifiable justification for investments in products, procedures, and people.

DEFINITIONS

Applying the appropriate lexicon in this process is critical. In the How to Use This Text section, a short dictionary of common terms is presented. You will note that words and terms have been carefully described and used quite specifically throughout the text. In this section, this careful use of words is also important.

When the concept of information states is presented, it is used to describe the three primary information states of transmission, storage, and processing. It has been argued by academics and researchers that more states exist. Some of these experts have posited additional information states, such as display. These distinctions and additions to the three primary states are unnecessary if not actually inaccurate.

It also has been argued that the processing state can ultimately be decomposed into minute permutations of transmission and storage. This is not worth the discussion to debate the merits of this assertion. Although this may be arguably true at a low level of abstraction (within the microprocessor), attempting to apply security requirements in this fashion is untenable. The processing state is vitally important to the assessment and implementation of security policy because, as we have discussed, it has completely changed the science of information security. The automated processing of data and other digital information has ushered in completely new requirements for technologies, procedures, and training that did not exist before the introduction of computer systems to the management of information resources.

The three primary states can easily accommodate all the security-relevant requirements for information systems security assessment and implementation. There is no need to add to or detract from the original model for either precision or clarity. So in this process we must always account for each of the three states of information and refer to them as such.

The elements of confidentiality, integrity, and availability are known and are referred to as security attributes. When we speak of information security, these are the elements to which we refer. As with information states, academics and researchers have argued that there could or should be additions and addenda. Some have made the case for the inclusion of other security attributes such as nonrepudiation and authentication. In the case of nonrepudiation, this is actually a class of safeguard mechanisms that ultimately help ensure data integrity. Classifying nonrepudiation as a unique security attribute is not only inaccurate, it is also unnecessary.

Endeavoring to make the case for other security safeguards such as authentication is also inaccurate and unnecessary. These are safeguards and do not belong as category headings for security attributes. In this way, some academics and researchers have tried to correlate technology-based models with the McCumber Cube information-based model. Although this may be conceptually possible, it does not appear to provide any advantage to the security analyst, because the technology-based model will have to be adapted and modified continually as technology evolves.

The three elements — technology, procedures, and human factors (people) — comprise the three primary categories of safeguards. Sometimes the terms *countermeasures* or *security measures* are used. Although we could debate the academic merits of each, I choose to use the more general term *safeguard* as it best encompasses the concept. Countermeasures may imply somewhat more active technical defenses and its use can be confusing depending on the application.

In this section, we will use the terms *states*, *attributes*, and *safeguards* rather specifically. It is important to point this out so that your comprehension will be aided as you apply the model. As we pointed out in a previous chapter, the term *security* means different things to different people; it is a term fraught with misunderstanding and misapplication. For analysts and practitioners engaged in assessing and implementing information systems security, accurate use and application of these terms is crucial.

THE McCUMBER CUBE METHODOLOGY

The first step of the McCumber Cube methodology process is to accurately map information flow as described in the Chapter 7. Each information state is then parsed out of the larger IT environment and examined for its security-relevant environment. We need to begin by reviewing the composition of the basic McCumber Cube (Figure 8.1).

The McCumber Cube methodology is ultimately based on decomposing the cube into the individual blocks that comprise it and using these blocks as the foundation for determining the appropriate safeguards for each information state. Across the Y-axis of the model are the information states of transmission, storage, and processing. Once these states are identified as outlined in the previous chapter, the analyst or practitioner is ready to analyze the security relevant aspects of the system impacting the information resources.

Now we must look at the other elements of the cube (Figure 8.2). The vertical axis comprises the information-centric security attributes

Figure 8.1   Basic McCumber Cube

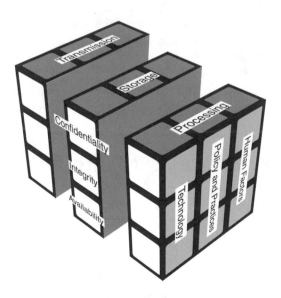

Figure 8.2   McCumber Cube Dissecting by Vertical Axis

of confidentiality, integrity, and availability. Simply looking at the cube on its face as a two-dimensional model, it is possible to create a matrix for defining the security requirements for each of the three information states.

THE TRANSMISSION STATE

The next step will be to separate a column based on the identified information state. For example, let us use one of the information states of transmission that we identified in Chapter 7. We can use the state that exists between an office computer (workstation) on the LAN and its connection to that network. Information is in its transmission state as it flows to and from this computer by an internal connection to a hub or switch. From there, information resources flow to and from various internal systems and even to an external router for access to the Internet. In this case, however, we need to define the transmission state as existing between the workstation and the hub. Information transmitted from the hub to other locations must be defined separately.

In this example, the transmission medium is Ethernet cabling that carries the information between the workstation and the hub. We must consider the entire transmission column (Figure 8.3) and assess all the security attributes we wish to enforce. Returning to the rows of security attributes, we see that confidentiality, integrity, and availability are all desirable security-relevant attributes we wish to maintain. Now it is time to assess what mechanisms we employ to maintain or enforce these requirements.

The Z-axis, or depth factor, of the cube defines the three primary categories of safeguards that can be employed to ensure the appropriate amount of security. If we begin with the first block, we can examine the security-relevant safeguards that ensure the appropriate amount of confidentiality assurance for the information in this transmission state. The value of the information (low, medium, or high) will help us determine to what degree these security requirements are enforced. It then becomes extremely useful for performing security cost-benefit trade-offs.

Transmission: Confidentiality

The first category to consider in the transmission-confidentiality square is technology. The safeguards we can employ for this transmission phase that also fall in the technology category begin with the medium itself. The fact the information flows through the wire means that a threat that can impact the confidentiality would require the ability to first access the data stream. Then the threat would need to be able to extract actual information (not simply data or electronic bits) and provide it to an unauthorized party. If your information valuation is relatively low or medium, you can review the library of vulnerabilities and determine that no special safeguards need to be employed to ensure confidentiality in this transmission state. If your information valuation is higher, you may wish to implement

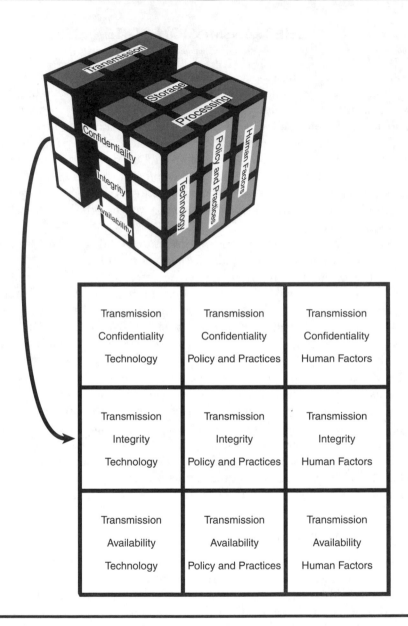

Figure 8.3 Transmission Column Separated

a physical technology safeguard such as protected conduits as a physical barrier to preclude wiretapping between the computer and the hub.

The next category of safeguard is policy. If you have a policy that only authorized, trusted personnel can access and modify the cabling that exists between the computer and the hub, you are using a policy safeguard.

The inherent value of the McCumber Cube methodology can clue you in to these requirements and provide you a basis for making these decisions.

The human factor is the final category to consider. In this case, it may not make sense to employ any human-based safeguards. Yet, for high-value information environments, there may be a case made to have periodic inspection of the cabling system itself to look for unauthorized taps or other possible violations of confidentiality.

Transmission: Integrity

After completely analyzing the three categories of safeguards used to maintain the confidentiality of the information resources in this transmission state, we move to integrity. You will find that many (certainly not all) of the safeguards considered to enforce confidentiality in transmission are also effective in helping maintain information integrity as well. This is not always the case, especially as we move on to the processing function. However, it is important to realize that security management and enforcement mechanisms overlap and can help maintain one, two, or all thee of the security attributes of confidentiality, integrity and availability. We now move to the next block — integrity.

We again apply our analysis to the transmission state in question. However, this time we look at controls and safeguards employed to maintain the accuracy of the information resources. In the transmission medium, most integrity controls are handled by the transmission protocol itself. In this case, depending on the protocol used, a variety of integrity checking mechanisms are employed to ensure that which is sent is that which is received. These security safeguards include checksums, hash and secure hash algorithms, and hamming codes.

At the security enforcement level of abstraction, it is also worth reviewing the list of vulnerabilities to determine if there are existing vulnerabilities in the protocols that can impact the integrity of the information during transmission in this specific technical environment. If one or more exists, then updates, patches, and modifications to mitigate or eliminate the risk should be examined. If none are available, then consider the full spectrum of add-on integrity safeguards depending on the value of the information. The value of the information and specific threat environment will help determine the amount of resources required to mitigate the risks.

Transmission: Availability

The next security attribute to consider is availability. This aspect of security is often critical for information in its transmission state and is many times overlooked. On-call support technicians provided by the host organization may adequately address maintaining the availability of the transmission function between this particular workstation and the hub. In any case, it is wise to determine how much downtime can be tolerated (based again on the value of the information and its application) and safeguards tailored to meet these empirical requirements.

From a technology perspective, redundant transmission paths (cables, hubs, and routers) can be used to achieve these availability requirements. Moving on to policies, we can employ service level agreements that dictate response time and uptime availability requirements. The human intervention dimension of safeguards may be a help desk capability that responds to the loss of or degradation of availability.

Now we have walked through the entire analytic process of the methodology for this specific transmission state. We will move on to the information state of storage and again apply the same process we just employed for the transmission state. For our example, we will use the organizational server in our architecture to outline the process for assessing and implementing security in the storage state.

THE STORAGE STATE

The storage function (Figure 8.4) will be highlighted by one of the database servers in our notional architecture. We will define the storage state as the function where information resides at rest within the server environment. Obviously, the applications supporting the database environment can process information and information is transmitted into and out of the database. However, for purposes of the methodology, we concentrate solely on the function of information at rest.

Storage: Confidentiality

As we did with the example of transmission state above, we begin by analyzing the block at the intersection of the storage state and the confidentiality attribute of security. The question to ask here is what is or should be done to ensure the confidentiality of the information in its storage state. We will begin with the first category of safeguard — technology.

Information in its storage state is, by definition, at rest. To compromise the information's confidentiality, unauthorized access is required. It is important to point out here that the concept of unauthorized access assumes that authorized users have appropriate granular levels of access. This concept supports principles outlined in models such as the Bell–LaPadula access model.

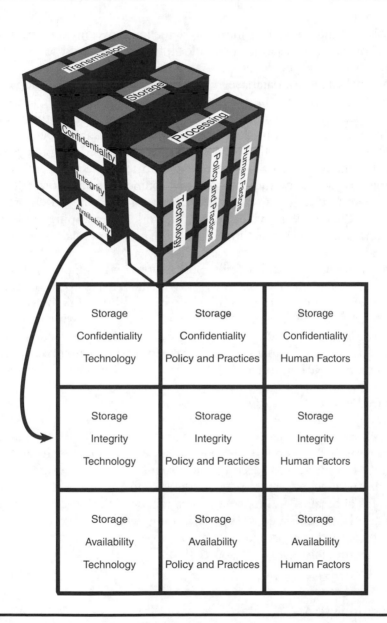

Storage Confidentiality Technology	Storage Confidentiality Policy and Practices	Storage Confidentiality Human Factors
Storage Integrity Technology	Storage Integrity Policy and Practices	Storage Integrity Human Factors
Storage Availability Technology	Storage Availability Policy and Practices	Storage Availability Human Factors

Figure 8.4   Storage Column Separated

Access control technology does not (and cannot) assume that authorized users may not abuse their privileges and exploit information resources. Granular access control methodologies employed in many database applications and operating system controls can provide appropriate technology-enforced safeguards. These safeguards then can be layered with technology solutions such as intrusion detection tools and auditing systems to monitor the activities of users and look for unauthorized or security-relevant activities and incidents.

The challenge in a database environment such as the one depicted in this example is the level of granularity of the technology safeguards. Here is good place to consider applying the McCumber Cube methodology to the database subsystem to develop security requirements specific to this technology. However, if the vendor has not performed this analysis, it is up to the implementer or system operator to make security enforcement decisions by evaluating the database environment as an information storage state and treating it as a composite unit for analysis and enforcement purposes. Chapter 9 provides the framework for mapping information states and applying the methodology for a more granular assessment, if one is appropriate.

After assessing the technology controls for confidentiality of the information in storage in the database server, the next step is to consider procedural controls. In this instance, there may be policy or procedural controls that dictate access rules regarding personnel who are allowed access (through a technology-based safeguard such as the database access control subsystem) for maintenance, upkeep, and management purposes. These controls will support and enhance the technical controls that actually enforce these policy requirements.

Procedural controls for protecting information resources in the storage state often will be employed in support of technology safeguards. When we next consider human factors safeguards, we will notice that these options also will often be an integral aspect of the technical control structure. For instance, a security or systems administrator may need to manually review output from an audit system or access control log to search for anomalies and make a determination if the procedural requirements are being enforced by the technology controls. For this example, all three categories of safeguards are employed to help provide confidentiality for the information resources in their storage state within the database server.

Storage: Integrity

The next step is to assess integrity controls for information in its storage state within the database server. We begin by moving to the block at the intersection of storage and integrity. Maintaining integrity of information in a database environment is usually the purview of controls within the database application or the applications that manage this information resource. The confidentiality controls we assessed above can also be considered for protecting information integrity in this example.

It is not important to create definitive and more granular boundaries between the transmission, storage, and processing states within the database environment unless you are performing a more detailed assessment of the database application or the application that supports and manages it. This will be covered in Chapter 9. At this level of abstraction (security enforcement) it is sufficient to apply the storage state label while understanding that more granular processing and transmission states exist within the database application environment.

Even though the technology safeguards to ensure integrity may be embedded within the application, they need to be enumerated and evaluated as an integral component of the security assessment process. These controls can then be considered and highlighted as key elements of the security program because they support the critical integrity attribute. In most current security processes, these key security-relevant technology safeguards are either assumed or not considered. In the McCumber Cube methodology, these requirements are called out by the methodic decomposition of the cube and need to be assessed.

Procedural safeguards for protecting the integrity of information in its storage state are the next area for consideration. As with confidentiality safeguards, many integrity controls will often be employed in support of technology safeguards embedded in the database applications and storage systems themselves. Specific procedural controls for integrity may also encompass ways in which the information (or data in this case) is acquired and evaluated before inclusion in the database itself. In other words, procedural controls for managing integrity for information at rest relies most heavily on preventing unauthorized modification of the resources.

These procedural (as well as technical) controls may be implemented during the processing state or even the transmission state. Some researchers have argued that when information is at rest, it is, by definition, immune from modification or alteration — authorized or not. Again, this is an issue of abstraction. If a granular assessment has been performed on the database environment for the purposes of security functionality, then this evaluation can comprise an integral part of the security enforcement analysis. If not, these issues then must be considered as part of the security enforcement analysis described in this chapter.

As with procedural safeguards, human factors safeguards for information integrity are often employed as an adjunct to both technology and procedural controls. However, the structured methodology makes you define and list them to ensure they adequately support your protection requirements. These safeguards may include human review of information prior to input, human oversight of the database environment, or flags to alert operators and users to suspicious data elements.

Storage: Availability

The availability of the information resources in the storage state is an area that is usually overlooked by vulnerability-centric security models. No one could seriously deny the importance of ensuring the availability of information in its storage state. This is an area of major concern to the author of this text. Most of us have been confronted with the security problem of nonavailability of information that has been stored. If you have stored important information on a diskette, CD, or external hard drive that is lost or damaged, you have experienced this problem. Perhaps you have also considered or even taken steps to mitigate the risk. You can make an additional copy of the media, store a copy of the information on another computer system, or retain the information in another medium such as a printed copy of the information. In each case, you have looked to mitigate the risk of loss of information in its storage state.

The next step of the methodology is to first consider technology safeguards for maintaining the availability of information in the storage state in our example. Many database systems have backup and recovery capabilities built into their applications that are representative of this safeguard category. When the value of the information warrants it (high or even medium), a "hot" backup or real-time journaling system may be required to meet the requirements of the availability attribute. This dynamic capability can ensure that the data remains available to users when the primary system is impacted. When the value of the information dictates, you can also consider additional technical solutions that include a mix of these techniques.

Procedural controls are the next category of safeguard for analysis. Procedures are a vital protective aspect of providing availability of information in storage. Most organizations have these controls, yet few consider them as security mechanisms. Most data centers and systems administrators have procedurally based requirements to back up data on a recurring basis. This may be on a nightly, weekly, or monthly basis. Critical systems may also have specialized procedures to actually restore the data within a specified time period.

It is readily obvious that these technology and procedural safeguards come with a cost. The function of availability is normally easier to calculate because empirical measurements exist for determining how much availability you can afford. These metrics are most frequently expressed as uptime requirements (as a percentage) and restoration time (in linear time as days, hours, and minutes). The safeguard costs logically increase as availability requirements become more stringent. For some information systems, being able to back up to the previous week's (or day's) data is adequate based on the dramatically increased costs associated with more immediate restoration.

The final step in the storage state is to assess the human factors category of safeguards. In this case, the human factors come into play predominantly to enact the requirements of the procedural safeguards. This may seem a trivial distinction, but it highlights one of the key strengths of this methodology. The McCumber Cube approach ensures all safeguard elements are properly considered and accounted for in the implementation. The procedural controls that need to be enacted in the event of a loss of availability incident are moot if the people assigned to implement them and restore the lost data are not available. The human factors safeguards also should consider training and testing to ensure people assigned these security-relevant duties have adequate knowledge and the skills necessary to implement the policies.

THE PROCESSING STATE

The processing state (Figure 8.5) is unique to modern computing environments. In How to Use This Text, I challenge the reader to apply the methodology to precomputer information systems such as the telegraph and Napoleonic military command and control. Those who take the challenge realize that processing is purely a human-based endeavor if computing systems are not involved. However, with modern computing technology the manipulation and reinterpretation of information can take place outside the human sphere.

Technically, the computer is only executing a preestablished set of instructions coded into it by a human. However, this information state is critical to understanding and applying security in IT systems. If the processing state did not exist, extensive use of cryptography would accommodate most of the security implementation requirements for confidentiality and many for integrity. However, the automated manipulation of data and the resultant changes in the information produced requires the identification and assessment of the processing state as a unique state of information. The processing state represents a critical function fraught with vulnerabilities and security exposures. Information during this stage is vulnerable to a wide variety of threats.

To walk through this next state, we will use an application server as the example. In fact, we will target specifically a financial application on this computer system that manages the accounts for a small business. This system takes input from various users and other applications and creates analysis reports for decision makers and outputs information for submission to auditing groups and regulatory agencies.

The security implications are fairly obvious. If the reports are inaccurate, the corporate decision makers will be basing their decisions on faulty data. Erroneous reporting to regulatory agencies could result in fines and

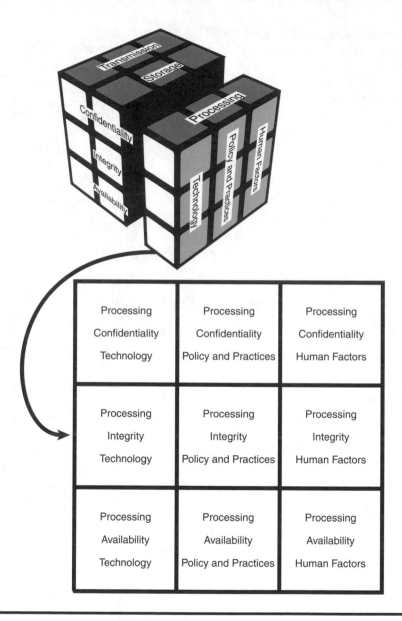

Figure 8.5 Processing Column Separated

penalties or even possible imprisonment for company executives. Ensuring appropriate protection for this processing state will be essential. The methodology instructs us to call out the next column representing the processing function.

Processing: Confidentiality

The first step is to call out the block that represents the intersection of the processing function and the confidentiality attribute. As we stated in previous chapters, encrypted information cannot be processed. To process information, it must be in plaintext. However, there are numerous safeguards that must be considered to ensure the confidentiality of information in the processing state. The set of safeguards to consider at this point are the technology safeguards. As with the storage state, we must begin with access control technologies.

To violate the confidentiality of information during the identified processing function, we need to somehow gain access to the information during this state. Because we know that information here must be processed in plaintext, we can be assured that vulnerabilities in cryptographic protections would not be an issue. The violation of confidentiality is most logically accomplished by gaining unauthorized access to the information during this vulnerable state. Even if the application has a solid access control mechanism, other programs and memory storage areas that retain data after the completion of processing can prove capable of allowing unauthorized exposure of the information.

System administrators and those with privileged access to operating systems can take advantage of their access rights to view data that has been sent to the application for processing. They can also intercept reports before they are transmitted to authorized users. The processing function requires a careful review of all possible exploitations of confidentiality — even as the states of transmission and processing are invoked during the processing state.

The next step is to analyze procedural options for ensuring the confidentiality of information in its processing state. This could be a requirement to allow only certain people physical access to systems that process information. If the information is accorded the appropriate amount of protection as it is in the transmission state entering a secured perimeter, the physical security control may preclude unauthorized users from potentially obtaining keyboard access to the application server and its environment.

Another policy safeguard could be aimed at preventing any changes to the application not authorized by the vendor or application development organization. There is often an assumption that confidentiality is assured in some measure by the application vendor's due diligence to create a product with a minimal amount of vulnerabilities. By maintaining the application in accordance with the vendor's recommendations, at least a small measure of assurance can be factored into the analysis. Each of these procedural safeguards represents an option for protecting information in the processing state.

After looking at procedural ways to enforce confidentiality, human factors are the next to be assessed. These safeguards can include background checks for application developers, system administrators, operators, and auditors. These checks would go a partial way in mitigating risks from those people with a criminal background or potential problems (financial, social, or psychological) who may seek to gain access to sensitive company information.

Personnel background checks, for example, have become an integral aspect of many security programs. In fact, they are often used as a basic preemployment screening mechanism in the hiring process of many companies and are a critical security component for many government operations. Even basic aspects of a prehire screening, such as the veracity of educational claims, can provide insight into a person's character.

These human factor security issues would work hand-in-hand with the procedural and technical controls to ensure the appropriate amount of protection is applied to information in the processing state. Again, the structured methodology approach ensures the complete spectrum of security safeguards are considered to provide a comprehensive look at all safeguards and how they interact.

Processing: Integrity

We next move to the block that represents the intersection of the processing state and the integrity attribute. As we did with the example of the confidentiality attribute above, we begin by analyzing what is or should be done to ensure the integrity of the information in its processing state. We will begin with the first category of safeguard — technology.

This is another block that represents significant vulnerabilities. The processing state is critical to maintaining the integrity (accuracy and robustness) of the information it manipulates. The first step is to consider technology safeguards for maintaining integrity.

In the application we are using for an example, much of the trust placed in the processing state is inherited from the people who coded the set of instructions that are performing the processing function. In many cases, the fact that an application is purchased from a major software vendor and is well respected in the industry counts for much. The various bugs and coding problems that crop up in most applications are a constant threat to the integrity of the information it manipulates. These programming errors are certainly just a part of operating automated processing systems, but technology safeguards exist.

Your processing state may require automated tools or software to preclude alteration to the programming code of the applications. Malicious code sentinels and anti-virus products help prevent changes to the application that can cause the processing function to act inappropriately. In the case of an e-mail application, it is instructive to look at the instance of malicious code that is programmed to cause an e-mail client to send out e-mail messages to everyone in the users address book that contains another iteration of the worm or virus. To protect the integrity of the information assets during the e-mail processing function, security products such as virus scanners and content filters are invaluable technology safeguards.

Automated checks that search for anomalies or bad data can be incorporated into the processing function. As with the transmission phase, checksums, hashes, and other processing techniques can be employed to ferret out potential integrity problems during the processing state. These types of controls may not be required for our example (based on the probable value of the information resources), but it still is part of the methodology to consciously examine each block of the cube using each of the three safeguard categories for assessment purposes. If you choose not to use a safeguard, you are still far ahead of those who did not even examine the processing state for possible vulnerabilities and potential safeguards to mitigate risks.

Procedural safeguards comprise the next category to assess. For integrity of processing, there are many possible procedural safeguards. One policy could be to only use an application from a certain known vendor with a track record of ensuring sound software with extensive quality assurance testing. Another policy may require only updates to the code by this same trusted vendor.

Other procedural safeguards to consider here include requirements on the review of data or information pre- and postprocessing. Integrity is also supported by physical access controls to the processing environment and assurance of only authorized and monitored modifications to software. By physically controlling access to the system, the list of possible threats to the integrity of the information in the processing function is dramatically reduced.

Human factors safeguards are the final assessment area for this section. As with confidentiality, human factors safeguards can include background checks for application developers, system administrators, operators, and auditors. Although the issue of integrity and confidentiality is closely related in the processing function, it is still important to uniquely assess the human factors safeguards that can affect each attribute. Confidentiality and integrity are two completely separate security attributes, and although a sound security enforcement program has many mutually supporting controls, failure to uniquely examine the impact to these attributes leaves the analysis open to overlooked vulnerabilities and possible safeguards.

Processing: Availability

The final step for this information state is looking at the vulnerabilities and safeguards for availability of the processing function. Again, we begin with the technology vulnerabilities and safeguard options. As with transmission, many processing availability safeguards are centered on redundant technology and backup capabilities. For our example, it may be adequate for our financial application to maintain a simple backup copy of the software to reload in case of loss of the processing function through any incident that precludes the application from performing its processing function. A backup host system also may be a technology safeguard.

Availability safeguards in this area tend to work in concert with other availability safeguards such as the ones that support transmission and storage. Many applications and other processing capabilities can cross-protect by working with safeguards that support and protect other information states through the use of redundant facilities, hardware, software, and support.

Procedural safeguards that can help maintain the processing capabilities of our application are recovery procedures and alternate processing sites that can provide backup in case of system failures, attacks, environmental degradation, and other incidents. Many of these security fallback options also have empirical requirements to assess the efficacy of the safeguards. As with the storage function, quicker and more comprehensive restoration comes with more cost. These may be based on the time value of the information or the requirement for timely access to make critical decisions in support of the organizational mission. The metric may be days, hours, or even minutes. If our financial application is used to pay employees, timely processing of the payroll is definitely critical to the effective operation of the organization as well as employee morale.

Human factors are now the final vulnerability and safeguards assessment area for the processing state. The technology and procedural controls that need to be enacted in the event of a loss of the processing capability are completely ineffective if the people assigned to implement them and restore the processing capability are not included. The human factors safeguards should also consider training and testing to ensure people assigned these security-relevant duties have adequate knowledge and the skills necessary to operate the technology solutions and implement the appropriate security policies under the appropriate circumstances.

RECAP OF THE METHODOLOGY

The general overview of the methodology is rather simple to espouse. The steps are:

1. Information flow mapping:
   a. Define the boundary.
   b. Make an inventory of all information resources and technology.
   c. Decompose and identify all information states.
2. Cube decomposition based on information states:
   a. Call out column from the cube — transmission, storage, or processing.
   b. Decompose blocks by the attributes of confidentiality, integrity, and availability.
   c. Identify existing and potential vulnerabilities:
      i. Use vulnerability library.
      ii. Develop or use safeguard library.
      iii. Factor information values — use valuation metrics.
      iv. Assign appropriate safeguards in each category.
3. Develop comprehensive architecture of safeguards (technology, procedures, human factors):
   a. Describe comprehensive security architecture components.
   b. Cost out architecture components (including procedural and human factor safeguards).
4. Perform comprehensive risk assessment for the specific environment (if necessary):
   a. Include threat and assets measurements.
   b. Add other implementation specific data.
   c. Perform cost trade-off and valuation analyses.

Although I have only included a short chapter on the risk assessment process, it is a critical aspect of ultimately making appropriate cost-benefit trade-offs for a security program and functions as the capstone for the implementation of specific elements of the security program. The McCumber Cube methodology allows the analyst or security practitioner to minutely examine the entire security environment outside of the actual implementation. Ultimately, the entire risk environment of the IT system must be included; that is where the elements of threat and asset valuation are ultimately employed to establish the trade-offs necessary for any security program. You can begin to approach perfect security (complete freedom from risk) only with unlimited resources. The risk assessment process will be able to use the safeguards developed with the McCumber Cube methodology and integrate that architectural environment into the risk assessment process to provide a solid underpinning to any information systems security program.

9

INFORMATION STATE ANALYSIS FOR COMPONENTS AND SUBSYSTEMS

INTRODUCTION

One of the most daunting challenges currently facing security researchers and practitioners is one of determining how secure a specific computer subsystem, product, or component may be. There have been numerous attempts to apply a variety of criteria to this problem so information systems implementers and purchasers can make judgments about security issues in the acquisition and implementation of specific products and architectures. This unrewarding pursuit finds its highest expression in the search for the secure computer out of the box.

Currently, the methodology in use for the government is known as the Common Criteria. This is the evaluation process that evolved from the NSA's Rainbow Series criteria. In an attempt to keep pace with rapid changes in technology, the criteria were changed and adapted to accommodate the concept of protection profiles instead of the more rigid and inflexible digraph categories of the Orange Book methodology. It will not benefit this text to delve into any detail of these criteria at this point; however, the reader unfamiliar with these efforts should make the time to understand the basics of this process and its evolution from the Orange Book criteria to the Common Criteria.

Although these approaches have been touted as the appropriate method for defining and implementing trusted or secure components and subsystems, they are really only able to make an assessment of the device's security-relevant functions and capabilities. As we have described in previous chapters, specific information system implementations require a comprehensive and dynamic risk assessment process to determine the adequacy of safeguards. I propose we actively acknowledge this fact and augment the Common Criteria approach with an assessment of each evaluated product by undertaking it as an assessment of its security functionality. This process could produce common security functionality assessments that would benefit purchasers, systems integrators, and security practitioners. These assessments of the product's security functionality would be drastically improved if they would employ the information-centric approach of the McCumber Cube and ensure the appropriate use of terminology for the security assessment it produces.

One of the major advantages of the McCumber Cube approach is the flexibility to apply the methodology to an even more minute and detailed assessment of individual components. If the purpose of a security assessment is to determine the requirements for the assessment or development of a specific IT component, subsystem, or even client system with rigorous internal security functionality, the evaluator need only refine the elements of this methodology to look at more minute state changes, specifically, those state changes that take place within the component under scrutiny.

Whether or not you or your organization uses the Common Criteria as an integral aspect of your information systems security program, you can still employ the state analysis of the McCumber Cube methodology at more discrete layers of abstraction when necessary to make decisions about security enforcement within specific subsystems or components. Products that can be assessed in this manner include applications, database systems, storage systems, and even protocols and information systems standards. By applying the same principles and procedures outlined in the previous chapter, you can perform state analysis and make judgments about the effectiveness of security controls for these components of your IT infrastructure.

SHORTCOMINGS OF CRITERIA STANDARDS FOR SECURITY ASSESSMENTS

Several approaches for performing security assessments for technology components have been advanced over the past three decades, but only a couple have made it into widespread use. Although there were several evaluation criteria developed in Canada and Europe, the most widely used have been the Rainbow Series criteria and Common Criteria that are referred to throughout this text. Both these evaluation criteria have their roots in the United States. The former was spawned from research at the NSA and the latter evolved from the original criteria and are now managed primarily for the U.S. government by the National Institute of Standards and Technology. It is not necessary for purposes of this text to delve into any great detail in the specifics, but it is important to note some of the serious shortcomings that preclude these processes from providing the types of security technology components they were designed to encourage and ultimately rate.

As we have already noted, the principal problem with these criteria is the fact they are both technology-based models. The original Orange Book digraphs were rigid criteria that had strict requirements for implementing assured security through the invocation and verification of concepts such as mandatory access controls, covert channel analysis, security domains, and verified designs. These requirements were intended to guide vendors, programmers, and developers in building their products to meet these security standards. Some subsystems were built, but it soon became obvious that the stringent requirements required years to build into the technology and the functionality was highly constrained as a result.

Another key factor was that computer systems of the late 1980s and early 1990s were quickly changing from stand-alone mainframe systems within tightly controlled environments to smaller, lighter, faster systems that were starting to reap the advantages of rapid advances in networking and interconnectivity. The PC revolution that began in the 1980s meant that processing systems were becoming ubiquitous, general purpose appliances rather than larger and more specialized mainframes including the secure systems originally envisioned by the security researchers of the period.

Computing and telecommunications technology had changed and the technology-based criteria could not adapt quickly enough. Both government and industry groups had already made major investments in implementing the criteria, so they sought to adapt the criteria to the changing technology environment by publishing a series of interpretations of the criteria that applied to databases, distributed systems, and even trusted recovery for these trusted systems. In the end, no amount of effort and expense could keep the criteria current with the pace of technology evolution.

Assumptions inherent in the criteria seem almost comical in hindsight. The original criteria bundled the concepts of security functionality and assurance in the enforcement of the criteria requirements. The Orange Book digraphs basically assumed that the environs of the system when deployed would naturally be more hostile the more secure you needed the system to be. This approach made a variety of assumptions regarding the threats, yet failed to even address the issues of information valuation. In short, the criteria were being applied to solve problems they could not define. It was a risk avoidance philosophy applied to a risk management problem.

The *Canadian Trusted Computer Product Evaluation Criteria* (CTCPEC), Version 3.0[1] was published in 1993 and did much better job by allowing functionality and assurance requirements to be analyzed and enforced separately. However, these criteria also suffered from a focus on a technology-based model. These criteria merged with the remnants of the Rainbow Series to create the Common Criteria now in use.

The Common Criteria seem doomed simply by the title alone — Common Criteria for IT Security Evaluation. Not only is the technology-based model cited in the title, the concept of trust was again replaced by the less precise term security. However, the Common Criteria have proven much more flexible in adapting to systems with varying applications and requirements. The assumed user establishes a protection profile that is evaluated against the criteria.

However, the central problem with these criteria remains. How much security do you achieve by connecting a firewall evaluated at EAL-2 to an unevaluated network to a commercial commodity, general-purpose laptop computer? Is that enough security? No one knows.

Although the process of developing and applying the criteria has helped spawn major advances in security technology, the results of the evaluation process have been mixed at best. It is still nearly impossible to quantify the value of demanding that vendors produce products that meet the criteria. This is accomplished by attempting to place requirements on government agencies to purchase only appropriately evaluated products. The criteria initiatives have created a cottage industry comprising evaluators and government technocrats, but whether or not they have helped protect our critical national information resources remains to be seen.

APPLYING THE McCUMBER CUBE METHODOLOGY FOR PRODUCT ASSESSMENTS

In Chapter 8, we applied the McCumber Cube methodology to a small organizational network that included such components as routers, hubs, workstations, PCs, and database servers. We began by defining the system boundaries, then made an inventory of the information resources and technology components within our determined boundary. We then decomposed this information system to determine the nature and location of the information states of transmission, storage, and processing.

After the states were identified and labeled, we began the process of calling out the appropriate column from the cube. The process then mandates the evaluation of each block where the information state intersects the security attribute of confidentiality, integrity, and availability. In each block, existing vulnerabilities are evaluated and safeguards are considered. Ultimately, as all safeguard categories are developed, a comprehensive, interwoven security policy enforcement program evolves from the methodology.

On a broad, global scale, this process can be used in a fashion nearly identical to the one outlined in Chapter 8. The information states can be identified and decomposed to assess the relative levels of risk in the environment. The methodology is applied at the level of abstraction that allows the analyst to make a judgment about the security environment by highlighting known vulnerabilities and looking at each of the three safeguard categories to determine the efficacy of the security systems in place. Although the outcome would not likely be the development of a security enforcement capability, the methodology provides a comprehensive and systematic approach for making an accurate (to a certain degree) security assessment. Because the boundaries for such a review could vary wildly, we will not cover that aspect of methodology in this text.

This chapter will take the methodology to a finer level of abstraction. The McCumber Cube can be applied to either assess or develop security functionality for subsystems and components that comprise an information system. In fact, following the methodology for this purpose creates an effective and consistent process for determining the effectiveness of the component or subsystem under review.

In each of these cases, the components and subsystems could be decomposed into the specific information state changes and the assessment methodology applied to these state changes within the technology component. This process would be superior to recent attempts to make security assessments of technology components and subsystems and making claims about their ability (or lack thereof) to enforce security policy requirements through the use of protection profiles.

STEPS FOR PRODUCT AND COMPONENT ASSESSMENT

The criteria for determining the environment is identical to the process we outlined in Chapter 7 on Mapping Information Flow. These steps are to define the boundary, inventory the information resources, then decompose and identify information states. In the case of these more defined entities, the first step is markedly easier although the subsequent steps may require a more abstract and perhaps somewhat tedious analysis. However, it is superior to other component and product assessments because of its information-centric approach.

INFORMATION FLOW MAPPING

Define the Boundary

Defining the boundary for this type of analysis is normally straightforward. The subsystem or component under review is most likely physically constrained by its form factor. In short, the box is your boundary. In this sense, however, the box may be a software program or other digital or virtual process that lacks a bounded physical embodiment. In either case, the boundary definition step is basically the same as we used in Chapter 7.

Take an Inventory of Information Resources and Components

In this step, you have to "look under the hood" to inventory the various components that make up a product, as well as look for the location and transmission paths of all information resources that will be manipulated by this subsystem. Carefully consider the degree of abstraction the product requires. There are no hard and fast rules; however, the management functions and various subsystems within the product will normally present themselves as information is moved through the product and functions are performed with the data entities.

Decompose and Identify All Information States

As with the network example, it is likely you will be able to accurately identify permutations of the three information states at this point. It is usually a good idea to make a topological map of the environment and label the information states as you would a network map that displays the location of servers, workstations, routers, hubs, and other equipment. The most important aspect of the process here is to ensure your identification of the information states is complete.

Let us take a router as an example. A router performs primarily a processing function: It reads headers on inbound packets, determines the best route to send the packet, then switches it back to its transmission state to move the packet on to the next location. The state of transmission is also represented in a simple router as communication paths direct the packets on their journey to their various wired or wireless connections. The storage state may not be present in the level of abstractions we are evaluating.

Another example would be a simple display terminal. If the device does not possess a processing function and merely accepts data from an external processor that it displays on a video screen, then defining it as a storage device is adequate. Although it may at first seem unusual to describe this as a storage device, that is exactly the function of the display. It stores the results of the processing function in some type of representational format for viewing by authorized users. Assessing whether or not to apply security protections to the device must be analyzed in relation to providing the confidentiality, integrity, and availability of the information in this storage state.

A modern, general-purpose desktop computer system will usually be assigned the two primary states of storage and processing, although it is usually unnecessary to decompose it below these two. A security analyst may wish to define the display as a separate storage function and individually assign storage states to each of the media within this desktop environment. For example, a hard disk is a storage device as well as any removable media and optical media. The wires or radio waves that bring data to and from the computer represent a change to the transmission state. Depending on the level of assessment, it may or may not be necessary to decompose the states into specific transmission states among the desktop system's interior components unless these pathways are being evaluated.

CUBE DECOMPOSITION BASED ON INFORMATION STATES

Here is where the real work begins. The functions performed are basically identical to the methodology we employed for networks, but the available information on vulnerabilities and safeguards at this level of abstraction is much more sparse. It is my hope that with use this process can generate a library of vulnerabilities and safeguards for the various subsystems that make up these products and information systems components.

However, we can again look at our router example. There are documented vulnerabilities within routers where information in a storage state has been compromised. In some cases, router tables can be exploited to locate protected devices and services. In this instance, a security practitioner would be best served to recognize the safeguard requirements for both the processing and storage functions of the router.

Call Out the Information State Column

The appropriate information state column is now separated from the cube; you now start by analyzing the block of the confidentiality and the information state intersect. This is the same as for the methodology at any level of abstraction. This will be repeated for each instantiation of an information state.

Decompose Blocks by Attribute

Here the methodology is applied in sequence to each of the attributes of confidentiality, integrity, and availability. The McCumber Cube is actually more accurate than most security criteria because the structured approach mandates that you assess every attribute of information security, not just confidentiality and not just confidentiality and integrity. Availability is a critical attribute that needs assurance even within specific products and components. Simply saying you can plug-and-replace the product in question is not a sound security strategy.

Many products and components have undergone rigorous analyses for confidentiality and integrity controls only to have availability assumed or ignored outright. This can result in the loss, delay, or even destruction of vital information resources that are subsequently attributed to a simple component malfunction. For many critical information resources, this can be at least as disastrous an outcome as unauthorized disclosure or loss of integrity.

Identify Existing and Potential Vulnerabilites

At this point, there may be little in the way of published vulnerabilities. Perhaps if a specific protocol is employed, there may be a known exploit or fault, but at this level, the analysis really calls for a structured look at safeguards employed to provide or enhance the security attributes. At first, it may appear difficult to determine how attributes like confidentiality could possibly be exploited with a specific box or subsystem. However, there is actual historical precedence for being concerned.

Confidentiality can be violated, for example, by the processing function itself when that function is made capable of passing information or data to unauthorized sources. In the original Orange Book, this was one of the vulnerabilities anticipated by the researchers and was identified as a covert channel in a computing system.

There are several definitions of what constitutes a covert channel. Perhaps the simplest definition is one that describes it as a communication channel that is neither designed nor intended to transfer information at all. A more focused description that uses the terminology of subjects and objects defines covert channels as those that use entities not normally viewed as data objects to transfer information from one subject to another. Although a transmission state is invoked, the confidentiality is actually compromised during the processing state by the presence of the covert channel.

This may at first appear to be an arcane or academic exercise, but a covert channel is perhaps the best depiction of hidden security vulnerabilities in the processing state of a subsystem. For those who would apply the McCumber Cube methodology to products and components, this type of assessment is precisely the level of detailed analysis required.

DEVELOP SECURITY ARCHITECTURE

Now the careful inspection of options for maintaining confidentiality, integrity, and availability are assessed. Within this product, there may be no need to ensure protection to assure confidentiality or perhaps it is a procedural one where there is a requirement for maintaining the product in a controlled environment. In the event that possible vulnerabilities such as covert channels are anticipated, specific technical modifications of design changes may be required to mitigate the risk from this low-level vulnerability.

The security architecture is developed and documented at this point by reviewing all the safeguard recommendations for each of the blocks and for each category of safeguard — technology, procedure, and human factors. Within precuts and components, human factors related safeguards may be in the small minority, because most design and enforcement functions should be enforced by technology and verified design requirements.

Describe Required Safeguards

The entire list of potential security safeguards for products and subsystems may be nonexistent. This application of the McCumber Cube methodology is aimed at establishing a design baseline for implementing security enforcement mechanisms or assessing the existence or lack of protection capabilities in the product design. The basic process as applied to the network or system environment is used.

The blocks at the intersection of information state and security attribute have been identified and the walk-through that follows will produce a spectrum of possible safeguard proposals to control the information resources as they change state within the product or subsystem. The technology safeguards will be evaluated along with possible supporting procedural and human factors safeguard elements to create a security architecture based on the use and application of the product.

At this point, it may or may not serve to attempt to factor in information valuation metrics. By its nature, a product evaluation is normally performed without regard to the ultimate deployment and use of the product in an operational environment. However, there could be numerous circumstances where the product or subsystem is being designed or evaluated with a specific implementation environment in mind. This would be the case for a product undergoing an evaluation for use in a secure environment or a technology component being designed with a known degree of assurance in mind. In each of these cases, the information valuation and anticipated threat environment can be factored directly in the safeguard assessment and architectural recommendations. These recommendations can be included in the cost-benefit step that follows.

Cost Out Architecture Components and Enforcement Mechanisms

This final step in the product evaluation process is essential to making the final judgment about the cost effectiveness of the recommended security architecture. This text has shown that all information security decisions are eventually about the management of risk. Processes and criteria that tout an uncompromising risk-avoidance approach will not be success because they fail to recognize and incorporate that reality. Risk-avoidance models are essentially making the cost benefit decision for the user with little or no consideration for different threat environments and information valuation metrics. This final stage of the McCumber Cube methodology is critical in that it recognizes and integrates the business of mission requirements as well as the necessary trade-offs between assurance and cost.

If the methodology were being applied to a proposed system yet to be built, an effective way to present this decision process at this level of abstraction would be to provide three or possibly more design options with their associated cost data. This approach allows the system developers and users to make security cost-benefit decisions before the product is built and deployed. Although it is reasonable to expect threat environments to evolve along with discovery of new vulnerabilities and changes in information value, this is an option we do not currently provide for most system purchasers.

The cost-benefit decision capabilities that are incorporated into this methodology provide an effective way to openly acknowledge the reality of all security safeguards decisions. Managers, system developers, and security architects all make these security cost-benefit decisions whether or not they are perceived as such. The structured methodology includes it as an integral part of the process.

RECAP OF THE METHODOLOGY FOR SUBSYSTEMS, PRODUCTS, AND COMPONENTS

The general overview of the methodology is only slightly different from the process used for policy enforcement. The steps are:

1. Information flow mapping:
   a. Define the boundary (the boundary of the box or the application).

    b. Make an inventory of all information resources and information handling subsystems within the boundary.

    c. Decompose and identify all information states.

2. Cube decomposition based on information states:

    a. Call out column from the cube — transmission, storage, or processing.

    b. Decompose blocks by the attributes of confidentiality, integrity, and availability.

    c. Identify existing and potential vulnerabilities:

       i. Use vulnerability library (to see if any have already been documented).

       ii. Develop safeguard inventory.

       iii. Factor information values — use valuation metrics if applicable.

       iv. Assign appropriate safeguards in each category.

3. Develop comprehensive architecture of safeguards (technology, procedures, human factors):

    a. Describe comprehensive security architecture components.

    b. Cost out architecture components (including procedural and human factor safeguards if they are necessary or desirable).

4. Perform cost-benefit analysis (not a full risk assessment *per se*):

    a. Include threat and assets measurements if known and applicable.

    b. Add other implementation specific data.

    c. Perform cost trade-off and valuation analyses.

REFERENCES

1. Canadian System Security Centre Communications Security Establishment, *The Canadian Trusted Computer Product Evaluation Criteria* (CTCPEC), Version 3, Canadian government, 1993.
2. National Institute of Standards and Technology, Common Criteria for IT Security Evaluation [updated 1998 and 1999; available at www.csrc.nist.gov/cc/index; accessed October 2003].

10

MANAGING THE SECURITY LIFE CYCLE

INTRODUCTION

The McCumber Cube methodology is not a process that needs to be replicated on a recurring basis; it is a methodology to use in the assessment and design phases of the security program. It also can be employed as a tool for design and assessment of individual products and system components. Invoking the use of the methodology is also called for when the information systems environment is significantly modified or upgraded. In keeping with the understanding of this process as an information-centric model, you can determine if the McCumber Cube methodology needs to be used by looking for new information flows, changes in asset (information) valuation, and the acquisition of new technologies. However, there are many security-relevant activities that take place on a day-to-day basis and we will cover the basics of that process here.

In this chapter, we will deal with the issues of security life-cycle management. Life-cycle management is the complete menu of organizational activities that are conducted on an ongoing basis to implement, enhance, and support the information systems security program. We address these issues here simply to introduce some of the major concepts in security life-cycle management. This chapter is not designed to be a comprehensive checklist for security practitioners. It is important, however, to lay out the underlying processes and principles that make up an information systems security program.

The process outlined in this chapter is taken primarily from Symantec Corporation's Lifecycle Security™ Model. I present it here because it complements the principles set forth in this text. It is a process that is centered on fundamentals that, like the McCumber Cube methodology,

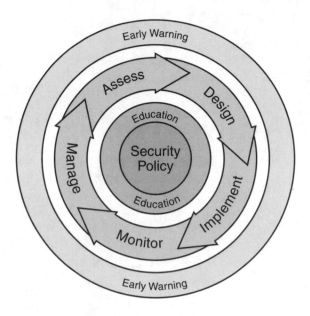

Figure 10.1   Information Security Life Cycle

do not change with the evolution of technology and systems. It provides practitioners, analysts, and IT implementers with an effective way to visualize and create strategies for managing the ongoing activities of security management.

The life-cycle security model is depicted as a circle (Figure 10.1). There is a sound reason for that. At any given time, there are a number of activities that are being pursued for the purpose of protecting an organization's information resources. Even if no information security program currently exists, there is still a need to conduct daily, weekly, and monthly recurring activities while performing the requisite assessment and implementation tasks. Few security practitioners have had the luxury of being able to design and implement a completely new program in a system yet to be deployed. Even the ones who have this experience are often severely constrained because they have lacked the tools to accurately quantify and express the value of the information security controls.

We will begin to look at the activities of the information security life cycle with the function labeled Assess (Figure 10.2). In this assessment phase, the elements of the complete information security program are laid out and evaluated. During this phase of the process, the McCumber Cube methodology provides a valuable tool for the evaluation and selection of security controls, the development of security policies, and the creation of training and awareness programs. By mapping the organization's

Figure 10.2 Information Security Life Cycle — Assess

information flows and creating the metrics that will be used to judge the value of critical information resources, the fundamental components of the information security program will be developed.

This is also the phase where the risk assessment process needs to be undertaken. While you are developing the metrics for the measurement of the value of your information resources and tracking its flow through the organization, you are creating some of the key inputs into your risk assessment process. To obtain all the data necessary for the risk assessment, you will also need to make a detailed catalog of threats to the information that includes all the aspects of both environmental and human-based categories.

Once the McCumber Cube analysis results are created along with the information resources valuation and threat data, you should have the entire catalogue of elements needed as input to your targeted operational risk assessment. The basic elements of the risk assessment process are threats, vulnerabilities, assets, and safeguards. You know you are complete when you have quantifiable information for each of these areas and you have used the risk assessment process to determine the security controls necessary to provide the protection required to meet mission and organizational objectives.

During the design phase (Figure 10.3), you take the proposed security architecture and create a technical and procedural blueprint for your entire

Figure 10.3 Information Security Life Cycle — Design

information security environment. The design phase is critical even for a currently deployed system undergoing a rigorous security review. In this case, your design should be able to highlight areas needing new components or upgrades to existing technology. Reviewing your risk assessment results as well as McCumber Cube analysis will provide you the necessary bases for the end-to-end design that is created as a result of the design phase.

The design phase also should include a complete review of security policies and procedures. Information security policies and procedures support and enhance the technical controls. They must be assessed in conjunction with the technical controls to ensure that the appropriate interoperability is considered. If you have walked through the structured methodology thoroughly and performed the decomposition stages correctly, this element of the life-cycle process should be quite easy. You should have a complete list of not only the proposed safeguards, but also all security policy requirements for the entire program.

Another key aspect of your security program that also should be available to you now is a comprehensive understanding of the training and awareness activities needed to complement the security program. The human factors component of the McCumber Cube methodology covers this critical area and the various places where this safeguard category was assessed and defined need to be gathered and developed into a human factors plan that supports the overall information security program.

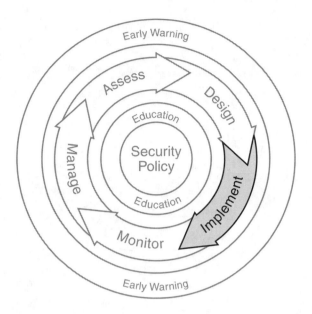

Figure 10.4   Information Security Life Cycle — Implement

The implementation phase is shown in Figure 10.4. This important phase of the life cycle encompasses all those activities associated with the selection, acquisition, and deployment of the technical and procedural security program. This is also the most difficult phase because significant costs of the security program must be justified and expended. However, if you have performed the structured methodology correctly, you will have most of the information you need at your fingertips.

The McCumber Cube analysis will provide a detailed description of your security requirements based on the asset valuation of the information resources for which the program provides assurance. By presenting this material to those responsible for financial and resources allocation decisions, you should have comprehensive, well-documented justification for all implementation requirements — technical, procedural, and human factors based. For those inevitable times when resources are constrained and trade-offs must be made, your analysis will remain an important part of your documentation for future use. You may be called on to provide justification when more resources become available or you may need to be able to show how your initial implementation plans were not fully executed after a undesirable consequence has been realized.

The implementation phase also may need to be accomplished over a period of time. The results of your structured methodology also will aid you in making a determination about what elements of the security

Figure 10.5   Information Security Life Cycle — Monitor

program are most critical and how they should be rolled out to protect the most sensitive information resources first. As with the design phase, having this information readily available makes the decision-making process for your information systems security program much easier and certainly justifiable.

Once the technology and procedural controls have been implemented, you have to plan and conduct monitoring of the security controls (Figure 10.5). Often this vital step is either overlooked or ignored in the assessment and design phase. An intrusion detection product or audit log will provide you with little or no protection if they are not monitored on a regular basis. The key question is always, What do I need to monitor?

Your inventory of security capabilities needs to be carefully evaluated for each entity that requires monitoring. Firewalls, intrusion detection systems, honeypots, audit logs, and malicious code sentinels all require a certain degree of monitoring for adequate security enforcement. In addition to the various security technologies you have deployed, the security procedures also need to be monitored for compliance.

You also will need to continually monitor the overall threat environment to maintain currency in the understanding of the evolution of the threats. Environmental threats, although daunting and far ranging, tend to remain relatively constant. The human threat, however, is changing and adapting. The motivations of those who would want to exploit your information resources are affected by everything from global events to personal needs and desires. New tools and techniques for exploiting information resources are developed daily. Keeping abreast of this dynamic environment is a primary responsibility for anyone charged with the protection of digital assets.

You also will notice that circumnavigating the life-cycle model is Early Warning, which has become increasingly important to information security. There are now many public and private organizations that can help you maintain an awareness of the threat and vulnerability environment that affects all IT resources. Central to the concept of early warning is access to information gathered from sensors both nationally and globally so you and those who support your efforts are aware of trends and changes that can affect information resources and IT. This can be achieved by allotting time and resources to monitor information sources or by subscribing to one of the many services now available to provide assessment and notification.

Within the center ring of the information security life cycle is a band representing education (Figure 10.6). Education represents the growth and nurturing of the human factors safeguard category. Education is a requirement not only for the person ultimately responsible for the information security program, but for everyone involved. At the broadest level of the organization, everyone who handles and uses information resources needs

Figure 10.6 Information Security Life Cycle — Education

to be aware of their personal responsibilities for maintaining confidentiality, integrity, and availability of these assets. However, the ultimate responsibility lies with the individual chartered with creating and managing the information security program.

For those who are new to this position, it makes sense to get some education right away. Taking classes offered by experts and attending relevant conferences and symposia is a good beginning. Make sure you ask plenty of questions and seek out proven methodologies. It is important to understand who is giving you advice and what their long-term goals are. Obviously, vendors who provide low- or no-cost information security courses would prefer you buy their products as a result of the education. They may also tailor the information in the course to target their solutions.

Consultants and service providers often promote free seminars and training materials to entice you to contract for their services. Their goal is not to educate you, as much as it is to impress you, with their understanding and skill. Usually it is worth the investment to take independent courses and even look for professional certification. The key point here is not to wait. Get pointed in the right direction and start making improvements.

There are many people involved in protecting information resources. The question has been asked, who are the smartest people in information security? Perhaps the smartest people are the penetration experts. In a recent article in an information security trade publication, the practice leader for a team of hackers-for-hire gushed, "… most of these guys [hackers] have an IQ that could boil water." Perhaps they are the smartest.

I personally stand in awe of cryptographers and cypherpunks. I have had the privilege of working with some extremely talented men and women for whom this intense and absorbing discipline was simply amusing. It is easy to feel humble while struggling through the mathematics and complex logic that comprises the study of modern cryptography.

Others may cry up the case for software and security product developers. Their ability to tackle a difficult problem, write the code to solve it, debug it, and release a working product is most admirable. As these products evolve to improve the security of systems, we can be assured of more accurate and scalable security solutions. These folks surely rate up there in smarts.

Ultimately, however, the question is as moot as it is silly. The information security profession is best described as multidisciplinary. There are experts in penetration testing, physical security of networks and systems, cryptography, security administration, intrusion detection, systems audit, and many other facets of our business. Some jobs are more technically oriented and others require management and people skills.

Those who aspire to grow in the profession may become a chief information security officer and assume responsibility for an entire information security program at a major corporation. In this capacity, they have to excel in the knowledge of how all these technologies and industry best practices work in harmony to achieve the most cost-effective protection. Yet they may not be able to hack their way out of a paper bag.

Everyone involved in building tools, creating products, designing architectures, developing policies, and assessing vulnerabilities is an important part of the whole. However, I believe the smartest person is the one who is able to provide the right amount of information and infrastructure protection for a reasonable investment and a minimum of overhead. This is truly the balancing act that deserves the highest recognition. Those who are able to apply just the right amount of security where it is needed should be heralded for their achievements. To become that person, you have to have a structured methodology that provides a solid, quantifiable approach that recognizes the interplay of technological, procedural, and human factors safeguards.

I have saved the management function (Figure 10.7) for last so we can conclude with some comments on the nature of the information security manager's function. The management of information systems security is a job without end. Just as the security environment or threats and vulnerabilities changes, so must the safeguards. Ongoing maintenance

Figure 10.7   Information Security Life Cycle — Manage

and configuration of technology components must keep pace with these changes. This management function is the key function of the person charged with the management and protection of information resources.

A key aspect of managing the security environment is creating and promoting that environment. Your program will be most successful only when it is most visible. Organizational decision makers must be keenly aware of the value of the information security program and its place in the overall corporate risk management program.

The first step in developing an effective information security program is to adapt an old Zen philosophy to your program. Understand that security is not a destination, but a journey. Applying and managing security controls is an ongoing process that reflects the values of the organization. If you believe information security is a critical aspect of your information systems and electronic commerce initiatives, you will find yourself and your colleagues actively promoting the confidentiality, integrity, and availability attributes of vital corporate data and technology systems both in operational use and in development.

Security is not simply something you implement and forget; it is a way of doing business. The journey mindset forces you to evaluate the value your organization places in its information and data. It also forces decision makers to consider the privacy and protection of the sensitive information of your company, your customers, and your collaborators.

Security programs are being recognized for their importance. Many large financial institutions and a rapidly growing number of other businesses have appointed a senior executive or corporate officer to specifically oversee the protection of all corporate information. They have realized that an effective information security program needs to be developed, implemented, and managed if they want retain their competitive advantages in an information-centric marketplace. Either you or someone you appoint must be the focal point for the entire information security program. The program will be their responsibility and it should form the basis for all or part of the annual performance evaluation. When the issue of information security is raised at a company meeting, everyone should be able to identify the key individual.

The management of information security is not simply an enforcement job. Far too many information security personnel perceive their job as that of an overzealous security guard or night watchman. They feel compelled to demand compliance from employees, look to either capture or chase away intruders, and aggressively enforce rules and regulations. The management of information security is something quite different.

Information security management is the art and science of assessing and implementing safeguards for the appropriate protection of information resources. To perform this difficult function, the information security manager and practitioners have to take on a consultative role that helps people throughout the organization meet their personal responsibilities for ensuring the confidentiality, integrity, and availability of the information that is the lifeblood of business and government.

11

SAFEGUARD ANALYSIS

INTRODUCTION

In the McCumber Cube, safeguards are categorized into three primary groups — technical, procedural, or human factors. Sometimes these safeguard categories are glibly defined as the Three Ps — products, procedures, and people.

Safeguards are most commonly defined as a concept synonymous with security controls and countermeasures. Technically, security controls are defined as the management, operational, and technical controls (safeguards or countermeasures) prescribed for an information system that, taken together, satisfy the specified security requirements and adequately protect the confidentiality, integrity, and availability of the system and its information. The problem with this definition is simply that the characteristics of confidentiality, integrity, and availability always apply strictly to the information, not to the underlying technology that effects the transmission, storage, and processing of the information. Additionally, that definition is far too broad to effectively manage a technical security program.

Security practitioners need to understand safeguards as any technical, procedural, or human factors control or countermeasure that can be employed to mitigate or eliminate risk in IT systems. Additionally, a safeguard may only address a portion of a vulnerability, a single vulnerability, or an entire class of vulnerabilities. The appropriate mix of safeguards is the cornerstone of an effective and cost-efficient security program for IT systems. Before we develop the safeguard analysis component of the model, it is important to review the categories of safeguards and more accurately define each one.

TECHNOLOGY SAFEGUARDS

Technology safeguards are those security controls and countermeasures that exist as IT components to enforce one or more security policy requirement. Technology safeguards can be hardware components, software, or any other type of direct, physical enforcement mechanism. In the realm of physical security, safeguards such as locks, doors, and fences are elements of physical (or by extension, technical) safeguards.

Technology safeguards for IT systems comprise a broad spectrum of physical products and software tools that mitigate risk by either eliminating vulnerabilities or enforcing a confidentiality, integrity, or availability requirement. Not all safeguards actually target specific technical vulnerabilities.

Many technology safeguards are designed and built to enforce one or more of the security attributes. For example, much of the functionality in modern firewalls is there to eliminate certain exposures, as defined by MITRE's CVE outlined in Appendix A. An exposure is different from a vulnerability by definition. An exposure refers to security-related facts that may not be considered to be vulnerabilities by everyone.

In the case of firewalls, the capability to proxy data transfer and to prevent unmonitored access to various ports on a server is not employed simply to eliminate what is commonly known as a vulnerability. Most of the blocked ports on a firewall-protected server are operating exactly as they were designed to. However, the firewall blocks access to defined ports by certain parties to prevent them from being probed and possibly used as a pathway for unauthorized access to information resources. This technology safeguard then mitigates the risk from numerous potential threats. Once this type of technology safeguard is implemented, it is then important to discern what related threats, vulnerabilities, and exposures remain.

Technology safeguards can also include physical safeguards used to support, enhance, supplement, or replace IT safeguards. For example, physical separation of IT systems and components is often used to enforce certain confidentiality controls. Defined physical spaces controlled by such safeguards as doors and locks are often to prevent the ability of information to either be viewed or moved outside a defined controlled area. The doors and locks are used to enforce some or all of the requirements for confidentiality.

These physical safeguards are sometimes referred to as air gaps, and they have been used effectively to either support or replace software or electronic controls that are often easier to subvert. When information resources need to be transferred to another system either within the controlled area or outside the area completely, a copy of the selected data are transferred to a portable medium such as a memory stick and physically brought to an appropriate device on the target information system.

Another example of physical safeguards supporting or enforcing IT security is the integration of access control badges or other physical security tools into the IT systems environment. The same access badges that can be used to unlock doors and raise the gate at the corporate garage can be used as a token at end points in a computer systems network as a form of authentication for access to information resources. Additionally, other identification and authentication devices used for control of physical access can often be adapted to complement IT access controls.

Technology safeguards are best considered in their broadest sense. They represent the most tangible and often the most effective security controls and countermeasures in the security practitioner's arsenal of tools. Ensuring that physical and other non-IT safeguards are considered as complementary to and supportive of an information security program ensures that the best possible mix of controls can be considered.

PROCEDURAL SAFEGUARDS

Procedural safeguards are critical countermeasure components and encompass a wide array of capabilities. Like technology safeguards, procedural safeguards also mitigate risk by either eliminating vulnerabilities or enforcing a confidentiality, integrity, or availability requirement. However, they do not take the form of a physical or technological product or component. They are normally best understood as denoting the way something is accomplished that meets the requirements of a security control or countermeasure.

Procedural safeguards are identified and implemented by their ability to mitigate risk through the enforcement of a way of effecting a desired security-relevant outcome. Many stand-alone procedural safeguards are used in the management of security requirements. For example, a procedural safeguard may dictate that only personnel obtaining an authorization form signed by a certain manager will be allowed access to information resources. This procedure in and of itself may not completely enforce the letter and intent of the confidentiality requirement, but it is a key part of the specific confidentiality controls.

Broadly speaking, procedural safeguards include almost any codified requirement designating a method or process for performing any action that enforces or supports the security policy. The easiest way to identify and assess procedural safeguards is to review all security policies and regulations that affect the organization's information resources. The difficulty of a comprehensive assessment of these controls is the fact these safeguards are usually codified in a variety of formats in a wide variety of corporate and even technical publications. Procedural safeguards for the enforcement of confidentiality, integrity, and availability requirements can run the gamut from simple user checklists to comprehensive manuals.

Physical security procedures are often procedural safeguards either used independently or in conjunction with other IT safeguards. For example, a procedural safeguard may be to ensure that all visitors in rooms containing network access points must be escorted to ensure that they are not allowed the opportunity to access IT resources and presumably gain access to sensitive information assets. This safeguard would also logically be invoked to provide security for all company assets, including office items or paperwork that could be pilfered by unaccompanied visitors. This type of common procedural safeguard, however, is a critical IT safeguard that supports the technical and human factors safeguards in a comprehensive program.

HUMAN FACTORS SAFEGUARDS

Human factors safeguards are often the most difficult to identify and the most difficult to quantify. As with both technical and procedural safeguards, human factors safeguards mitigate risk by either eliminating vulnerabilities or enforcing a confidentiality, integrity, or availability requirement. Human factors are often defined as the study of how humans behave physically and psychologically in relation to particular environments, products, or services. In our case, it would be the information security program. Often the term is used as a synonym for ergonomics, but in the case of a safeguard category, this is not accurate. A more refined and focused definition is required.

Human factors study primarily focuses on general human behavior in relation to technology (such as studies of how people react to various form factors of technology), on a generic type of product, on specific environment or product designs as a whole, or on some specific design aspects of a particular environment or product. Using this more traditional definition of human factors engineering, the result of human factors study can include suggestions on how to redesign an object of study or a general guideline for designing such an object or technology. In addition to relatively formal human factors study, human factors can be said to be underway any time a designer thinks about the effects of the design on the end user.

In understanding and implementing human factors safeguards, it is important to recognize that many of these controls may not directly appear to be safeguards or they may appear as a separate component of a technical or procedural safeguard. Technology safeguards are things and procedural safeguards are plans, processes, and policies. Human factors safeguards are tied directly to people and their performance in enforcing or supporting security requirements. Rarely is it easy to quickly identify human factor safeguards.

Human factors safeguards can be used to mitigate risk through the influence of organizational members such as system users, security analysts, system administrators, company partners, visitors, and auditors. An example of a human factor safeguard is the keen eye of an auditor searching records and logs for malicious activities and anomalies. This uniquely human activity relies on the ability of the auditor to filter this information through his or her personal knowledge and training to recognize potential breaches and other security violations.

Human factors safeguards can also be employed to influence the security relevant activities of outsiders and even potential attackers. In cases such as this, human factors safeguards are used as psychological enforcement mechanisms. Take the case of a security warning banner on a government owned and operated Web site. It may serve primarily a legal purpose in providing the required warnings and disclaimers so that people who violate the system rules cannot claim they were unaware of their responsibilities if they are prosecuted for their actions. However, it can also serve a key purpose as a warning that the site owner treats potential threats seriously and is willing and able to take legal steps to protect its sensitive information resources. This warning, then, works just like a sticker in the front window of a home or a placard on a residential lawn proclaiming the fact that the house has a monitored alarm system. The sign not only provides inexpensive advertising for the alarm company, but also provides the homeowner a means to encourage potential burglars to seek out a less well protected home.

Human factors safeguards are often the least costly and most effective components of a sound security program. In many ways, the overall security program itself is a form of macro-safeguard. The fact that a structured methodology is being used to build and manage the security program ensures that the appropriate people and tools are integrated to create a comprehensive security framework. This is turn involves technologists, administrators, executives, and security personnel who contribute and share in supporting the security objectives. This broad involvement in turn provides a scaffold of support structures to ensure the continued effectiveness of the overall protection program.

VULNERABILITY–SAFEGUARD PAIRING

An important aspect for understanding safeguards is the ability to map your proposed or existing safeguards against potential threats. Safeguard analysis for IT systems is a critical aspect of providing both enforcement and management of security policy. Safeguards are employed to either completely or partially mitigate risks from vulnerabilities. When applying the McCumber Cube methodology, it is important to map the safeguards against their corresponding vulnerabilities. By compiling a complete list of potential system vulnerabilities, you can more easily determine the safeguard suites necessary to cost-effectively implement your security requirements.

We have already outlined the effectiveness mapping threat–vulnerability pairs. At this point, it is also beneficial to map the vulnerabilities to safeguards. These security safeguards should be considered in the broadest sense of the term. Even physical security safeguards and organizational procedures are effective aspects of your security program and should not be overlooked in favor of purely technical safeguards. Each safeguard contributes to the greater program and many safeguards can mitigate risks across a broad spectrum of vulnerabilities.

Just as threat–vulnerability pairs are used to comprehensively identify vulnerabilities, there is great value in performing a similar analysis by developing a comprehensive vulnerability–safeguard pairing. This pairing is performed in the same manner of the threat–vulnerability pairing exercise. Identified vulnerabilities (either using the CVE or other methodology) are placed down the left-hand side of a chart and appropriate safeguards for these relevant vulnerabilities are then paired by cross-reference. As in threat–vulnerability pairs, there are often one-to-many and many-to-one relationships. This type of analysis is portrayed in Table 11.1.

Although such an exercise may be impractical for a large IT system, this type of analysis can be used effectively in smaller subsets and with discreet technology elements to foster critical thinking and a perspective on the comprehensive set of potential safeguards. As with any safeguard analysis, it is appropriate to consider safeguards that span all three categories. Your analysis will be easier and more effective if you ensure that these safeguards are also categorized as technological, procedural, or human factors.

HIERARCHICAL DEPENDENCIES OF SAFEGUARDS

One of the most important attributes of safeguards is their hierarchical dependency. The McCumber Cube categorizes safeguards into technical, procedural, and human factors. These categories are identified separately and can be conveniently placed in one category or another. However, there is an important feature of the model that recognizes this hierarchical dependency. These dependencies are depicted in Table 11.2.

The dependency attribute shows that for each technical safeguard, there are supporting procedural and human factors safeguards. If the safeguard is purely a procedural one, there is at least one supporting

Table 11.1 Vulnerability–Safeguard Pairing

Vulnerability	Safeguards
CVE-2002-00-43 Sudo (superuser do) allows a system administrator to give certain users (or groups of users) the ability to run some (or all) commands as root or another user while logging the commands and arguments. Sudo 1.6.0 through 1.6.3p7 does not properly clear the environment before calling the mail program, which could allow local users to gain root privileges by modifying environment variables and changing how the mail program is invoked.	Technical: None Procedural: Do not install and use Sudo 1.6.0 through 1.6.3p7; upgrade to Sudo 1.6.4 or higher which runs the mail program with a clean environment. Admins wishing to run the mailer as the invoking user and not as root should use the *–disable-root-mailer* configure option in Sudo.1.6.5. Human Factors: Ensure technical staff and BSD UNIX system administrators are aware of this requirement.

Table 11.2 Hierarchical Dependencies of Safeguards

Technical safeguards	
Procedural safeguards	Procedural safeguards
Human factors safeguards	Human factors safeguards
Human factors safeguards	

human factors safeguard associated with it. Human factors safeguards often stand alone as singular entities.

To clarify this concept, let us begin with a fairly common technical safeguard — a firewall. The firewall is logically a technical safeguard; it exists (minimally) as software. The firewall can perform several security-relevant functions. An *Internet* firewall examines all traffic routed between an organizational network and the open Internet to determine if it conforms to certain criteria. If it does, the data is passed from outside (the Internet) to inside the corporate network. Traffic that does not meet the explicit criteria is stopped. A *network* firewall filters both inbound and outbound traffic. The firewall can be employed to log all attempts to enter the private network and be set up to trigger alarms when unauthorized or potentially hostile entry is attempted. Firewalls can perform this security function by filtering packets based on their source, destination addresses, and port numbers. This aspect of firewall management is known as address filtering. Firewalls can also be configured to filter specific types of network traffic. This capability is known as protocol filtering because the decision to forward or reject traffic depends on the protocol used, for example, HTTP (Hypertext Transfer Protocol), FTP (File Transfer Protocol), or Telnet. Firewalls can also filter traffic by packet attribute or state.

The firewall's ability to perform these important network security functions is obviously supported by an established set of procedures that identify the types of security functions it must perform. Out-of-the-box configurations are almost universally inadequate. The firewall must be manually configured to perform the required security functions such as filtering and logging that support the security requirements of the organization that acquires and implements the firewall technology. The technical safeguard implements these procedural safeguards.

To develop, implement, and monitor these firewall procedures and requirements, human factors safeguards are necessarily employed. Ultimately, a human must make an initial risk management determination about what security functions the firewall must perform and determine which firewall best meets the organization's requirements. Also, a firewall produces logs and other output that often require human oversight to review, and possibly human intercession to enforce, a security policy with the firewall technology. In the case of the firewall, it quickly becomes obvious that the technology safeguard itself must be supported by at least one (and often many) procedural safeguards. The same is true for human factors safeguards.

When assessing procedural safeguards, it is critical to remember that at least one and possibly several human factors safeguards in turn support them. We can again look to the example of the physical security procedure that requires an escort for visitors in rooms containing IT and network access points. The human factors safeguards supporting the actual procedure are actually fundamental to the efficacy of the procedure itself. As always, this safeguard was developed and enforced as the result of a corporate risk management decision — whether it was off-the-cuff, copied from another company's policies, or the result of an in-depth, tailored risk analysis.

There are also several other explicit or implicit human factors safeguards directly supporting this procedural safeguard. The fact that visitors are required to obtain an escort actively discourages visitors from innumerable suspicious or malicious activities. It also dramatically displays to visitors that the organization has valuable assets that it is willing to protect even if it requires pulling someone from their normal duties to act as an escort. Conversely, the procedure affects the employees by making the escorts personally responsible for protecting assets even though their primary duty may not be security. This relatively simple and inexpensive procedural safeguard then is not only the product of human factors safeguard analysis, but is supported by human factors safeguards that impact the security-relevant activities of employees and visitors alike.

Although a human factors safeguard may support one or many procedural or technical safeguards, they are often defined and analyzed in their own context. Many human factors safeguards are employed by themselves to influence human behavior. Human factors safeguards always support procedural safeguards, including procedural safeguards that support technical safeguards. In this context, it is easy to see that each and every safeguard — technical, procedural, or human factors — has at least one human factors component.

The hierarchical nature of IT safeguards is a critical aspect of the McCumber Cube. It recognizes and highlights the important aspect of supporting and interrelated safeguards. Procedural and human factors safeguards support all technical safeguards. Human factors safeguards support all procedural safeguards. And human factors safeguards can stand independently or can support the other safeguards as noted above.

This hierarchical dependency applies to all types of safeguards, not just those associated with IT security. For example, physical security practitioners may define the need for a fence to control access to a certain area. The fence itself represents the purely technical solution. However, there will be a procedural need to monitor, lock, and unlock doors or gates. There will also be procedural components to the upkeep and maintenance of the fence. The fence also provides a human factors safeguard by physically partitioning the enclosed area and serving notice to potential human threats that the area is protected property.

Every type of safeguard, irrespective of its application, has the hierarchical dependency trait that is highlighted by the McCumber Cube. In the case of physical security safeguards, the elements of confidentiality, integrity, and availability do not apply directly to physical assets, but the three-tier structure of the safeguard component directly applies to any type of safeguard. Applying this reasoning to any safeguard or countermeasure application provides practitioners with a categorization capability to fully assess the security impact to their safeguard deployment and management.

SECURITY POLICIES AND PROCEDURAL SAFEGUARDS

There is an important distinction to make at this point: Security policies are not the same as procedural safeguards. A security policy is a document that defines in writing how a company plans to protect its physical, personnel, and information assets. A security policy is often classified as a living document, meaning that the document is never finished, but is continuously updated as technology and employee requirements change. A company's security policy should include a description of how the company plans to educate its employees regarding protecting the company's assets, an explanation of how security measurements will be carried out and enforced, and a procedure for evaluating the effectiveness of the security policy to ensure that necessary safeguards are implemented, enforced, and managed.

A security policy must also define the consequences for knowing violations of organizational security policy. Many policies are drafted and promulgated without any consequences outlined. When consequences are outlined, often they state simply that any violation could result in penalties up to and including termination of the employee. To effectively provide a human factors safeguard element to the policy, detailed consequences should be included.

Policies need not overlap procedural safeguards. Policies define the assets, the associated security requirements, and the consequences and remedial actions necessary to return to an acceptable level of risk. They are the genesis for a risk analysis, whereas procedural safeguards are tools chosen as a result of that same analysis.

Defining the difference between the two concepts is relatively easy. Procedural safeguards are tied to specific vulnerabilities as described in the section on vulnerability–safeguard pairing. These codified policies are not the same as a procedural safeguard. Procedural safeguards implement policies, but are not, of themselves, policies. This distinction is important when creating both policies and procedural safeguards. By identifying the appropriate characteristics of both, the security practitioner can be assured of a more effective policy as well as appropriately targeted safeguards.

DEVELOPING COMPREHENSIVE SAFEGUARDS: THE LESSONS OF THE SHOGUN

In 1975, author James Clavell wrote a momentous piece of historical fiction called *Shogun*. The book can teach us some important lessons about the use of safeguards and their application to IT security as well. At the dawn of the Information Age, simple computer access controls were coupled with physical security measures to ensure adequate control over digital assets. The thought and execution was simple. If people could not gain access to the information, they could not exploit it. This was the primary rule of the Shogun: If possible enemies could not even approach your assets, they could not kill them or steal them.

Another clever security tactic employed in the novel was the law of centralization. For example, all the national treasure of Japan at that period was gathered and then stored in a single fortress location. The logic behind that activity was simple, yet elegant. If you had to protect a significant quantity of valuable assets, you could gain a significant economic advantage by keeping your security forces focused on a single collection point. This was more effective than trying to distribute your security forces across a broad geographic area where travel was difficult. Anyone who would deign to steal the treasure was faced with an extensive and interwoven security system composed of numerous armed guards, secret passageways, alarms, and an impregnable vault. This analogy has also not been lost in the Information Age.

Historically, information and computer security was much more effective when the information could be gathered and stored in a single location. All the security technology needed to control and protect the data could be centrally purchased, configured, and managed by a tight group of specialists at a single location. An added value was a fact that the security tools could work in concert to interoperate to create a seamless secure boundary with interlocking layers of protection.

As the Internet revolution swept the IT industry along in its wake, people began to realize that, unlike gold and jewels, most information actually increased in value as it was shared and used across distributed systems. A good example would be your credit card. You can better protect your financial information from misuse if you refuse to share the number with anyone over the telephone, Internet, or even in person. However, you cannot gain the full advantage of catalog sales and Internet shopping unless you share it with vendors and service providers through these media. What you need, therefore, is an ability to share your credit card information with a degree of confidence that you can limit or eliminate risks to your personal assets.

Although you want the ability to share your information, you know you cannot relinquish your right to control it. The requirement for distributed security emerged directly from this basic characteristic of information asset management. Unfortunately, many safeguard technologies are simply the software equivalent of the samurai warrior.

My favorite example of samurai software includes most popular versions of antiviral programs. Every month or so, they recommend you upload something known as the virus definition files. These updates are nothing more than software signatures of possible viruses and malicious code. For each and every possible new virus, a new samurai has to be dispatched that can kill the offending program. As the number of viruses and variants grows, the size of the signature file grows in direct proportion. Because this dated security technology cannot prevent the undesirable actions of viruses, it is forced to identify and eliminate any code that could be a virus.

Because distributed security often means little or no security, another common practice in the security industry is based on the law of centralization. Internet portals and large databases are often used to put data in one place so it can be effectively controlled with an interoperating security system. To create a portal that stores and manages the data, all the data has to be converted to a format consistent with the portal technology. Usually this would be in the form of a large database or HTML (Hypertext Markup Language) files. This cumbersome task is exacerbated by the fact that this data now needs centralized mediation to ensure that the information's asset value is controlled. Managing this problem can limit the value your data can realize because it must be centrally retained and managed. This central storage system may ultimately be several steps removed from where the information is originally created and updated.

The lessons of the Shogun that were effective at the dawn of the 17th century may not be easy to apply at the dawn of the Information Age. New ways to share information while controlling its use need to be developed. This is important in the planning and application of safeguards and controls. One of the most telling examples involves the problems associated with peer-to-peer software technology.

The peer-to-peer concept of sharing information resources among users is straightforward. It takes advantage of all the interconnected computers to freely share and distribute files among users. Sometimes a common location or portal is used to act as a mediator by identifying the location of information resources and facilitating its transfer. By facilitating the unlimited flow of digitized assets, however, the peer-to-peer solution denies data owners a way to control their information or realize revenue from its use.

However, it makes little sense to refrain from making the best use of information through a medium such as peer-to-peer technology. An acceptable answer to this dilemma lies with the appropriate use of safeguards. When control and use policies can be applied directly to data assets, such as music recordings and other digitized content, it becomes possible to use portal systems and databases to mediate and enforce the policies established by the owners and users of the information resources. Such an arrangement would benefit both the producers of digital content and the consumers thereof. Content could be made available in a variety of digital formats and the owners and information producers could be assured of fair compensation for their investments.

The characters represented in the *Shogun* saga understood the value of their assets and protected them accordingly. As the threats increased, they had only a limited number of options to exercise. They could call for more samurai guards and they could also shift their assets to locations that increased the likelihood of better security. With data, intellectual property, and other information and other digital assets, we have to harness the power of new technology safeguards to mediate, monitor, and control to ensure that we realize their true value. Simply acquiring and deploying more samurai is no longer sufficient. And keeping your assets locked in the dungeon prevents your organization from getting the best ROI.

IDENTIFYING AND APPLYING APPROPRIATE SAFEGUARDS

Determining which safeguards to employ is a critical task. That is the reason a sound approach is to carefully juxtapose your safeguards against a comprehensive list of technical vulnerabilities. Acquiring, developing, and implementing a collection of safeguards based on their marketing description (e.g., firewall, intrusion detection system, honeypot, authentication, etc.) is an inadequate process. Safeguards need to be assessed and implemented as a means to cost-effectively reduce risk exposure to information assets. As an example, we will examine a specific technical class of safeguard — authentication tools.

Authentication tools consist of tokens and biometric devices that allow administrators to definitively determine someone's unique identity. They go far beyond the more common identification and passwords that account for most authentication schemes. Although rapid advances in this area are necessary, the specific security functions authentication products provide are actually quite limited. Once you determine who someone is, the next big issue is figuring out what they have permission to do with your data.

Most IT authentication safeguards have the ability to enforce a limited number of permissions. Permissions are simply binary decisions about what is and is not allowed. In the case of a safeguard such as a firewall, there is an assortment of permissions that define what connections and processes are allowed to pass through from the Internet to the company's internal network. Once a program, a piece of data, or a request is allowed pass through to the internal network, the firewall no longer exercises any control over the activities of a user or remote process. For that job, you need to be able to intercept any call for data and evaluate it against a policy that states what that person or program can do and under what conditions.

With an authentication technology, you first require a policy to determine what a person or process can do with specific pieces of information and under what conditions. Although the authentication safeguard may provide sound access control, it often cannot enforce the actual authorization requirements of the policy. Unfortunately, data security authorization technologies have received significantly less attention than the more basic authentication process. Biometric devices like thumbprint readers and retina scanners have an ability to uniquely identify an individual and ensure that person alone is accessing the resources protected by the authentication safeguard. The more granular (and often more critical) aspect of authorization goes beyond simple access control.

Authorization is the process of enforcing the policy of what information a person can access, modify, or create along with a set of conditions that constrains their activities based on a nearly unlimited number of potential factors such as time of day, location, and primary job function, among others. These attributes should be captured in the security policy and need to be enforced by the appropriate safeguards.

This can present a serious problem to identifying and implementing safeguards as security products companies are often tied to a product roadmap that focuses almost entirely on network security. Network security is important, but relying solely on network security technologies has meant that data protection can only be enforced at the network boundaries and normally only with network (not information) resources. Insiders on the local network can still easily misuse company information and data that must travel outside the local network is usually left without any protection whatsoever.

Expensive and complex technologies like public key infrastructure and host-based intrusion detection can provide your organization with today's most advanced network security products. However, it is important to determine precisely what protection you expect from your investment in these large-scale network security tools. The security practitioner must define specifically which vulnerabilities are either fully or partially mitigated with the safeguards under review. This brings us back to the simple basics of security policy and risk assessment.

The best way to determine if you are using the right tools is to start by reevaluating your most recent corporate security policies and your risk assessment documents. The safeguards you select and employ to protect your company's data should directly provide the control and audit functions that support fundamental security policy. If you find it difficult to connect the policy with the tool, you should carefully analyze the functionality of the product you are planning to acquire and employ.

If your organization is one of many that have emerging requirements for sharing information and allowing corporate data to be selectively distributed, you will need to find the right tools for the job. Although network security technology continues to be an important component of the corporate IT landscape, security authentication and authorization solutions are rapidly becoming critical to meet evolving business needs. It is no longer sufficient to provide for security enforcement solely at the network boundaries. For organizations to find and exploit new revenue channels and to seek out new customers, they will need to share their information in a controlled manner. Make sure you are using the right tools for the job.

COMPREHENSIVE SAFEGUARD MANAGEMENT: APPLYING THE McCUMBER CUBE

Ultimately, all your safeguards — technical, procedural, and human factors — must interoperate as a whole to provide the required amount of protection. Once the risk assessment process is complete, you have a roadmap for determining how much protection is required and an in-depth analysis of the key assets you are trying to protect and manage. Now you can again go back to the McCumber Cube methodology and apply the Cube to map the safeguards against vulnerabilities as they apply specifically to information resources.

As with any adaptation and use of the McCumber Cube methodology, the focus is on the information states — attributes of data and information. In other words, it is not effective to try to apply the safeguards to a specific technical specification; instead you need to target the safeguards as they support the appropriate information attributes of confidentiality, integrity, and availability. Any safeguard should be tied directly to these factors to assess efficacy and cost-effectiveness.

After evaluating safeguards in this manner, it is necessary to also ensure you have considered the hierarchical properties of the safeguards. Procedural and human factors safeguards support all technical safeguards. Human factors safeguards support all procedural safeguards. Only human factors safeguards can operate as stand-alone countermeasures.

The McCumber Cube methodology is based on information attributes and not technical criteria. However, safeguard assessments should ultimately move from their application to information resources to the risks from the specific vulnerabilities they mitigate. This process may at first appear cumbersome and difficult; however, it can reap significant benefits to the security practitioner.

The most obvious and perhaps the most significant value to be realized from following the structured process of tying safeguards to their specific vulnerabilities (as defined in the CVE or through penetration testing and other means) is the ability to accurately justify and defend the investment in appropriate safeguards. This is sometimes referred to as the ROI or security.

THE ROI OF SAFEGUARDS:
DO SECURITY SAFEGUARDS HAVE A PAYOFF?

Sound security has always made common sense. Cars have seatbelts, buildings have fire sprinklers, and access badges are commonplace. No one seems to question these fundamental technical security safeguards. However, the value of security safeguards for information is, for better or worse, somewhat less obvious. Decision makers and resource planners often demand to know what they can expect in return from an investment in information security safeguards.

One of the most elusive goals of all security practitioners is the security ROI calculator. Often, security experts are called on to justify security expenses. And many decision makers like to look at every corporate investment in light of how soon the investment will pay for itself. Calculating ROI is the most widely accepted way to measure anticipated savings or increased revenue generated from expenditures. There are a variety of metrics used to assess the value received from the investment. For security, the ROI is normally built around the consequences of the risks that are averted.

Most numbers currently in use by proponents of ROI calculations for security fall in the FUD category — fear, uncertainty, and doubt. This approach is aimed at trying to scare the decision maker into making the necessary investment. The approach seeks to instill fear by showing the potential security losses as astronomical and highly likely. Inexperienced or newly minted security practitioners seek to create an aura of immediacy with these inflated numbers, yet they most often tend to alienate the people they are meant to impress.

For many years, an industry trade association has published the numbers used by so many security practitioners hoping to make a point. These numbers are purposely so large as to be almost meaningless. By describing something on so vast a scale, you are basically trying the end the point in your favor simply by using the biggest number you have in your list of supposed facts. However, little or no academic rigor was actually applied. The numbers are an amalgam of estimates compiled from estimates made by other people. On top of that, many if not most of the respondents who provided these numbers in the survey had a vested interested in seeing the possible or projected loss from threats to be as large as possible. Basically, the numbers have absolutely no statistical validity.

There are still numerous ongoing efforts aimed at developing a ROI model for information security safeguards. However, ensure that you have evaluated the statistical underpinnings and various assumptions and estimates that may be included. Often security practitioners hurt their case by inappropriate use of inaccurate numbers.

Another problem exists when it assumed that all vulnerabilities are holes or software bugs. Such is not the case. This concept was developed and presented in the chapter on vulnerabilities and would be valuable to review in light of understanding ROI for safeguards. Fixing software errors and other problems can certainly have a positive impact on security, but does not provide the security practitioner with all the safeguards required.

One significant area of safeguard ROI that has been proven is the value of incorporating security safeguards into the systems design process. Estimates range from improvement in the low double digits to orders of magnitude depending on the study in question and the type of system under study. The lower estimates are usually derived from the analysis of software development efforts that place an emphasis on safeguards and the larger for complex, large-scale systems that ultimately require a comprehensive risk assessment and safeguard upgrade to maintain confidentiality, integrity, and availability attributes of the information to transmit, store, and process.

There has even been one ROI study that established a baseline by leaving a system without safeguards and running a series of attacks replicating an external, hostile, structured threat. Then they added safeguards to the system and ran the same series of attacks. After several iterations of the test, they arrived at a security ROI represented by a curve. The curve supposedly represented the trade-off between what an organization would spend on security and an estimate of the amount of security provided for the information resources.

Assessing these types of parameters will produce data that are more defensible than speculation; however, a quick comparison to a broader risk assessment will show that this approach is also fundamentally flawed. The attacks are simulating only one type of attack. The external, hostile, structured threat (or hacker) is not representative of the full spectrum of human threat. Insider threats as well as nonmalicious threats are completely ignored or are assumed to represent no risk.

Another fundamental flaw of this approach is an overreliance on technical safeguards. Without explicitly citing procedural and human factors safeguards, it can be easy to assume that these add little or no risk mitigation value. The procedural and human factors safeguards associated with the technical safeguards that are priced for this study are either included as a cost factor or simply assumed to exist with the associated technical safeguard. Because the hierarchical dependencies of the safeguards are not explicitly included in the analysis, a comprehensive safeguard implementation cannot be specified.

One affiliated aspect of this approach is that the term survivability is used in place of the word security. Although this may seem a minor semantic difference, it actually represents a significant departure from the more classical understanding of security. As we have already defined security, a recap is unnecessary here. The term survivability implies an overreliance on the security component of availability at the expense of confidentiality. It also patently ignores the vital attribute of information integrity.

Another fuzzy metric used as an alternative to the security ROI calculation is the subjective comparison to similar industry or organization. This can also be referred to as industry best practices. Many decision makers prefer to conservatively follow the trails blazed by their industry leaders. These people rely on replicating those programs with a proven track record for success.

When searching for appropriate industry best practices with regard to safeguard implementation, it is critical to assure the organization behind the information. Many best practices guides are vendor-produced roadmaps that, not surprisingly, feature the vendor's products as the centerpiece of the standard. Organizations that have highly effective programs, especially security programs, are usually unwilling to share that information, because they can no longer control its distribution and use. The most problematic aspect of industry best practices for information security is that often, simple knowledge of the safeguards employed can encourage attackers.

Fundamentally, information security safeguards lend themselves more easily to analogies to insurance policies. If you have paid for life insurance the past 20 years and you have not yet died, does that mean the monies you used to pay for that insurance were a wasted investment? Security safeguards are analogous to exercising, eating right, and taking out a good family insurance policy. You buy it, use it, and manage it to prevent and deal with undesirable consequences. Sometimes the threat never materializes and sometimes you are rewarded for your investment.

Ultimately, it will be the insurance industry that finally drives more effective metrics for IT safeguards. Insurance companies seeking customers will be able to sell risk-sharing products that will cover their customers in the event of information compromise. Recently, this has come to be known as hacker insurance. However, actuarially driven insurance companies will be able to define metrics that capture a comprehensive view of threats as well as the complete understanding of the value of information.

As organizations with valuable information assets see the value in these insurance products, insurance companies will competitively strive to provide the best product for the best price. To do so, they will need to accurately assess the amount of risk mitigation provided by various safeguards and combinations of safeguards. Discounts will be provided to customers who follow certain standards or use certain products. Only then will the true science of risk management metrics be achieved and be able to accurately define an effective ROI for security safeguards.

12

PRACTICAL APPLICATIONS OF McCUMBER CUBE ANALYSIS

INTRODUCTION

The theoretical underpinnings of the information-centric McCumber Cube model have been explored in depth. The application of this methodology for security enforcement is now a straightforward process of defining and evaluating the elements of the model and applying it to the information security design problem at hand. The actual implementation of a structured analysis is admittedly a tedious and detail-oriented process, but without a structured methodology to follow, it becomes difficult to both justify and implement a comprehensive program. There are several aspects of a practical implementation of the model that will be discussed in this chapter.

An in-depth understanding of the theory that supports the McCumber Cube model is important to effectively implement the principles of the model to develop and enhance security for any type of information resources or assets. The universal nature of the model is such that it has direct applicability to almost every information security challenge. It can provide a basis for an enterprisewide security program, an assessment of select safeguards, or the detailed analysis of an information security product.

In this chapter, we will review a number of ways the McCumber Cube can be employed. We will start at the global level of abstraction and then briefly discuss various targeted applications of the model. Because the model is independent of technology, it can be used as a basis for analysis and decision making with the understanding that the principles of the model will not change with the evolution of technology. In other words, the McCumber Cube application technique you learn and employ today will be the same one you can use in the future. That is certainly more than you can say for programming techniques or technology roadmaps.

For anyone performing any type of information security analysis, the model is applicable and often enlightening. By focusing on information as the foundation of information security, it opens up new avenues of research and development for capabilities to provide confidentiality, integrity, and availability of information resources. The technology-centric approach is always self-limiting. Technology changes and new products and processes are introduced with startling frequency. By working at a level of abstraction above the technology layer, security practitioners can more efficiently design security safeguards and security programs that provide cost-effective protection.

When evaluating or assessing the analyses of others, applying McCumber Cube logic to the information security problem forces the security practitioner or analyst to focus on the information security attributes and reconsider the conclusions. Too often, security analyses are developed around faulty assumptions. Sometimes, the technology-centric approach means that any definitive results will be obsolete with the next evolution of technology and that may be only weeks away. The model is an excellent reference to apply when the topic is the protection of data and information resources of any kind.

APPLYING THE MODEL TO GLOBAL AND NATIONAL SECURITY ISSUES

The McCumber Cube model is an effective basis for any security analysis. There are several reports and analyses in recent years that are aimed at assessing security incidents and their impact on a global or national level. These reports and studies often make assumptions about threats, vulnerabilities, and safeguards that are obsolete or inaccurate. When a threat is presented on this level of abstraction, it is almost entirely focused on malicious attackers who have extensive IT skills. Safeguards and best practices are almost always tied to the existing state-of-the-art technology and conclusions are based on conjecture at best and fear mongering at worst.

In February 2003, the Office of the President of the United States published the *National Strategy to Secure Cyberspace*.[1] This was a nonregulatory publication. It did not have the effect of law. The strategy was developed after several years of intense consultations among thousands of individuals — officials at all levels of government, experts from the private sector, and other concerned citizens. It was published to establish priorities and recommendations for providing the appropriate protection of cyberspace functionality. Initially, the document contained some rather pointed observations about serious vulnerabilities of specific technologies such as wireless Internet access and Internet service providers' (ISPs) infrastructure. Through its various iterations, the drafters eventually dropped some of the more controversial statements made about whether these ISPs or even universities could be doing more on behalf of cyber-space security. Instead, the *National Strategy to Secure Cyberspace* was toned down and was published simply to encourage industry, government agencies, and the public to reduce risks wherever practical.

Those aspects of the national strategy that focus on best practices, of course, will be outdated soon enough. So will the references to specific technologies and the references to the emerging wireless environment. This will hardly be the foundation of the cybersecurity the way the U.S. Constitution represents the foundation for our national government. That is because the U.S. Constitution is built on sound principles for a consti-tutional republic and not designed to capture all the specific detail on how that is accomplished. Had the *National Strategy to Secure Cyberspace* been developed around the basic principles and imperatives of protecting our national information resources, it would make a bigger impact.

The other option would be to focus such a document on the need to protect the technology infrastructure. In this case, the approach would be different and the model may not apply because information is not the subject of the strategy. In either case, a sound understanding of the model necessary would have provided a superior foundation worthy of the amount of effort it takes to create and publish such a document.

National-level debates and mandates over the protection of information resources revolve around two fundamental elements — the technical infrastructure used to transmit, store, and process data and the information itself. If the foundation is specifically on the information, the McCumber Cube model applies. In the case of an information-centric requirement, it provides the basis for understanding the information attributes of the concept of security. We defined security in an earlier chapter and the definition is quite apt in this case. Security is not a binary concept and any analyses, proposals, or guidelines that imply that it is can often be more confusing than enlightening.

When depicting risk to information resources on a global or national scale, the essentials of the risk management process also apply directly to the risk issue under review. The elements of threat, vulnerability, asset, and safeguard are juxtaposed to assess the amount of risk. Any decrease in the threat, the number and severity, and the value of the information assets will decrease the amount of risk. Conversely, any increase in the number and nature of the threat, the number or severity of vulnerabilities, and the value of the assets requiring protection will increase risk. Referring to these variables in any discussion of risk to information makes it easier to analyze, model, and interpret the results or conclusions.

Applying the McCumber Cube model to these large-scale issues can dramatically simplify the analysis and provide a common context for evaluating various options. The essential elements of information security and the ability to decompose complex technical infrastructures into state changes of transmission, storage, and processing requires analysts and decision makers alike to work from a common palette. This feature alone demands the use of the Cube for effective communication about complex technologies and the valuable information they handle.

PROGRAMMING AND SOFTWARE DEVELOPMENT

The McCumber Cube also lends itself to use in programming of applications and other software development activities. Just like the decomposition and assessment of components, software not only facilitates the processing of information, but its transmission and storage as well. Because the model is information-centric, creating an information flow map of the software design can assess security attributes of computer programs. The emphasis for this type of project is not on the code itself, but on the information that is manipulated by the software.

The information flow map for a software development program would be created to identify the state changes of transmission, storage, and processing. This would then be used to track the information flow through the program. Security attributes are then overlaid to create a security management map of the program or application.

At each identified state, the appropriate attributes of confidentiality, integrity, and availability can be analyzed and assessed. Necessary security-relevant issues are quickly highlighted as vulnerable information states are identified. These vulnerabilities may be exposed by identifying information that can be unintentionally modified by outside processes, human interaction with the program, or simple loss of data.

USING THE McCUMBER CUBE IN AN ORGANIZATIONAL INFORMATION SECURITY PROGRAM

The McCumber Cube is most effective when applied to an organizational information security program. It provides numerous practical applications for use by the security program manager, the security practitioner, and all decision makers involved in information security issues. For starters, the McCumber Cube provides a common lexicon for discussing and analyzing information security issues. Instead of a tedious and unproductive debate over technical vulnerabilities and safeguard specifications, security practitioners and decision makers have a common framework to discuss both the concept of security and the trade-offs involved in acquiring, deploying, and managing security safeguards.

Before security practitioners and decision makers can even begin to wrangle about the merits of various options for protecting information, they need to agree on a common definition of security and the amount and nature of that protection. Security is an ideal state not unlike the concept of love. We may feel secure just as we may feel love, but for professionals to discuss the practicalities of this ideal state, certain common ground must be achieved. If the decision maker simply demands that his or her information be secure, it is left to the security practitioner to define how much security is adequate. This ages old problem has resulted in more than one security expert getting sacked.

The first step in any organizational security program is to explicitly define what it means to be secure. One person's definition of security is not usually the same definition perceived by another. The McCumber Cube immediately identifies the basic elements that comprise the definition of security as it is applied to information and data. To effectively communicate regarding the security attributes of information, all parties to the discussion must define that security on terms of confidentiality, integrity, and availability. Although there have been those who have sought to expand the number of security-relevant attributes, the basic three provide adequate and comprehensive categorization to meet the needs of organizational security programs.

The next important elements of the model are the information states that force the user to abstract the information security problem to a level above the technical infrastructure and its associated components, computers, protocols, and media. By employing the information states of transmission, storage, and processing, the primary security analyses are performed to determine a comprehensive strategy before these plans and procedures must be translated into specific technical solutions and safeguards.

The value of the information state aspect of the model is difficult to underestimate. Too many times and in many situations, technologists and those responsible for business or mission requirements fail to agree on the value of security. It is common knowledge that many senior corporate leaders and government executives perceive security controls as a necessary evil. There is always the temptation to skimp on security spending when more revenue-generating investments beckon. In many cases, the final verdict on how much to invest in security is based solely on how much risk the decision maker feels. Although there is something to be said for gut-level instincts, security for corporate data is not one of the areas where this approach is particularly successful.

Information state abstraction allows security policies and standards to transcend the volatile and dynamic technology infrastructure that actually transmits, stores, and processes the data. This means that CxO-level guidance and corporate governance requirements do not need to change with changes in the technology. This is an important feature that allows organizational security practitioners the ability to obtain an accurate agreement on how much security is enough and yet leave the specifics of implementation to the technologists who can best deploy it.

Another key aspect of information state analysis is that it more effectively facilitates the development and enforcement of the broader security program. Many information security programs have standards and policies that must be rewritten or at best updated at least annually to account for technology evolution. By applying security policies and requirements to information states as opposed to specific technologies such as a PCs, compact disks, or hard drives, the policy will most likely remain current for any foreseen or unforeseen changes in technology. However, it is important to note here that changes will still be necessary for significant changes in the value, location, or nature of information resources.

Information state analysis is the heart of the McCumber Cube and is its most valuable commodity. Security practitioners will soon find that approaching information security problems by defining information states and tracing the flow of information throughout its life cycle will uncover previously unknown vulnerabilities and also help to quickly assess new and innovative safeguards to mitigate risk. This process is much more efficient and ultimately more effective than the more common probe for vulnerabilities and subsequent search for technical safeguards.

Just as the technology infrastructure changes, so do the technical safeguards. Instead of mandating a corporate firewall requirement, the policy should be one of controlling the flow of information into and out of the organizational environment. Certainly a modern firewall is a logical and effective safeguard in an existing infrastructure. Over time, however, products will undoubtedly emerge that may provide enhanced security functionality with a different name or safeguard nomenclature.

Information flow maps using the transmission, storage, and processing convention are valuable resources for assessing risk in IT systems. By tracking and mapping the flow of information from its creation or accession to its deletion of long-term storage can be an eye-opening experience. The McCumber Cube model provides this level of abstraction specifically for the security practitioners. System architects and administrators may rely on maps or blueprints depicting the location of components and wiring, but a state map can overlay these elements with a picture of the information states that can then be correlated with the security requirements.

There are several other ways the model can be used by organizational security practitioners that we will cover in the next sections. Notice how the value of the model increases with greater application. If the model is employed accurately and consistently throughout the IT security program, the effort required to adapt and use the model will be saved many times over in repetitious or unproductive activities.

USING THE McCUMBER CUBE FOR PRODUCT OR SUBSYSTEM ASSESSMENT

Chapter 9 on Information State Analysis for Components and Subsystems is primarily targeted toward using the model as a replacement for existing government and industry criteria for evaluating and assessing security in specific technology devices or software applications. To understand information security, it must be in context. In other words, the relative security of a piece of information is dependent not only on the device or medium that is currently transmitting, storing, or processing it, but also on factors such as the value of the information, the location of the component, and the nature of the threat.

However, the McCumber Cube can be effectively used in assessing various proposed technologies for organizational use. By creating an information flow map for the product under review, the same security assessment process can be mapped within the security component, application, or subsystem. The security attributes of confidentiality, integrity, and availability can be estimated if not absolutely defined for the changing information states.

An example of using the model for this purpose could be a data storage system. By decomposing the various parts of the storage device into state changes, you can identify where information flows in, where it is stored, and any processing functions required to store, retrieve, or move the data. Once these are identified, the security practitioner can then apply the appropriate security attributes of confidentiality, integrity, and availability to make a quick determination of the existence and efficacy of security controls and safeguards within the storage system.

The focus, as always, is on the organizational information resources requiring protection. The degree of protection required and the investment necessary to provide that level of protection are calculated through the same basic risk assessment process outlined in the appendix. The McCumber Cube provides the security relevancy attributes and state analysis capabilities necessary to identify potential product or subsystem vulnerabilities and possible safeguards.

USING THE McCUMBER CUBE FOR SAFEGUARD PLANNING AND DEPLOYMENT

Perhaps one of the most consistently useful aspects of the McCumber Cube methodology is its adaptability to use as a safeguard planning and deployment tool. As we showed in Chapter 11 on safeguard assessment, the model depicts not only the three primary safeguard categories of technical, procedural, and human factors, it also highlights the law of safeguard dependency. Both procedural and human factors safeguards support any and all technical safeguards by definition. Human factors safeguards are always present when a procedural safeguard is invoked. Human factors safeguards are present in all safeguard configurations, but they are the only safeguards that can stand independently.

Safeguard planning is the key to an effective security program. Just as it is important to consider all possible threat categories and carefully evaluate the value of information assets, the security practitioner must accurately track safeguard assessment, accession, and deployment. As we have stated in Chapter 11, it is not effective to try to apply the safeguards to a specific technical specification, but to target the safeguards as they support the appropriate information attributes of confidentiality, integrity, and availability. Any safeguard should be tied directly to these factors to assess efficacy and cost-effectiveness.

These security attributes, in turn, are predicated on the seminal information flow map. This is the primary document to work from to define the security attributes. Once these attributes have been defined, it will be necessary to then change the level of abstraction to the technical vulnerabilities within the technology infrastructure. These vulnerabilities can then be mapped to safeguards that mitigate the risk from these vulnerabilities either by eliminating the vulnerability itself or rendering it either partially or completely risk free by changes to its environment.

The McCumber Cube model aids this entire process by forcing the security practitioner to consider and evaluate all three categories of safeguard. It also ensures that the safeguard dependencies are considered for a comprehensive understanding of how the technical, procedural, and human factors safeguards interoperate. These interactions may consist of a software product supported by a procedure that ensures its use and a human factors element that overtly influences users to be more security conscious.

Security practitioners who employ this safeguard model are assured of developing a comprehensive program that recognizes the interrelationships of their safeguards in ensuring the information attributes of confidentiality, integrity, and availability. This is important for any organizational security program. A penetration-and-patch approach to safeguards is not effective and does not provide an understanding and evaluation of the dependencies of safeguards.

TIPS AND TECHNIQUES FOR BUILDING YOUR SECURITY PROGRAM

As we present the many practical ways the McCumber Cube model can be used in assessing and developing security for information resources, it is also just as important to have other key elements in place. In this section we will provide some helpful tips and techniques for your use in building, growing, and maintaining an organizational security program.

ESTABLISHING THE SECURITY PROGRAM: DEFINING YOU

Establishing (or assuming) an information security program is a daunting task. The most important ingredient in the task, quite simply, is the security practitioner. As the security practitioner, you are called on to assess, justify, analyze, monitor, and react to the entire range of potential security related incidents and environments. Your role is that of the consultant, whether you are in a corporate environment, in a government agency, an IT contractor, or actually working as a consultant. Decision makers and colleagues alike will look to you for advice and guidance on the risks to vital information resources.

The first step is educating yourself. Sure, there are self-taught security gurus, system crackers, and even cryptographers. But the art and science of information security is changing every day and it is impossible to be personally aware of every possible vulnerability and available safeguard. That means you have to start with a solid grounding in the basics. If you employ the proper fundamental models and tools, the changes in the IT industry and the products it creates will pose no real problems.

Information security experts were originally computer users or IT workers who developed an interest in the security attributes of early computing systems. Perhaps some of them even exploited these systems either out of curiosity or from malicious intent. There were no schools, classes, or even standards that guided them. They were the pioneers.

Over the years, information security has become a recognized profession within the IT domain. Yet even information security personnel have a wide variety or interdisciplinary skills and many people choose to specialize. Some pursue penetration testing as a career; others are skilled at policy evaluation and development. Still others choose to build security products and some prefer security management. It is important to define you and your role in information security.

For those willing to tackle the big problems such as enterprisewide security program management and leading-edge security systems development, the challenges are manifest. You will be called on to justify and defend your recommendations. You will be forced to validate your conclusions. Most importantly, your work will be tested every day by environmental and human threats that seek to compromise the confidentiality, integrity, and availability of the information resources you seek to protect.

By defining you, I mean it is incumbent on you to gain the proper training and foundational skills to be an effective information security professional. The days of the ersatz hacker or computer hobbyist being picked up as a corporate computer security expert are over — if they every existed at all. Many security and technical certifications are now available to complement traditional educational programs. Also, many colleges and universities now offer certificate and degree programs in information security. These programs represent a sea of change in the industry and are a great opportunity for anyone seeking to enter this career field.

Identifying yourself as an information security professional will require formal education, testing, certification, and experience. Although these efforts are time-consuming and difficult, they can never be expunged from your records. They are yours to keep. Your attainment will show your customers, bosses, and colleagues your commitment and dedication to this critical field of endeavor.

How many vulnerabilities does a system attacker need to exploit an organization's information assets? The answer is only one. How many vulnerabilities does the defender need to consider? The obvious answer here is all of them. It takes much more time, effort, and commitment to play defense in this business than it does to play offense.

In almost every organizational situation the security professional is best perceived as a consultant — even if they have a lofty position such as the chief information security officer. The unique set of interdisciplinary skills, technical knowledge, and interpersonal skills demands someone willing to take on the role of an outsider looking in. Successful security programs are built and led by men and women who can place themselves in others' shoes and look at information as both a malicious outsider and an internal bumbler who can bring down the system. They need to be able to convey abstract concepts to senior managers who must make difficult decisions about resources and funding for security.

Ultimately, they are the advocates for a speechless and amorphic entity — information. In that role, they must be able to cogently evaluate and express the nature of the risks that are faced by the organization and be able to design, defend, and build a comprehensive set of interoperating safeguards to guard against potential consequences that may never be realized. It is not a job for the quiet, unassuming personality.

AVOIDING THE SECURITY COP LABEL

One of the most common problems of IT security practitioners is the perception or adoption of the security cop label within the organization. Without tangible senior-level support for an organizational information security program, the practitioner (and the security staff) is often left to develop policies, analyze the infrastructure, design the security program, and enforce compliance. In such an environment, even the most talented and politically astute security professional can easily fail.

You can obtain the security cop label when you are perceived as a security policy enforcer. This identity can be fatal for your program and ultimately your career. The security cop is someone everyone else in the organization tries to avoid. To them, no good can come from a visit with the security practitioner. Yet many information security professionals bemoan the fact that they do not feel like an integral member of the business team, but an outsider charged with punishing security offenders and creating roadblocks and security hurdles for employees and managers simply trying to perform their duties. This phenomenon is so common, it needs to be addressed here.

The woeful situation of the security cop arises when management does not support the security professional, but leaves them alone to build and manage the information security program. When the inevitable conflicts arise between expediency and security, the security practitioner is always left defending the unpopular position.

There is only one tried and true method for avoiding this unenviable fate. You must have full support and backing from your organizational leadership. Your approach and attitude about security must reflect theirs. For any security program to be effective, the security program manager and their staff must be supporting the rest of the organization in meeting the risk mitigation requirements of the leadership. In this capacity, the security manager is perceived as a helpmate and supporter in meeting corporate requirements. Obtaining that support and then becoming an integral member of the leadership team is covered in the next section.

OBTAINING CORPORATE APPROVAL AND SUPPORT

The most effective IT security programs are structured as a corporate commitment, not simply the brainchild of a security practitioner or information security group. If you or your security group is solely responsible for developing, implementing, and enforcing the security program, you will be held personally responsible for all related security violations and any security technology problems. You will also be held to account for the use of any and all resources related to your area of responsibility. Inevitably, you will also be held responsible for slowing up surefire moneymaking projects and preventing honest work from being accomplished.

An effective and successful security program begins with obtaining corporate or organizational support for security. The ideal situation is to seek a position where there is a stated organizational security requirement that is supported by everyone. These situations are not really rare, but they are fairly easy to identify. Security conscious organizations leave clues.

After the terrorist attacks of September 11, 2001, I took a keen interest in airline security. In the airline industry, there exists a glaring difference in the security programs of two of our nation's largest airlines. I fly them both and have personally witnessed the dramatic differences. Airline A has obviously returned to a pre-9/11 security posture. Aside from the installation of reinforced cockpit doors, the flight attendants and cockpit personnel are back to moving casually between the flight deck and the main cabin. Passengers are allowed to idly stretch their legs around the forward galley and people move freely between the different cabins. There are no preflight security announcements. This cavalier attitude toward in-flight security encourages passengers and crew alike to disregard seemingly commonsense safeguards.

Airline B is markedly different. Flight attendants block the aisle to the forward galley and the flight deck with a beverage cart every time flight deck personnel need to use the head. The aircraft commander makes security announcements and passengers are prevented from moving between cabins. Travelers who congregate near the cockpit door are quickly dispatched back to their assigned seats. Although many may view these safeguards as an overreaction, they certainly provide a sense that at least one major airline is taking security seriously; however, Airline A gives the perception that security is unimportant, even in this era. Whoever is responsible for the security program at this airline needs to quickly reevaluate their program or find another field of employment.

You can quickly discern which airlines are described here by keeping an eye on security procedures next time you fly. See which airline has their employees taking security seriously. Listen for security announcements and watch as flight attendants, flight crew members, and even ground crew personnel go about their duties. The sense of (or lack of) security quickly becomes obvious.

You will find it is actually quite easy to determine which organization has the superior security program. Although each airline may have identical security requirements, Airline B has taken the rules to heart and treats security issues appropriately. You can witness it by seeing first-hand how these rules are enforced and through the everyday actions of their employees. Just like cleanliness at Walt Disney World, support for security within Airline B helps ensure everyone, including passengers, take security precautions more seriously, and thus make it a significantly more effective program.

An information security program is no different. I can usually tell within an hour of on-site analysis which organizations have effective information security programs. It is easy to determine. You can look for visible signs like:

- Security notices posted near computer systems and access points to computer and network resources
- Locked workstations
- Warning banners on sensitive applications
- Security checklists
- Security responsibilities spelled out in position descriptions for all employees with access to sensitive information

You can also divine the effectiveness of a security program from talking with employees:

- Those with access to sensitive information can easily explain their security responsibilities.
- Everyone can quickly identify those responsible for information security.
- Asking about information security does not merit a shoulder shrug or a giggle for a response.
- Senior decision makers know without prompting how information security is implemented and by whom.

These are the signs of an effective information security program. Look for the verbal and nonverbal clues that quickly show how seriously an organization takes information security. If you are the one responsible, ask someone outside your sphere of influence to give you some unbiased feedback. Security is as security does.

Ideally, you want to work where the sense of the importance of security is important. If you are unfortunate enough to get the task of creating an organizational environment, your most immediate priority will be to establish that security-conscious environment.

The McCumber Cube provides an excellent tool to start making the organizational leadership aware of the value of a sound security program. Perhaps someone already soured their interest in information security by providing tedious technical lectures about technology vulnerabilities. You can use the McCumber Cube to define the elements of security and seek their guidance and leadership in creating an effective risk management program that includes your information security requirements.

The best place to start is with a common language to discuss the elements of risk and security. By using the security attributes of confidentiality, integrity, and availability as well as the information states in lieu of technical jargon, you will be well on your way to creating an atmosphere of mutual respect that can be the beginning of this security-conscious environment.

CREATING PEARL HARBOR FILES

One of the interesting aspects of becoming a computer security professional is the inevitable requirements to create your own Pearl Harbor file. What are those? I can explain it best with a story.

I have a good friend who finally achieved some of the recognition he has so richly deserved. Tim had worked in numerous physical security positions over the years and had always worked after hours to improve his superior professional capabilities. When he had a government job, he sweated through years of evening college classes to obtain a baccalaureate degree and then went on to receive his masters as well. While others spent their free time pursuing relaxation or hobbies, Tim taught security classes for others and wrote articles and technical papers. He has always been a go-getter and I was truly pleased for Tim and his family when I found out he successfully competed for the position of Vice President and Director of Security for a Fortune 100 company.

Because I was in the same town as Tim's company on a recent business trip, I decided to make an appointment to see him. I called his secretary two weeks in advance to schedule an audience with the new vice president. She said Tim was currently on a business trip overseas, but he would be back in town for my visit. I was just able to squeeze in for a short luncheon meeting because his schedule was already booked for the entire next month. I asked for directions to the downtown skyscraper that housed the company's headquarters and offered to meet him at his office.

On the appointed day, I arrived nearly 20 minutes before our scheduled lunch and rode the elevator to the 32nd floor. I was directed to a plush lounge area just outside his closed office door that enjoyed an unobstructed view of the busy waterfront. I glanced around while I thumbed through the professional magazines and corporate literature that littered the coffee table. The office environment was the perfect depiction of corporate efficiency. Administrative people moved quietly between fax machines, printers, and computers. Telephones with muted ringing tones were quickly answered by courteous employees wearing tasteful dress business attire. I was impressed.

When his office door opened several minutes later, two individuals with date books and cumbersome folders walked quickly past me toward the elevators and pressed the down button. Tim emerged moments later and leaned over to say something to his secretary. As his eye scanned the waiting area, I was pleased to note the look of warm familiarity when he recognized me.

"John, how ya been?" he called out.

"Just great, Tim," I answered as I jumped to my feet. "It looks like the home boy has done well for himself. Congratulations on the new job."

"Thanks for stopping by while you were in town. I'm sorry I don't have more time to give you. I've asked my secretary to have our lunch brought here to my office so we don't have to waste time riding the elevators. Besides, it will be more comfortable here," he said while escorting me past the secretary and into his office.

As I crossed the threshold, I noted the change in flooring. The functional office-grade carpeting of the waiting area changed to plush thickly padded rugs in colors that complemented the drapes and upholstered chairs. The large desk and other wood furnishings were all made of matching fruitwood with granite surfaces. Recessed lights provided soft, indirect illumination.

"Hey, man, this is a long way from government working conditions. Not battleship gray desk. No 1940s era rotating fan pushing around the fetid air. How do you manage to get any work accomplished in these surroundings?" I asked.

"I make do," he smirked. Then he opened an armoire to reveal a large wet bar complete with glassware and carafes for hot beverages. "Coffee or tea?" he asked smugly.

"I'll take some black coffee and you can cut the act now that the door is closed. No need to play the big executive role with an old buddy."

As Tim smiled and poured, I exercised one of my bad habits. I started pawing around his office checking out cabinets, files, and shelves around his desk while making comments like:

"Where do you hide your booze?" and "Nice joinery work."

I took mementos and awards off the shelves and felt their heft. I peered into coffee cups. As I was closing a file cabinet, a title on one of the files caught my eye. It simply said "Pearl Harbor."

"What's this 'Pearl Harbor' file?" I asked picking up the weighty stack of papers.

"Hey, stop rummaging the place. You must think you still work for NSA. And for Pete's sake, put that file back. It's one of the most important ones I possess. I've used that file for years, now."

"If it is that important, why is it called Pearl Harbor and what's in it?" I queried trying to sound innocently curious. His answer was quickly stifled by a knock at the door. He opened it and allowed the white-coated attendant to push in and unload the cart with our salads and iced tea. As we started eating, he said he would tell me about the file if I did not laugh. Here is what he told me:

"Early in my career, I was responsible for the physical security for a small group of government buildings. When I took over the job from a retiring civil servant, I had to reassess the security measures currently in place and make recommendations for security enhancements and other improvements. Any time the building managers would propose changes or additions to the buildings, they had to seek my input and approval for any necessary security enhancements. I also had to justify all the current and projected costs for security including salaries for guards, fences, lights, and anything else in the security budget.

"As my job responsibilities slowly grew, the government housed more people and more expensive equipment in the buildings. Of course, newer and better security equipment was being developed and the government security requirements evolved as well. In addition, the area around the buildings became a little more threatening. When I felt it was necessary, I would approach the facility director with a proposal to purchase newer security technologies such as cipher locks, surveillance cameras, and extra lighting. Each time he would ask me to write up a lengthy report to justify the expenditure so he could disapprove it."

"You just said, '... so he could disapprove it,'" I interrupted. "Surely he didn't always disapprove your proposals?"

"Of course he always disapproved them. In bureaucratic circles, you open yourself up to criticism from your seniors for approving new spending projects and God forbid you ever exceed your budget. If he approved or endorsed any new spending project not specifically directed by our agency heads, he became vulnerable. However, he never heard a peep from the headquarters if he simply disapproved the proposal at his level. And when it comes to security, it can be difficult to justify the expenditures because more often that not, you are spending money to guard against something that may never happen. However, I didn't get discouraged. I always did a thorough job writing up the proposal and kept them in a file."

"That makes sense; but what would happen if a security breach did occur — like equipment theft or a parking lot mugging after you had proposed something which could have prevented it?" I urged.

"There you have it!" he exclaimed. "That's his Pearl Harbor — the unexpected attack! When a security violation resulted in a loss, we would resolve the problem and then have a *post mortem* meeting about it. For that interview, I would dig out a couple relevant proposals I had made over the preceding years and finally win approval for some needed enhancements."

"Did he approve all of them?" I asked.

"Of course not, but I was usually able to push through some of the more urgent upgrades. It happened enough that I just started calling this my Pearl Harbor file." His voice softened, then he asked, "You're a consultant in the network security business. Don't you recommend a Pearl Harbor file for your clients?"

"No, I don't think so ... hey, come to think of it, I guess I may have made recommendations to that effect. I never called them Pearl Harbor files before, but I have suggested to IT security managers to fully document all their proposed security enhancements, even if they're not ultimately approved. This is an important part of any IT risk management program. Any security program upgrade — whether it is for the IT infrastructure or the buildings, people, and equipment — must be viewed in light of risk mitigation. It's ultimately a business decision and not all of your recommendations will be accepted and implemented. The cure should never be worse than the disease."

"But you must admit there are times even for you computer geeks when you are forced to say 'I told you so.'"

"I've never been an I-told-you-so type of consultant," I replied. "It sounds churlish and it's not good for repeat business. I can only advise. However, I did make a mental note to rename some old files I have lying around."

As we exchanged business cards and regards to each other's families, I mused over a recent incident with one of my financial services clients. We had made recommendations last year regarding their e-mail server that were never implemented. The client phoned me just last week to ask for help. Someone had used their server to relay harassing e-mails and spam while disguising the real origin of the abusive communication. The sheer number of e-mails not only caused tie-ups with their Internet service, they also forced corporate communications personnel to deal with a flood of calls from angry recipients. Had they heeded our recommendations, they could have caught the problem before they were wrongly blamed for sending out abusive and indecent e-mails.

As Tim saw me to the elevator, we shook hands and I buttoned my overcoat. As we waited for the door to open, I said, "Do you know why I was prompted to ask you about the Pearl Harbor file I saw in your cabinet?"

"Not really," he replied.

"Because the one in your file cabinet was the second one I had happened to see today. I earlier noticed that one of the two people leaving your office while I was in the waiting area was carrying out a file with that same name written on the tab."

DEFINING YOUR SECURITY POLICY

To effectively develop and implement any security program, the first (and some would argue most important) aspect is to define your security policy. Developing security policy is not the subject of this book, so the presentation of policy development will be confined to significant aspects that are required to be able to effectively allow the security practitioner to apply the structured methodology.

In the most simplistic terms, security policy is defining what needs protection and to what degree. Because the IT security policy is one of risk management, it is critical to determine how these requirements interact with other corporate and organizational risk mitigation strategies.

In most medium- to large-size organizations, security or risk management policies are rarely, if ever, found in one convenient document or set of documents. Security and risk management policies are often divided into areas of responsibility or among functional groups. There is most likely a set of physical security requirements that are logically associated with specific buildings or organizational facilities. These policies are the responsibility of the group or individuals chartered to manage and enforce the physical security of the facility and provide protection for its occupants and guests.

The human relations unit at a company is often the caretaker for organizational personnel security policies. These requirements are used to limit the organizational risk associated with personnel actions. Every personnel policy from employee prehire screening to exit interviews is simply a procedure or action to handle personnel activities in such a fashion as to limit the risk associated with the human element. By definition, these, too, are technically security policies.

Depending on the size of the organization and its business or mission objectives, there may also be a comprehensive risk management team. These standing committees often meet on an as-needed basis and require the involvement of corporate legal staff, senior decision makers, financial planners, technical experts, and others. These groups usually use the risk assessment process to determine the organization's risk exposure for a variety of critical decisions. The results of their planning sessions are often policies and procedures formulated to effectively manage risk for key company initiatives. By definition, that is then a type of security policy.

Given this environment, the most effective way to manage IT security policy is to also frame it in its basic risk management context. In fact, IT security is just the type of strategic issue that should be dealt with at the higher levels of abstraction by decision-making bodies like the organizational risk management committee. By structuring the security investment and management decisions into either-or risk management language, the security program manager has the ability to achieve the commitment, support, and resources to be more effective.

The key to obtaining this support can be found in the proper use of security language. This book has already laid out the appropriate lexicon and a strict adherence to the use of words like threat, vulnerability, and asset ensures everyone is accurately communicating the issues at hand. Security can sometimes be an emotionally charged subject. Company executives can be offended when the insider threat is portrayed as a company leader with access to sensitive information resources. By sticking to metrics like the ones outlined in Appendix B, the security practitioner can focus on statistics and analyses devoid of presumptions and suppositions.

Another important aspect of this approach is the absence of complex technical information that most senior executives find challenging. If your security plan calls for you to request resources to purchase a new intrusion prevention capability, it may impress your superiors that you can describe the product's response to intrusions or denial-of-service attacks based on the type and location of the event within the network and providing session termination, traffic recording and playback, combined with e-mail and SNMP (Simple Network Management Protocol) notifications. However, you are more likely to gain the support you need if you can put the problem in risk management terms and describe the risk mitigation capabilities of the proposed investment.

Being able to communicate in these risk management terms is central to an effective IT security program. To do so, some patient education may be required. Organizations that support a risk management committee are more likely to be able to quickly adapt to risk management analyses, but without such a group, grounding in the basics of risk management is necessary. However, a security practitioner will undoubtedly find the value in creating an environment where the issues can be discussed and decisions made with the least stress. This process is necessary to avoid the common pitfall cited in the next section.

DEFINING WHAT VERSUS HOW

For security practitioners, one of the keys to success is being able to successfully describe the the elements of information security. The McCumber Cube model supports this important philosophy. Historically, information security was centered on managerially imposing the How to the detriment of the What. In information security, almost all the enforcement technology we currently have available is based on process, the How.

Firewalls, encryption, access control, and even security administration are all built around telling the information systems how to implement a convoluted process that is supposed to enforce the dictums of the security policy. Currently, most of these technologies and point solutions are designed to simply prevent certain activities from taking place. For example, a firewall is designed to keep unauthorized users and data from entering an organization's network. The firewall administrator must then go through a detailed and difficult process of defining specifically which processes and data are authorized and then programming the firewall to keep everything else out.

Every comprehensive review of information security describes the importance of having a security policy. Every computer security consultant worth his or her salt patiently explains to clients why they need this policy to accurately determine the efficacy of their security program. The policy forms the basis of all the discussions of What. Unfortunately, the consultant then must determine the degree to which the many components of security that make up the process (the How) effectively implement the policy (the What). This difficult game of abstraction is how the best consultants earn their high fees.

By now you might be asking yourself: Why not opt for products and tools that let you apply the What instead of expending all the effort to implement the How? Unfortunately, most security safeguard technologies are designed to be another link in the security process chain. These tools cannot enforce the What because they simply cannot implement an information-centric security policy. They can only implement binary technology-based security policies.

Take your medical records as an example. There are policies or rules regarding the use of this sensitive information that may be as simple as this:

■ The patient may request and be allowed access to all information in their file at any time.
■ The Records Department must document all access requests and use of these records. They must keep these records accurate.
■ The hospital Finance Department may see and update charges, payments, insurance information, and other relevant fields, but must not have access to sensitive medical information.
■ An authorized physician can gain access to your record (and may do so without your approval if you are incapacitated), but may not have access to your financial data.
■ The medical insurance company may gain access with your approval for doctors' diagnoses and other relevant data. If you refuse to grant this access, you may be denied reimbursement of your medical fees.

Now, think about all the IT security technologies and safeguards you may be aware of and try to imagine enforcing these five simple rules with complex network technologies like firewalls, public key encryption, access control systems, operating system tools, and application security products. After a few moments' reflection, it is easy to see the difficulties of defining security technology processes for even a few simple security policy requirements in a limited systems environment.

Defining the What of security policies becomes a possibility only when we can develop the ability to apply these policies directly to the information assets themselves. In the example above, we would need to be able to assign these policies to the medical record itself. This is not only the most efficient way to translate information management requirements to functional implementation; it is also the most effective way to secure the information or data assets. If the security and management policies were thus tightly coupled with the record itself, then a centrally managed policy enforcement controller would be able to mediate any attempts by a person or other program to affect that asset.

Current access control and network-based security technology is already proving unable to adapt to the demands of the digital marketplace. Valuable information and digital assets such as music recordings and art are most effectively used when they can be shared with others. However, companies, copyright owners, inventors, artists, musicians, designers, and others must be the ones to set the rules to enforce their digital rights. These new information-based security technologies will finally allow us to realize the profits and cost savings promised by a worldwide Internet.

Information-based policy enforcement technologies like the one described here are just emerging. These new capabilities will open up completely new ways to share information and data, collaborate with others, and organize the cacophony of information that exists in most organizations. People will be able to feel comfortable opening up their networks, because they will have the ability to enforce exactly how each bit of data is used regardless of where it is being transmitted, stored, or processed.

Most creative and intelligent workers prefer the freedom that comes from defining the What as opposed to enforcing the How. Slavish adherence to processes over results is the domain of bureaucrats and assembly lines. The new digital economy demands that information security professionals create and manage ways to share valuable information and data assets while ensuring that they continue to play by the rules their owners have defined.

SECURITY POLICY:
DEVELOPMENT AND IMPLEMENTATION

I recently visited two colleagues of mine who noted they were extremely busy. They both manage large IT security projects: one for a large U.S. government agency and the other for a commercial financial services firm. Each of these friends stressed how busy they were. Each of my lunch partners claimed a 60 plus hour work week and sleepless nights worrying about deadlines and requirements. I was intrigued to hear what efforts kept them so busy. Protecting company networks and data assets is certainly an important job and these guys must be getting nailed daily by bad guys to be this busy.

Over lunch, I asked them if the threats to their information systems had raised so dramatically as to force them and their staff members to adapt by putting in Herculean efforts to deal with the crises. Perhaps there was a new round of insidious viruses that were attacking their desktop systems or a rash of insider activity that was jeopardizing corporate data. As it turned out, the answers were surprising. In one case the flurry of extended hours and months-long effort was directed at completing a new round of risk analyses. In the other, the big crush was the development of the IT security policies that were required because of a company merger.

I asked why there should be such a significant work crunch in an organization to complete common risk analyses for its corporate IT systems. I naively asked if that was not a standard, albeit time-consuming aspect of the job for IT security experts. Both my guests rolled their eyes and said I must have been out of the corporate loop for too long. They both told horror stories of tedious documents of enormous size that had to be completed by teams of people incorporating reams and reams of hard-copy information. I was amazed. If it took months of dedicated effort to write these tomes, I asked, what could you possibly do with them?

This was where they both grew a bit sheepish. It seems these great analytical documents were ultimately used to prove to higher-ups and outside government agencies that their organizations cared about the protection of sensitive information. Apparently, the mindset was the bigger the document the more you cared. Little was being done to actually define and implement appropriate security controls.

I followed up by asking about the development of security policies — again, another fairly standard task for IT security managers and their staffs. They both claimed the policy development efforts were major undertakings that absorbed the work of dozens of employees as they teamed up with lawyers and managers to define how information needed to be protected. In each of my colleagues' cases, these policies ended up being published in large binders. I again asked about implementation issues.

In both organizations, it seemed policies were considered the domain of lawyers and managers looking to cover their assets in case of an errant or malicious employee's exploitation of their computer systems. If something went wrong, the lawyers and senior managers could sanctimoniously proclaim that they had developed and published appropriate regulations that emphatically stated those activities that were considered unacceptable.

Even though I could foresee the response, I had to ask if they had planned to actually use these policies to implement the necessary authentication and authorization technologies that would enforce and monitor these security policies. Neither of my friends was able to define any such activity. It appeared that both were expected to exert strenuous, long-term efforts to publish documents about the state of their IT security in their respective organizations without any follow-up on plans to deploy enhanced security technology.

They went on to explain that security policies do not always translate easily into improved security and it is not always possible to interpret how targeted point solutions like firewalls, intrusion detection, and operating system controls will actually be able to implement the organization's business rules. In other words, they were both working extremely hard writing documents about security, rather than investing these vital efforts into actually improving the technical capabilities to monitor, control, and react to security relevant events.

Most all of us are extremely busy. We expend the greater part of our working lives trying diligently to accomplish the difficult tasks laid out before us. For these security experts, it appeared that most of this busy time was devoted to doing little to improve the state of their organizations' security programs. If you are going to invest all that hard work into your information security program, consider the end result of all your company's exertion.

Developing and promulgating security policy is a critical and fundamental element of any security program. However, it must be an ongoing process that is interleaved with the myriad of other aspects of the program that include threat monitoring, vulnerability analysis, and safeguard implementation and management.

REFERENCE

1. Office of the President of the United States, *National Strategy to Secure Cyberspace,* February 2003 [available at www.whitehouse.gov/pcipb].

III

APPENDICES

Appendix A

VULNERABILITIES

INTRODUCTION

Vulnerabilities and security exposures are at the heart of the science of information security. They are not employed directly in the McCumber Cube methodology, because they are technology-based artifacts that are ultimately juxtaposed against various safeguards to ensure appropriate risk mitigation in the risk assessment process. However, the definitions and complete library of vulnerabilities have been admirably defined and addressed in the CVE library such that any detailed analysis outside this effort would be futile at best and conflicting at worst. With this in mind, I have included here several sections of the CVE library[1] that define the issue of vulnerabilities and exposures.

These sections have been inserted directly from the CVE Web site that is available at www.cve.mitre.org. I felt it important to include this information in this section to show how it can be employed in conjunction with the McCumber Cube methodology to build, tailor, and maintain a comprehensive and cost-effective information systems security program.

THE PROBLEM: VULNERABILITY MEANS DIFFERENT THINGS

CVE aspires to describe and name all publicly known facts about computer systems that could allow somebody to violate a reasonable security policy for that system. Often, these things are referred to as vulnerabilities. However, Editorial Board discussions have revealed that there are at least two common uses of the term *vulnerability*.

The broad use of vulnerability refers to any fact about a computer system that is a legitimate security concern, but only within some contexts. For example, because the finger service reveals user information, there are reasonable security policies that disallow finger from being run on some systems. Thus, finger may be regarded as a vulnerability according to this usage of the word.

A narrower view holds that some security-related facts fall short of being true vulnerabilities. With respect to the presence of the finger service, it may be argued that because finger behaves as it was designed to behave, it should not be considered to be a vulnerability in this narrower view.

THE APPROACH: INTRODUCING A NEW TERM — EXPOSURE

Because the term *vulnerability* has several different uses, there needs to be a way of making the distinction when it is appropriate. For this reason, we have introduced the term *exposure* to allow us to refer to security-related facts that may not be considered to be vulnerabilities by everyone. Relative to this narrower view of vulnerability, we would say that finger is an exposure.

DISTINGUISHING BETWEEN VULNERABILITIES AND EXPOSURES

At present, CVE provides no mechanism to distinguish between vulnerabilities and exposures, although the Editorial Board accepted a content decision that may provide a basis for later discussion. The primary focus of the Editorial Board is to add new entries to CVE. Users of CVE are encouraged to distinguish between CVE entries in any manner that best supports their own particular objectives.

Until the security community develops a better language to describe such things, you are encouraged to infer from the context whether vulnerability is being used in the broad sense, the narrow sense, or even in some other manner. For example, we might see this broad usage of the word when we see references to vulnerability databases and vulnerability assessment tools. A reference to a vulnerability database should not automatically imply that all entries in that database will meet the standard of the narrow use of vulnerability.

DEFINITION

In August 1999, the Editorial Board voted to accept the following *content decision* (CD), which describes terminology to be used in CVE. Note that these definitions are imprecise. It is expected that the language will evolve with usage.

SHORT DESCRIPTION

In an attempt to remain independent of the multiple perspectives of what a vulnerability is, the CVE identifies both universal vulnerabilities (i.e., those problems that are normally regarded as vulnerabilities within the context of all reasonable security policies) and exposures (i.e., problems that are only violations of some reasonable security policies).

DEFINITIONS

A universal vulnerability is one that is considered a vulnerability under any commonly used security policy that includes at least some requirements for minimizing the threat from an attacker. (This excludes entirely open security policies in which all users are trusted or where there is no consideration of risk to the system.)

The following guidelines, although imprecise, provide the basis of a universal vulnerability definition. A universal vulnerability is a state in a computing system (or set of systems) that either:

- Allows an attacker to execute commands as another user
- Allows an attacker to access data that is contrary to the specified access restrictions for that data
- Allows an attacker to pose as another entity
- Allows an attacker to conduct a denial of service

The following guidelines provide the basis for a definition of an exposure. An exposure is a state in a computing system (or set of systems) that is not a universal vulnerability, but either:

- Allows an attacker to conduct information-gathering activities
- Allows an attacker to hide activities
- Includes a capability that behaves as expected, but can be easily compromised
- Is a primary point of entry that an attacker may attempt to use to gain access to the system or data
- Is considered a problem according to some reasonable security policy

RATIONALE

Discussions on the Editorial Board mailing list and during the CVE Review meetings indicate that there is no definition for a vulnerability that is acceptable to the entire community. At least two different definitions of vulnerability have arisen and been discussed. There appears to be a universally accepted, historically grounded core definition that deals primarily with specific flaws that directly allow some compromise of the system (a universal definition). A broader definition includes problems that do not directly allow compromise, but could be an important component of a successful attack and are a violation of some security policies (a contingent definition).

In accordance with the original stated requirements for CVE, the CVE list should remain independent of multiple perspectives. Because the definition of vulnerability varies so widely depending on context and policy, CVE should avoid imposing an overly restrictive perspective on the vulnerability definition itself. Therefore, the term *universal vulnerability* is to be applied to those CVE entries that are considered vulnerabilities under any security policy (and thus by any perspective), and *exposure* is to be applied to the remaining CVE entries that include violations of some reasonable security policy.

EXAMPLES

Examples of universal vulnerabilities include:

- A phf (remote command execution as user "nobody")
- An rpc.ttdbserverd (remote command execution as root)
- World-writeable password file (modification of system-critical data)
- Default password (remote command execution or other access)
- Denial-of-service problems that allow an attacker to cause the Blue Screen of Death
- A smurf (denial of service by flooding a network)

Examples of exposures include:

- Running services such as finger (useful for information gathering, though it works as advertised)
- Inappropriate settings for Windows® NT auditing policies (where inappropriate is enterprise-specific)
- Running services that are common attack points (e.g., HTTP, FTP, or SMTP)
- Use of applications or services that can be successfully attacked by brute force methods (e.g., use of trivially broken encryption or a small key space)

WHAT IS A CVE CANDIDATE?

CVE candidates are those vulnerabilities or exposures under consideration for acceptance into CVE. Candidates are assigned special numbers to distinguish them from CVE entries. Each candidate has three primary items associated with it:

1. Number (also referred to as a name)
2. Description
3. References

The number (or name) is an encoding of the year that the candidate number was assigned and a unique number N for the Nth candidate assigned that year, e.g., CAN-1999-0067.

If the Editorial Board accepts the candidate, an official CVE entry is created that includes the description and reference and the candidate number is converted into a CVE name by replacing the "CAN" with "CVE." For example, when the Editorial Board accepted the candidate CAN-1999-0067, the candidate number was converted to CVE-1999-0067 and the resulting new entry was added to CVE. Note that the assignment of a candidate number is not a guarantee that it will become an official CVE entry.

THE TWO WAYS NEW SECURITY ISSUES BECOME CANDIDATES

Candidate numbers get assigned to specific issues in two different ways — as data sources or candidate numbering authorities (CNAs).

Data Sources

In most cases, we on the Editorial Board assign candidate numbers to issues that have already been publicized (e.g., on Bugtraq or in a security advisory). We rely on other data sources to feed us with vulnerability information that they regularly collect and summarize.

We collect and integrate the information from these multiple sources and create candidates from them. As a result of this process, it takes a minimum of two weeks after the initial public announcement of the problem before the candidates become available to the public. (Our data sources publish their summaries once a week, then it takes us at least a week to process their summaries.)

Candidate Numbering Authorities

Organizations or individuals reserve candidate numbers from MITRE for issues that have not yet been publicized. These entities, called CNAs, then include the candidate number in their initial public announcement. As such, the candidate number is immediately available. The CVE Initiative is working to do this more regularly across the industry. One effort involves providing blocks of candidates to key parties (like CERT/CC or major operating system vendors like Microsoft). These CNAs can then assign the candidates to incoming issues, independently of MITRE. This addresses some other concerns besides timing, but it requires that the CNAs know how to assign the proper number of candidates and it also requires close coordination across all parties.

Once a candidate has been created and assigned to a specific issue, it is proposed to the CVE Editorial Board. Board members review and vote on the candidates. In general, at least three Board members must accept the candidate before it can be promoted to an official CVE entry.

HOW LONG IT TAKES FOR CANDIDATES TO BECOME OFFICIAL CVE ENTRIES

In general it takes one day to one month to assign a candidate number and one to six months for the typical candidate to become an official CVE entry. The review process by the Editorial Board allows a minimum of two weeks from proposal to final acceptance and conversion to an official CVE entry. However, this only happens in certain relatively rare circumstances when the candidate identifies a well-known issue that has been publicly acknowledged by the vendor.

If the candidate is for an obscure issue, or Board members do not have a minimum level of confidence that the reported issue is real, then it can take months or even years before enough Board members cast the required number of Accept votes. Some candidates may never obtain enough Accept votes, but they may not be inaccurate either; these situations are currently handled by the CVE Editor.

During the review process for candidates, an Editorial Board member may find a possible inconsistency or ask a question that requires more detailed research. This can delay a candidate further while the questions are dealt with because some questions are, technically speaking, difficult to answer. Some candidates may also be further delayed by certain CVE CDs.

We currently release new CVE versions about once per quarter. This simplifies maintenance for people who maintain CVE-compatible databases, products, and services. These new versions are announced on the

News and Events page and in our free e-newsletters, "CVE-Announce" and "CVE-Data-Update."

HOW CANDIDATES ARE AFFECTED BY CVE CDS

CVE CDs are the criteria and consistency rules that determine:

- What security issues become CVE candidates for eventual inclusion in the CVE list
- How we distinguish between similar or related security issues

Approximately 15 percent of all candidates are affected by one or more CDs.

Generally, the CVE approach is to create separate candidates for:

- Vulnerabilities of different types
- Vulnerabilities of the same type that appear in different versions
- Vulnerabilities that appear in different code bases (i.e., by vendor; however, this also includes vendors who share the same code such as Linux/UNIX® vendors)

CDs are difficult to document and formalize, partly because of the variety and complexity of vulnerabilities, and partly because of the variety and quality of available information. In effect, CDs also represent areas in which security experts may differ on the proper way of distinguishing between security issues. As a result of these factors, CDs also can change over time. Because CDs directly affect which issues go into CVE and how they are counted, it is important that CDs be stable before an issue can be promoted to an official CVE entry. As such, if a candidate is affected by an incomplete or unverified CD, it will not be accepted as an official entry until the CD is stable — even if it has enough Accept votes.

Although we have stabilized some CDs, others have not received sufficient discussion and verification. This is especially the case with respect to configuration problems, which are not well-studied in the community in general, and are often areas of sharp disagreement between CVE Editorial Board members (for example, some reported configuration errors fall in the area of best practices, which some members do not think belong in CVE; also, there is wide variety in how people count configuration errors). The instability of content decisions is one of the biggest factors in the delays of certain candidates. But as we further stabilize CDs, that will allow a number of candidates to be promoted to official entries.

THE CANDIDATE NUMBERING PROCESS

CVE Candidates

CVE candidates are those vulnerabilities or exposures under consideration for acceptance into CVE. Candidates are assigned special numbers to distinguish them from CVE entries. Each candidate has three primary items associated with it:

1. Number (also referred to as a name)
2. Description
3. References

The number, also referred to as a name, is an encoding of the year that the candidate number was assigned and a unique number N for the Nth candidate assigned that year, e.g., CAN-1999-0067.

Established practices are followed when a candidate is created. If the Editorial Board accepts the candidate, an official CVE entry is created that includes the description and references. The candidate number is converted into a CVE name by replacing the "CAN" with "CVE." For example, when the Editorial Board accepted the candidate CAN-1999-0067, the candidate number was converted to CVE-1999-0067 and the resulting new entry was added to CVE.

The assignment of a candidate number is not a guarantee that it will become an official CVE entry.

Candidate Numbering Authority

Once a potential security vulnerability or exposure is discovered, it is assigned a CVE candidate number by the CVE CNA. Only the CNA can assign candidate numbers. As part of its role of managing CVE, MITRE functions as the CNA.

CVE Editor

After the candidate number is assigned, the CVE Editor proposes the candidate to the Editorial Board. Members discuss the candidate, modify it, and vote on whether to accept or reject the candidate for inclusion in CVE. If accepted, the candidate becomes an official CVE entry and is added to the CVE list on the Web site. In addition to its role as CNA, MITRE also functions as the CVE Editor.

Phases of a CVE Candidate

An overview of the phases of a candidate as it moves toward being accepted or rejected as a CVE entry is included below:

- Discovery — a potential vulnerability or exposure is discovered. Or an analysis of legacy vulnerabilities across various public sources is performed.
- Public announcement — a public announcement is made about the potential vulnerability or exposure through postings to mailing lists, newsgroups, security advisories, etc. After the announcement, the information is submitted to the CVE CNA by an Editorial Board member or by the CNA itself.
- Assignment — the CNA first verifies that the vulnerability or exposure is not already an entry or candidate and if it is not, assigns a candidate number. Only the CNA can assign candidate numbers. Occasionally, the CNA may provide a candidate number to an organization prior to a public announcement so that the candidate number may be included in the announcement. Currently, The MITRE Corporation functions as both CNA and Editor for CVE.
- Proposal — the Editor proposes the potential vulnerability or exposure to the Editorial Board, using the candidate number obtained during Assignment. It then becomes a candidate for CVE acceptance. Members discuss the candidate and vote on it. They may Accept, Reject, Recast (signifying the need for a major change), Modify (signifying the need for a minor change), Have No Opinion, or say that they are actively Reviewing the candidate. Note: Editorial Board members' votes and comments are recorded on the CVE Web site.
- Modification — when a candidate receives a vote to Modify or Recast, it means that it may need to be altered in order to be accepted. The Editor decides on what alterations need to be made (if any), then resubmits the altered candidate to the Board for additional voting. When only minor changes are necessary, additional voting will not be required and the Editor will simply move the candidate to the Interim Decision phase after making the change. Note: Modification history is recorded on the CVE Web site.
- Interim Decision — the Editor decides when it is appropriate to determine whether debate about the candidate is complete or has come to a standstill. The Editor casts a single Accept or Reject vote, then gives the Board the opportunity to post any final comments or objections. Votes with extensive comments or objections may result in a requirement for additional voting, which may return the candidate

to the Modification phase. If no change is needed, the candidate may advance to the Final Decision phase.

■ Final Decision — if the Editor determines that no sufficient grounds exist for changing the vote made in the Interim Decision, the decision becomes final. If the candidate is Accepted, the Editor announces to all Board members that the candidate will be placed into CVE and identifies the CVE name (or names) that will be assigned to the new entry. If the candidate is Rejected, the Editor notes the reason for rejection.

■ Publication — once a candidate is Accepted, the CVE name (or names) is assigned and the candidate is added to CVE. It then becomes a CVE entry and a new version of CVE is published via the CVE Web site.

■ Reassessment— occasionally, a CVE entry may need to be reassessed and possibly modified (for example, when there is increased under-standing of the vulnerability or exposure). Reassessment of a CVE entry involves the same phases as a new candidate, from modification through voting to final decision.

■ Deprecation — in some rare cases, the Editorial Board may decide that a CVE entry should no longer remain active in CVE. For example, the Board may decide to modify the level of abstraction by splitting the entry into lower-level entries or merging it with others. In such cases, the vulnerability will be annotated with a status of Deprecated.

FROM CANDIDATE TO CVE ENTRY

Once the Editorial Board accepts a candidate, it is now part of CVE and is published on the CVE Web site. CVE entries include the name (also referred to as the CVE number), a brief description of the security vulnerability or exposure, and any pertinent references. The CVE name, for example CVE-1999-0067, is an encoding of the year that the candidate number was assigned and a unique number N for the Nth candidate assigned that year.

CVE names make it possible for your databases and tools to speak to each other and share data across separate databases and tools. For example, if a report from a security tool incorporates CVE names, you may then quickly and accurately access fix information in one or more separate CVE-compatible databases to remediate the problem. Also, you will know exactly what each tool covers because CVE provides you with a baseline for evaluating the coverage of your tools. This means you can determine which tools are most effective and appropriate for your orga-nization's needs. These benefits make CVE the key to information sharing.

TO LEARN MORE

CVE is freely available for review or download from the Internet at www.cve.mitre.org.

MITRE

The MITRE Corporation maintains CVE and provides neutral guidance to the Editorial Board on all matters related to the ongoing development of CVE. In partnership with government, MITRE is an independent, not-for-profit corporation working in the public interest. It addresses issues of critical national importance, combining systems engineering and IT to develop innovative solutions that make a difference.

REFERENCE

1. Mitre Corporation, *Common Vulnerabilities and Exposures*, www.cve.mitre.org [accessed October 2003].

Appendix B

RISK ASSESSMENT METRICS

This appendix will propose and define a set of quantifiable metrics that can be used to mathematically calculate risk. Most of this material evolved out the Trident-Risk Assessment process (T-RAP) that was published under the title *Risk Management Theory and Practice*.[1] This study was sponsored by the U.S. Air Force Information Warfare Center. Subsequent work with the theories and concepts therein produced a set of equations and analytical tools that was incorporated into a series of technology offerings. I cite these modeling processes here as a complement to the McCumber Cube methodology and the basis for the risk management assessment methodology presented in Chapter 5.

This risk assessment process captured the major elements of what specific information needed to be gathered, quantified, and analyzed in order to calculate a measurement of baseline and residual risk elements. Baseline risk is the sum total of the anticipated adverse impact that can result if a threat exploits a vulnerability of the assets under review. The residual risk is that risk that remains after the application of chosen safeguards. These are the key elements of understanding security in an operational environment.

OVERVIEW OF THE BASIC RISK ASSESSMENT PROCESS

The basic risk assessment process (Figure B.1) is an iterative methodology where the operational environment is a key component. This aspect sets it apart from the McCumber Cube methodology. The three major activities associated with this process are the policy and data capture, risk analysis, and decision support phase. During the first activity, the various data elements are gathered and quantified. These data are captured and categorized as three separate lists of threats, vulnerabilities, and assets. Ultimately, they will create sets of triplets that will be used to rank order the

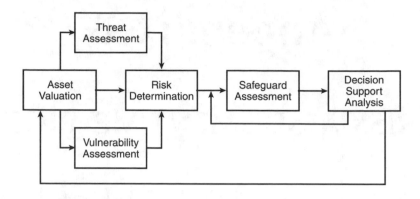

Figure B.1 Basic Risk Assessment Process

risk to the information assets. The result of this phase will be the creation of a baseline risk measurement — the risk to the information resources that exists before safeguards are employed to mitigate risk.

Once the baseline risk is calculated, safeguards will be selected to mitigate these risks. The measurement at this phase of the process is to determine to what degree the selected safeguards mitigate the risk. This calculation will produce a metric known as residual risk. Residual risk is the risk that remains after the application of the selected safeguards. This is the mathematics that recognizes the fact that no security program provides 100 percent risk mitigation. Such a risk avoidance capability is not achievable in information systems environments.

With these metrics to manipulate, the security analyst or practitioner can then run through a series of analyses to assess the effectiveness different safeguard options and compare the impact on residual risk while keeping track of the investment required for each set of options. In this way, different decision support methodologies can be applied to select and implement the most cost-effective security architecture based on the value of the information resources. Decision support methodologies such as weak link analysis, cost–benefit analysis, linear programming, and goal programming can be employed.

RISK ASSESSMENT METRICS

Now that you have an overview of the overall risk assessment process, we need to take a closer look at the empirical data that needs to be gathered to make this process work mathematically. We will also present a quick overview of the various decision support calculations that can be used to determine the most effective security architecture for the environment under review. Finally, we will show where data can be located to support this process.

THREAT METRICS

In Chapter 4, we showed how threat was decomposed as environmental and human. We also decomposed the human threat element into eight categories to better capture and understand all possible human-based threats.

To quantifiably capture the elements of human threat, various data sources need to be analyzed. The threat factors can be gathered by analyzing historical data and projections of trends in human threat experience. Also, statistical and expert analysis can be incorporated to provide a starting point for developing a custom or more tailored threat analysis. The purpose of this analysis is to identify and rank those threats that apply specifically to the assets under review or the organization itself.

There are three primary areas of human threat data that need to be factored in the risk assessment process:

1. System connectivity
2. Motivation and capability of the threat
3. Occurrence measurement for a threat class

We will look at each of these three areas.

System connectivity or access is the first element. It is designed to measure the amount of presence the human threat has to an organization. Obviously a trusted insider would represent more of threat to the organization's information than someone without these physical access rights. Physical access measures the amount of physical presence a threat could have to the organization. Electronic access measures the amount of electronic or logical presence a threat could have to the organization.

The motivation and capabilities of the human threat can be measured by a threat profile to determine the relative motivation and technical capability of a threat. Motivation measures the degree to which a threat wants to cause harm to the organization. Capability measures the knowledge that a threat possesses about the use of the information infrastructure and technology systems of an organization.

The occurrence measurement ranks the historical data and projected likelihood of a similar occurrence the way an insurance company actuarial table projects the likelihood of a person having an accident. The occurrence measurement is the approximation of the probability of occurrence. The occurrence measurement takes into account the number of incidents attributable to threat classes and the population size of sample.

The human threat measurement then is a function of the three primary elements of degree and mode of access, the threat profile, and the occurrence measurement. The threat measurement of the risk assessment process then is mathematically:

Threat measurement = f (access, threat profile, occurrence measurement)

VULNERABILITY METRICS

The chapter on vulnerabilities presents the state-of-the-art in vulnerability and exposures libraries. Vulnerabilities are those specific technical weaknesses that can be exploited to impact an asset. Vulnerabilities exist in system and network hardware, system and network operating systems, system and network applications, network protocols, connectivity, current safeguards, and even the physical environment. To use this information in the risk assessment process, specific quantifiable analyses need to be performed. There are aspects to the vulnerabilities that can be measured and they are necessary to identify and rank these vulnerabilities. The elements of the vulnerability measurement are exposure and the vulnerability subcomponent.

The exposure metric provides a way to determine if vulnerability can be exploited via physical or electronic exposure to the vulnerability. Physical exposure can be defined as a binary value that determines if the vulnerability can be exploited via physical access to the system with the vulnerability. Electronic exposure can also be a binary value that determines if the vulnerability can be exploited via electronic access to the system with the vulnerability.

The next measurable vulnerability metric is what is called the *vulnerability subcomponent*. It consists of several elements. The vulnerability subcomponent is the measurement of the severity of the vulnerability by measuring these factors:

- Potential damage — a measurement of the potential damage caused by exploitation of this vulnerability.
- Relative age — a measurement of when the vulnerability was discovered.
- Information available — a measurement of the amount of information available for the vulnerability.
- Area of impact to operations — these are binary values to determine the operational concerns that are impacted by the vulnerability.

Once these elements are captured and quantified, the mathematical function for the vulnerability component of the risk assessment process is:

Vulnerability measurement = f (exposure, vulnerability subcomponent)

ASSET METRICS

Most of the concepts of asset metrics were covered in Chapter 3. However, in the risk assessment process outlined here, certain aspects of the information valuation need to be accurately captured to perform the mathematical and analytical functions necessary for a risk assessment. These asset measurement functions for this process are part of a comprehensive analysis that includes the elements of:

■ Sensitivity
■ Criticality
■ Perishability
■ Recoverability
■ Quantity
■ Quality
■ Economic value

These are the elements of asset valuation that were developed for this risk assessment process and are listed here as a guide.

Sensitivity is the relative measurement of what the organization can expect regarding the degree of damage to the organization if the existence or disclosure of the information was realized. Various values (on a numerical scale or relative scale such as high, medium, and low) can be assigned to reflect this information asset measurement.

Criticality is also a relative measurement and indicates the degree to how vital this information resource is to the performance (or mission) of the organization. Lower values are assigned if loss or degradation of the information does little to impact the ability of the organization to accomplish its mission. If the information asset is absolutely critical to mission accomplishment, the highest value is assigned.

The concept of perishability is central to determining the time value of the information. There have been entire books dedicated to presenting the concept of the perishable nature of many information resources. Suffice it to say, the imputed value of information can change as it ages, so this element of valuation must be taken into account.

In the risk assessment process, it may be necessary to have an additional measurement for recoverability. In the McCumber Cube methodology, this element is primarily accounted for by the availability attribute, however, this risk assessment methodology may refine this attribute by also assigning value to the relative measurement of how easy it is to recover the asset in the event it is destroyed, damaged, or distorted.

Quantity and quality are two values that may need to be computed as well. For certain information assets, the more you possess, the greater the value. An example could be a potential client mailing list. For obvious reasons, a company would generally pay more for a larger list of names than for a much smaller list, unless specific targeted clients are called for. In the case where the information asset value is determined based on the rarity of the information, it may make sense to assign higher values for more specific or targeted information. Quality is a subjective attribute of information assets that is based on the level or degree of excellence.

Finally, a more specific economic value can be assigned based on the procurement or replacement cost of the information resources. If your organization has specific data on how much it costs to obtain, maintain, and replace information assets, you can use these empirical measurements at this point.

Once these elements are captured and quantified, the mathematical function for the asset component of the risk assessment process is:

Asset Measurement = f (sensitivity + criticality + perishability + recoverability + quantity + quality + economic value)

BASELINE RISK FACTORS

Once you have captured and calculated these elements, you can then create a quantifiable baseline risk measurement. Remember, a baseline risk measurement is the sum total of the anticipated adverse impact that can result if a threat exploits a vulnerability of the assets under review. This risk measurement is computed thus:

Risk Measurement = Threat Measurement × Vulnerability Measurement × Asset Measurement

Obviously, this simplistic formula is reiterated for each triple that is created by parsing the threat, technical vulnerabilities, and various assets. This can make for a large chain of computations, but it does provide the structured, empirical analysis necessary to determine what is meant by the concepts of risk and security in IT systems. Only when the elements of risk assessment are quantified can we create the tools necessary to help the security practitioner or analyst determine how much security is enough.

SAFEGUARD CALCULATIONS

Safeguard values are quantified by determining the risks that are mitigated by each safeguard proposed. A safeguard can mitigate risk for any of the factors that comprise the elements of the threat measurement, vulnerability measurement, or asset measurement. To accurately account for the entire spectrum of safeguards, technical, procedural, and human factors safeguards should all be considered.

Most technologists are familiar with the technical risk mitigation aspects of safeguards. In other words, they consider only those safeguards that can impact technical vulnerabilities. This is part of the vulnerability-centric security model. However, the McCumber Cube methodology indicates that safeguards can also be procedural and human factors based. In the risk assessment process, it is critical to consider safeguards in each of these categories as you do when employing the McCumber Cube methodology.

To fully analyze the entire complement of safeguards it is also important to remember that safeguards can impact more than just vulnerability measurement factors. Safeguards can be used that reduce the risk from threats and can also be used to change elements of assets to reduce the risk. For example, by adding logon screens that warn users of their legal liabilities, the security practitioner may cause potential attackers to reconsider an attack, thereby potentially influencing (mitigating) the risk from specific human threat categories. In the case of asset risk mitigation, some organizations segregate information resources based on its calculated value to provide enhanced security or to limit access paths. In this case, by moving assets, this procedural safeguard is employed to mitigate risk to the asset variables.

To capture the degree or the extent to which safeguards mitigate risk, this risk assessment process uses the term *counter values*. Counter values (depicted as CV in the equations) are used to reduce the impact of risk on the affected factors for each of the threat, vulnerability, and asset measurements. They are the aspects of the safeguard as applied to the appropriate risk elements. They are included mathematically in each of the equations of baseline risk in a manner that allows us to determine the residual risk. Remember, residual risk is the risk that remains after the application of the selected safeguards; this is how we calculate it using counter values for each of the measurements:

Threat measurement with safeguards included is now defined as:

((Physical access – CV) + (electronic access – CV)) *
((capability – CV) + (motivation – CV) * (occurrence
measurement – CV))

Vulnerability measurement with safeguards included is now defined as:

(Physical exposure + electronic exposure) *
((potential damage – CV) + age + (information – CV) +
confidentiality + integrity + availability + reliability + usability))

Asset measurement with safeguards included is now defined as:

(Sensitivity – CV + criticality – CV + perishability – CV +
recoverability – CV + quantity – CV + quality – CV +
economic value – CV)

The calculations are now run with the counter value (safeguard)
factored into the equation to help determine the residual risk. If the
baseline risk has been calculated with relative accuracy and the counter
values have been developed consistently, you now have both baseline
and residual risk calculations to perform a variety of analyses to provide
decision-making capabilities for your risk management (security) program.
Before we cover these analyses, it is important to look at how the type
of raw data needed in the previous calculations should be gathered and
applied.

OBTAINING RISK ASSESSMENT DATA

This risk assessment process may at first appear daunting or even merely
a hypothetical exercise if there is no way to determine and rate the various
factors and counter values. The data necessary to perform this type of
analysis is not currently in popular use either in technical or policy circles.
However, this data is not dissimilar to actuarial data used in the insurance
industry.

Some of the factors presented above would need to be created by the
analyst using information generated by the organization. This would
primarily be an assessment based on the information systems and on the
relative value of information assets they transmit, store, and process. These
values could use broad categories like low, medium, and high that could
be simply quantified as 1, 2, and 3. They could be defined more granularly
on a much larger scale and could include weighted values. In any case,
this data could be compiled as an integral part of the McCumber Cube

methodology or used as an adjunct for the operational risk assessment process alone.

To obtain more objective, and hence more accurate, data for such aspects as threat factors and vulnerability components, the analyst can employ statistical data collected by the organization, outside agencies, trade or industry groups, or even insurance companies. Another source for this data would be the expert opinion of professionals in IT operations, security, or technology management for use in developing weighting factors. All of these sources could be used for input to make valuation judgments regarding the various risk measurement variables of threats, vulnerabilities, and assets.

Some security professionals have sneered at the need to collect and employ such data. These are often the same people who appear to prefer the seat-of-the-pants approach to security. Unfortunately, the simpler days when a security professional had to merely deploy a considered collection of point solutions to create a security program are fast coming to an end. The information systems technology environment for most organizations is far too complex and the cost to design, acquire, deploy, and maintain the information security systems is too significant to use a unstructured, qualitative approach. To determine the elements of a complex albeit comprehensive security program, a structured analysis like the McCumber Cube methodology is called for. To answer the questions about how much and what type of security is required in an operational environment, an empirical risk management process is required. We can now examine some analyses that can be performed with the data generated by the risk assessment process.

RISK ASSESSMENT DECISION SUPPORT TOOLS

Granted, the effort required to perform a quantitative risk assessment can be onerous. However, once you have cranked through the data gathering and calculations required in the risk assessment process, you have all the raw data required to perform a variety of extremely valuable decision support analyses. The results of these analyses can give you the hard facts needed to define, develop, justify, and implement an operational information security program for any type of application or organization. Although there are numerous techniques and analyses to perform, I will cover four of the more important ones.

The first possible use of the risk assessment data is for weak link analysis. Weak link analysis in the case of information security is based on the assumption that greatest baseline risk measurement represents the greatest information security risk to the organization. As you calculate the baseline risks, those with the highest risk measurement are those that require the application of targeted safeguards (technical, procedural, and human factors). As successive iterations of the analysis are performed, you can apply safeguards to the highest risk measurement and repeat until a constraint (such as overall cost) is reached.

The second analysis is a cost–benefit analysis using the risk assessment data. In this decision support analysis, you can use the risk assessment process to compare residual risks using comparable security safeguard solution sets. The set of most cost-effective safeguards can then be selected based on its ability to meet the quantitative risk mitigation criteria established for the information resources under review. These are the cost–benefit ratios that allow you to select the suite of safeguards that provide the best protection for the least cost.

Two other decision support methodologies that could be employed with this data are linear programming and goal-oriented programming. In linear programming, you can allow for the optimization of multiple security variables using different safeguard solution sets. Goal-oriented programming allows the analyst to set goals or constraints and allows the system to select a safeguard set that meets the security requirements of the system within these constraints.

Whatever decision support tools you choose to employ, the risk assessment metrics described here can provide you with the raw data necessary to make critical decisions about your information security program. It provides a structured, empirical approach that works hand-in-hand with the McCumber Cube methodology to define, justify, acquire, deploy, and maintain a cost-effective security program in any systems environment.

REFERENCE

1. Trident Data Systems, *Risk Management Theory and Practice: An Operational and Engineering Support Process* [report], March 30, 1995

Appendix C

DIAGRAMS AND TABLES

INTRODUCTION

The McCumber Cube methodology is a structured approach to analyzing all facets of information security requirements. However, it also provides a common information security lexicon that can be employed for specifying requirements, making risk mitigation decisions, and developing and deploying safeguards. Additionally, many aspects of the model allow us to use the categorization and mapping to greatly expand the value of following this approach.

In this appendix, we will provide a compendium of helpful diagrams, charts, and tables that can be employed in information security programs or reports of any kind. These charts are presented as ideas and templates for your use. They can also be adapted or modified easily to meet specific needs.

TABLE C.1 — HUMAN THREAT CATEGORIZATION

This chart outlines the various threat categories. It was adapted from Trident Data Systems' report, *Risk Management Theory and Practice*.[1] It is helpful in mapping and evaluating human threat categories. It can be used to ensure that you are considering all the possible human threat categories and not simply external, hostile threats. This chart can be expanded or blocked to use as headings and subheadings to expand on the many sources of exploitation and loss.

TABLE C.2 — THREAT–VULNERABILITY PAIRING

This chart allows you place the same human threat categories outlined in the previous chart down the X-axis and map them against specific

Table C.1 Human Threat Categorization

• External	• Internal
– Hostile	– Hostile
• Structured	• Structured
• Nonstructured	• Nonstructured
– Nonhostile	– Nonhostile
• Structured	• Structured
• Nonstructured	• Nonstructured

Table C.2 Threat–Vulnerability Pairing

Human Threat Categories	Vulnerabilities
Internal-hostile-structured	CVE-XXXX-01
Internal-hostile-unstructured	Description:
Internal-nonhostile-structured	CVE-XXXX-01
Internal-nonhostile-unstructured	Description:
External-hostile-structured	CVE-XXXX-01
External-hostile-unstructured	Description:
External-nonhostile-structured	CVE-XXXX-01
External-nonhostile-unstructured	Description:

vulnerabilities. This chart is helpful for identifying and explaining which threats can exploit which vulnerabilities. You can also place the technical vulnerabilities down the X-axis and chart them against the threats that can exploit them. I used the CVE codes as an example, but you can use whatever vulnerability designation system you choose.

TABLE C.3 — VULNERABILITY–SAFEGUARD PAIRING EXAMPLE

This is simple one-to-one pairing of a vulnerability and a safeguard. However, in many circumstances, a safeguard may mitigate risk from a number of vulnerabilities and certain vulnerabilities may require more than one safeguard. It is best to always seek out possible one-to-many and many-to-many relationships.

Table C.3   Vulnerability–Safeguard Pairing (Example)

Vulnerability	*Safeguards*
CVE-2002-00-43 Sudo (superuser do) allows a system administrator to give certain users (or groups of users) the ability to run some (or all) commands as root or another user while logging the commands and arguments. Sudo 1.6.0 through 1.6.3p7 does not properly clear the environment before calling the mail program, which could allow local users to gain root privileges by modifying environment variables and changing how the mail program is invoked.	**Technical:** None **Procedural:** Do not install and use Sudo 1.6.0 through 1.6.3p7; upgrade to Sudo 1.6.4 or higher which runs the mail program with a clean environment. Admins wishing to run the mailer as the invoking user and not as root should use the *–disable-root-mailer* configure option in Sudo.1.6.5. **Human Factors:** Ensure technical staff and BSD UNIX system administrators are aware of this requirement.

TABLE C.4 — EXPANDED VULNERABILITY– SAFEGUARD CHARTING

This chart is similar to the previous threat–vulnerability pairing, but maps vulnerabilities to safeguards. The important thing to remember with this approach is that certain safeguards may only partially mitigate the risk associated with the vulnerability, so the fact they can be connected by a link between the vulnerability and the safeguard does not automatically mean the safeguard eliminates the vulnerability.

TABLE C.5 — SAFEGUARD HIERARCHICAL DEPENDENCIES

Safeguard hierarchical dependencies are important to understand when evaluating any type of safeguard. Remember, a technical safeguard is always supported by both procedural and human factors safeguards. A procedural safeguard is always supported by at least one human factors safeguard. Human factors safeguards are the only ones that can stand alone. I have greatly simplified these safeguards to highlight the use of the dependency attribute.

Table C.4 Expanded Vulnerability–Safeguard Pairing

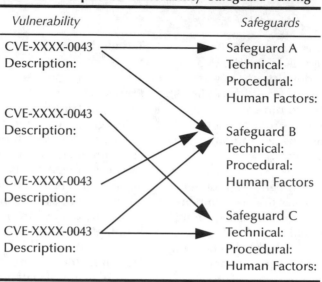

Vulnerability	Safeguards
CVE-XXXX-0043 Description:	Safeguard A Technical: Procedural: Human Factors:
CVE-XXXX-0043 Description:	Safeguard B Technical: Procedural: Human Factors
CVE-XXXX-0043 Description:	
CVE-XXXX-0043 Description:	Safeguard C Technical: Procedural: Human Factors:

Table C.5 Safeguard Hierarchical Dependencies

Safeguard: Intrusion detection system	**Safeguard:** Password development and management requirements
Technical: Software, hardware, enforcement capabilities, etc. **Procedural:** Security policy, configuration, technology management, etc. **Human Factors:** Security management, training, audit & review, user awareness, etc.	**Technical:** None (other than system enforcement) **Procedural:** Security policy, password assignment procedures, etc. **Human Factors:** User awareness, password management oversight, human-based anomaly detection, training.
Safeguard: Login warning banner	
Technical: None **Procedural:** None **Human Factors:** User awareness, effect on external threats, legal support, etc.	

FIGURE C.1 — NETWORK INFORMATION STATE MAPPING EXAMPLE

This notional diagram outlines the labeling necessary to identify information states in network environments. Obviously, this is a simple example. Identifying and mapping information states in network systems is central to applying the McCumber Cube methodology. More complex systems can be broken down into subsystems roughly the complexity of this example.

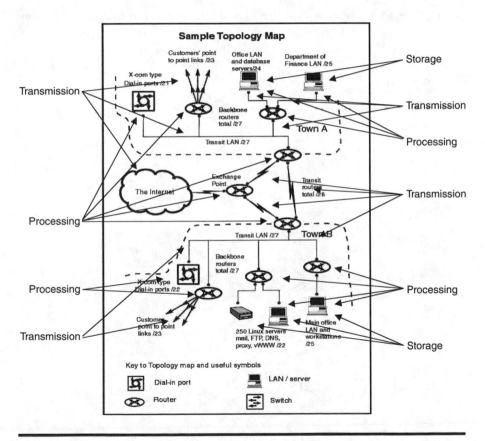

Figure C.1   Network Information State Mapping Example

FIGURE C.2 — COMPONENT INFORMATION STATE MAPPING EXAMPLE

This notional diagram shows an exploded view of a notebook computer. It represents a component or device that can be decomposed into its parts to identify and map the information states within the technology components. This process is effective for detailed information security analysis for IT components.

REFERENCE

1. Trident Data Systems, *Risk Management Theory and Practice: An Operational and Engineering Support Process* [report], March 30, 1995.

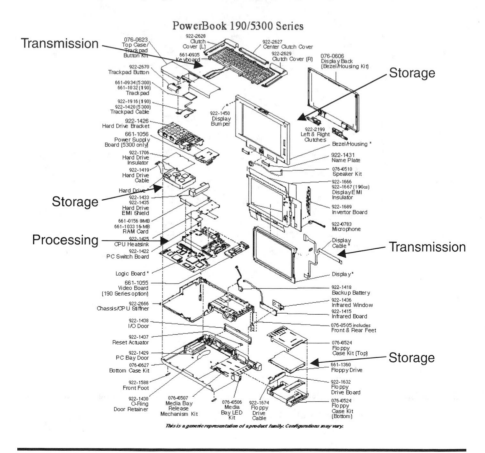

Figure C.2   Component Information State Mapping Example

Appendix D

OTHER RESOURCES

INTRODUCTION

When researching and analyzing references for IT security, it is also best to continue using a structured methodology. The categorization of security elements found in the risk assessment methodology provides us with a way to group and assess the key aspects of any security program. If, in fact, an information security program is founded on the essential risk management exemplar, it already possesses a process to define the primary categories — threat, vulnerabilities, assets, and safeguards. Additionally, the McCumber Cube methodology has also structured the elements of the safeguards into technology, procedures, and human factors. With this starting point, you can more easily search and discover the many data elements required for an effective security environment.

As with any reference section such as this, many of these starting points will evolve and change. However, as with the McCumber Cube methodology, the categories and structure of the references will remain relatively constant. By searching within these categories, you can gather the basic information required to meet the needs of your security evaluation and risk assessment processes. I have only listed a few of the major resources in each of these areas. Broader research is strongly advised.

The information in this section is not intended to be a complete listing of all available products and services; it is only representational of the types of resources and data repositories available to security practitioners. This list is not meant to endorse any specific vendor nor provide any type of ranking. Any omissions, errors, or oversights are unintentional.

THREAT INFORMATION

Threat information is perhaps the most dynamic element of your security program. Historically, it factored little in the static programs used for those implementing risk avoidance or penetration-and-patch methodologies. For the future, however, an effective security program will require access to continually updated incident and trend data. This type of data requires significant resources to gather, analyze, and maintain. Fortunately, several services have been developed to meet this need. Most provide this service for a fee.

The largest repository of relevant threat data is currently maintained by Symantec Corporation (www.symantec.com) and is provided to subscribers in the form of DeepSight Threat Management and DeepSight Alert Services.

Other threat services include:

■ www.idefense.com
■ www.redsiren.com

VULNERABILITY AND SAFEGUARD INFORMATION

The chapter on vulnerability information cited MITRE's CVE library. This is the best place to begin assessing technical vulnerabilities. Safeguard information is often comingled with vulnerability resources, so I have chosen to list several key resources here under the heading of vulnerability and safeguards. However, it is critical to consider all elements of safeguards — technical, procedural, and human factors. These may require some more detailed research to uncover. Other repositories of related information are also mentioned here:

■ www.cve.mitre.org
■ www.cert.org
■ www.csrc.nist.gov
■ www.sans.org
■ www.securityfocus.com

There are innumerable vendors, integrators, and technology firms that provide information security products and services to implement your chosen safeguards. Many of these entities offer a wide range of both products and services. Any compilation cited here will undoubtedly change dramatically over time, so they are not included here.

There are also numerous information resources for specific technical vulnerability and safeguard information. These are most often organized and disseminated based on the computing platform or operating system in question.

ASSET INFORMATION

Processes, methods, and techniques for the evaluation and management of information assets is the area most lacking in technical guidance and resources. More applied research is required in this soft science area. As the burgeoning requirements for the enforcement of confidentiality, integrity, and availability of information resources continue to be elevated, it is hoped that this discipline will receive the attention it deserves from academicians and practitioners alike. The chapter on information as an asset constitutes some of the major issues. The chapter on risk management metrics provides a starting point for your efforts at defining the empirical objective.

Most of the primary research needed to evaluate an organization's information resources is to be found within the organization of operational environment itself. Many of the evaluation criteria for information are relative. In other words, the metrics you develop to determine the value of the information are tied to the missions and functions that information supports. All information is gathered, analyzed, and maintained to support some type of decision-making process. If not, there would be no need to possess it. So determining how much value to attach to specific elements of information is usually relative to the business function the information supports. This vital data is already contained with the business processes of the operational environment and requires extraction and analysis by the security practitioner. Without such data, the security and risk management environment will be a game of guesswork and approximation.

INDEX

NOTE: Page numbers in bold refer to figures.

N